The Social Archaeology
of Houses

edited by
ROSS SAMSON

EDINBURGH UNIVERSITY PRESS

© Edinburgh University Press 1990
22 George Square, Edinburgh

Set in Baskerville
by ASAP, 197 Great Western Road, Glasgow, and
printed in Great Britain
by Alden Press, Oxford

British Library Cataloguing
  in Publication Data
The social archaeology of houses.
  I. Samson, Ross
  307.309

ISBN 0-7486-0290-9

Contents

Contributors

Douglass W. Bailey
is a research student in the Department of Archaeology, University of Cambridge. His doctoral dissertation is entitled 'The social reality of figurines from Chalcolithic Bulgaria'.

Dr Frank Brown
is a lecturer in the School of Architecture at the University of Manchester. He has a special interest in architectural and urban morphology, on which he has done research at University College London, Cambridge, and the Open University. His doctoral thesis involved an historical analysis and computer simulation of the spatial development of medieval London. He has also collaborated with J. P. Steadman on S.E.R.C.-funded projects investigating the morphology of the contemporary British building stock, both domestic and non-domestic.

Dr John Chapman
is a lecturer in European prehistory at the Department of Archaeology, University of Newcastle-upon-Tyne. His research interests are archaeological theory and the Mesolithic, Neolithic, and Copper Age, especially in south-eastern Europe. He is co-director of both 'The Neothermal Dalmatia Project, an Anglo-Yugoslav co-operative fieldwork and excavation project, and 'The Upper Tisza Project', a collaborative Anglo-Hungarian project started in 1991.

Dr Richard Hingley
is an assistant inspector of ancient monuments for Historic Scotland, Edinburgh. He read archaeology at the University of Durham and undertook research at the University of Southampton. He has published works concerning the social analysis of Iron Age and Romano-British settlements and has an interest in the study of artefacts, ritual, and ideology.

Dr Matthew Johnson   is a temporary lecturer in the Archaeology Department at the University of Durham. He read archae-
ology and anthropology at St John's College, Cambridge. His doctoral research was on early modern
houses in Cambridgeshire and his current research
interests include traditional architecture and social
and archaeological theory. He is currently pursuing
fieldwork in Wales, Durham, and the Alpes-Mari-
times in France.

Colin Richards   is a research Fellow in the Archaeology Department
at the University of Glasgow. He read archaeology
at the University of Reading and his doctoral
research on late Neolithic Orkney was undertaken
at the University of Glasgow. He is presently direct-
ing major excavation projects at Barnhouse and
Maes Howe, Mainland, Orkney. His research interests include material culture studies in Bali and prehistoric religion.

Ross Samson   is the director of Cruithne Press, an academic press,
and Archaeological Services and Publishing, a type-
setting business, at 197 Great Western Road, Glasgow G4 9EB. He also commissions archaeological
books for Avebury of the Academic Publishing
Group. He read medieval history at St. Andrews
University and completed his doctoral research on
Dark Age villas in Gaul and Germania at the University of Glasgow.

Dr Tom Saunders   is a part-time lecturer in medieval archaeology in
the Department of External Studies, University of
Leeds and in the Department of Archaeology, University of York. He read archaeology at the University of York and there completed his doctoral thesis,
entitled, 'Marxism and archaeology: the origins of
feudalism in early medieval England'.

Dr Eleanor Scott   works for the Royal Commission on the Historical
Monuments of England on the Hadrian's Wall Arch-
ive Project. She read archaeology at the University
of Newcastle and there completed her doctoral
research on Romano-British villas. She organised the
Theoretical Roman Archaeology Conference held at
Newcastle in 1991 and her research interests include the life and work of Gertrude Bell.

One

Introduction

ROSS SAMSON

> In Fiji the east wall is for the chiefs. In China, although the whole house is sacred the northwest corner is the most sacred. The Mongol Yurt is divided into four parts: to the right of the door the husband and wife, facing them the guest of honor, and to the left the other guests in descending order of importance. The altar is always on the left of the bed as one enters. In the Arab tent there is also a ritual space distribution which differs among tribes; as one example, the entry in the Touareg tent is always on the south, with the men on the east side and the women on the west. This ritual space distribution is found in houses in India, in Lapland, and among the Northwest Indians. . . . The radial plan of the Eskimo, which is the most characteristic feature of their dwelling, is closely related to the ceremonial and hierarchic aspects of dance. (RAPOPORT 1969, 54–5.)

Archaeology has often been characterised as the study of the past's refuse. A more representative maxim of what archaeology studies might be this trilogy: the dead, the dross, and the domicile. Studies on the burial of bodies abound and we are as likely to hear from archaeologists about the house of the dead as the house of the living. No aspect of the past has been as thoroughly imbued with the life and blood of anthropological and socio-logical ideas as death and mortuary practices. Despite the colourful anec-dotes that are to be gleaned from anthropology relating to domestic arrangements, British archaeologists have been little inspired to write an anthropology or sociology of the houses they excavate. We hope this book will go some way to encouraging more thought on the social aspects of what is arguably the single most important artefact for reconstructing past societies, the houses in which people dwelt.

This volume is the product of two sessions of the Theoretical Archaeology Group (TAG) conference held at Newcastle, 18-20 December 1989. One, entitled 'The social archaeology of houses', was organised by me, the other, 'Making sense of space', was organised by Frank Brown. The two sessions represented two trends found in present-day archaeological work on architecture in Britain.

One approach, spatial analysis, is quite distinct and involves methods of representing, measuring, and analysing the organisation and configuration of space. The key contributors to this field are, without doubt, Bill Hillier and Julienne Hanson. The two chapters by Frank Brown and the chapter by John Chapman are heavily indebted to their work on spatial analysis. Thus we find gamma and alpha analysis, convex and axial articulation, grid convexity and axiality, convex and axial ringiness, the building space index, real relative asymmetry, built:unbuilt space, inter-house space analysis, house dimension analysis, and rectangular dissection.

The other trend is more amorphous and involves applying to architecture a strand of social theory developed elsewhere. Thus there is traditional structuralist cosmology in Richard Hingley's chapter, Marxism in Tom Saunders', and straightforward social history in my own.

The application of social theory derived largely from sociology and anthropology to houses remains *ad hoc* for the greater part. There are as many social archaeologies of houses as there are schools of social theory. And of all this theory, none is especially well suited to architecture. One possible exception is structuration theory: the theory of social practice. It has not, however, been used as widely as it might be, with a few excellent exceptions (e.g. GRAVES 1989). Other borrowings are occasionally quite successful. Matthew Johnson mentions French work that relies heavily on the ideas of Claude Lévi-Strauss, father of structuralism. Although these French theorists are not cited by other contributors in this book, French structuralism is now commonplace in cognitive archaeology; many archaeologists feel comfortable using it in their own way without relying on schools to point them in the right direction. This is particularly true of cosmological studies. Johnson also mentions the American classic, *Folk Housing in Middle Virginia*, by Henry Glassie. Glassie, too, has relied heavily on pure structuralism. Johnson situates this North American school in the tradition of the 'ethnography of everyday life' which receives its impetus from symbolic anthropologists, like Clifford Geertz. The success of Glassie and Mark Leone can be measured in the extent to which some treat their works and interpretations almost as a body of social theory specifically created for understanding architecture.

The study of architecture comes closest to producing its own unique social archaeology of houses when it combines Hillier and Hanson's extrapolated theory of the social logic of space and Glassie and Leone's symbolic anthropology of world views. If not a well thought-out theory, this approach is largely the product of reading the most exciting theoretical writing on architecture that archaeologists have come across, outside of cosmological interpretations.

Architectural studies and the archaeology of houses

Studies on domestic architecture inspires archaeologists in Britain only little. This is all the more remarkable given the close proximity in which archaeologists and architects or architectural historians often work. Before its new name, English Heritage, and after its old name, Ministry of Works, the Commission for Historic Buildings and Ancient Monuments neatly expressed in its name the two disciplinary branches it united.

Architectural studies themselves cover huge territory. Practical architecture, architectural study for would-be architects, is something of which most archaeologists are blissfully ignorant. So it is that most reconstruction drawings are based heavily on an eye of faith, and copying other drawings found in books. The amount of practical knowledge that is brought to bear on such an exercise is usually minimal.

Architectural history has long been dominated by art history. My own experience of reading about English Elizabethan and Jacobean architecture as a background to looking at Scottish post-Reformation tower-houses brought home to me how little social history has been written. Instead most books spoke vaguely about the 'weight' of Elizabethan architecture, which caused it to sink in face of the new neo-Classicism, or about the skilful interplay of horizontal and vertical lines. The pretentious, and often meaningless, vocabulary of the art critic that surrounds much of architectural history really only helps the reader to understand what it is that the author likes about certain styles.

Architectural interest has also been the concern of folk studies and ethnographers, of anthropology and sociologists. We might expect to find archaeologists trying to make use of this work. Some indication of how little use they do make of architectural studies can be had from a glance through the bibliographies at the end of each chapter, and of papers written elsewhere by archaeologists on houses. Henry Glassie's *Folk Housing in Middle Virginia* is a clear favourite, and to this I shall return. Oddly, one finds the name Amos Rapoport cited on a few times. His *House Form and Culture* has made it to classic status. This is revealed by the constant reference to it in the recently published *Vernacular Architecture* (TURAN 1990). The book has been dubbed 'an intellectual guidepost' for scholars (DUNCAN 1981, 2). Given the near seminal status of *House Form and Culture* among American architectural historians – and the important fact that it is shorter and easier to read than *Folk Housing in Middle Virginia* – we might ask why it is not the better known to British archaeologists interested in architecture. To answer this question we would have to go some way towards understanding the directions taken by American architectural historians in their explanations of architecture. This is the route we would have to take because, as I believe, Rapoport and his successors have thrown up so many analytical frameworks, so many paradigms, so many categories of study that their work seems to lack coherence. On offer is not a powerful analytical or methodological tool, but a plethora of interesting ways of thinking about houses.

Lawrence (1990, 220-1) details seven basic frameworks in which American, English, and French scholars have worked to explain vernacular houses: 1) the aesthetic/formalist interpretation, primarily concerned with the formal composition of buildings rather than analysing what these buildings mean or who occupied them; 2) the typological approach, focusing upon the geometrical and compositional rules that can be attributed to the floor plan of extant dwellings, notably the size and shape of rooms, and the location of doors, windows, and chimneys; 3) the evolutionary theory; 4) social and geographical diffusionism, the introduction of new building designs and construction techniques from foreigners or social diffusion; 5) physical explanations, such as the constraints of materials and technology, site and climate; 6) social explanations, including economics, household structure, and defence; 7) cultural factors including collective spatial images and religious practices.

The first of these is the old art historical approach. The second in the list is discussed in Johnson's chapter where he concentrates on the use of typologies for diffusionist and evolutionary explanations. But in its pure state it can be joined with the formalist interpretation as the methodological foundation for describing and measuring buildings. This is a necessary precondition of talking about houses and will be dealt with separately in the next section of this introduction.

The third and fourth in the list are as tried, true, and traditional as one could find in archaeology. The spread of ideas and people scarcely needs further comment, except perhaps to say that diffusionism has so long been deemed 'a bad thing' as a theoretical explanatory tool, that it surely must be poised for rehabilitation in the next round of new theories. The evolutionary explanation is, to my mind, much more insidious. Diffusion at least explains change in terms of human action, the evolutionary explanation of things almost implies that houses can grow, change, and reproduce of their own accord. Houses appear to follow the dictates of Darwinian survival of the fittest. Evolutionary theory is less a theory than it is a facile way of ordering what we see as systematic changes in the past.

The fifth in the list is without doubt the least inspiring. Despite its promising name, *House Form and Culture* only talks about the cultural content of house form in one chapter. In chapter four, 'Climate as a modifying factor', we learn on page 85 that 'the need for shelter varies with the severity of the forces to be overcome' and that they are 'those natural forces known as *the weather*.' However, it is intrinsically uninteresting to know that igloos of the Inuit are not made of sun-dried bricks and that Hopi Indians do not use ice and snow for their adobe houses. It is dull to discover that brick is common as a building material in the stone- and tree-poor North German Plain. But is the replacement of thatch by tiles simply functional? At a greater cost, did tiled roofs really become common as emulation of the wealthy? Did a move away from the need for rebuilding or refurbishing every new generation mark the beginnings of houses as commodities?

Interesting questions can come out of the most boring discussion of material constraints. This can be seen in what I can only describe as an obsession with 'vernacular' as a concept in much of the work done in the USA. Throughout *Vernacular Architecture* the question surfaces in one guise or another time and time again. Primitive, vernacular, popular, and high-style are the categories Rapoport ascribes to architecture. By defining and defending each concept, each category, scholars invariably analyse their subject. Thus the obsession with carving out vernacular's 'proper' niche has led to full discussion, if not necessarily study, of how knowledge of building, knowledge of how to go about, knowledge of world order and social propriety operates in the building process.

In short, the attempt to distinguish 'vernacular' from 'popular' has become a vehicle to better understand how and where knowledge of building resides or how popular perceptions and desires impinge on building design. Similarly a study of material or climatic constraints can become a vehicle for understanding the rise of capitalism and the commoditisation of even the essentials of every day life.

The problem with using such 'vehicles' is that the mundane questions of defining what is high-style or how great are the physical constraints of building in wood remain central. The really interesting social questions are dragged in only willy-nilly. And they are the truly difficult to explain questions.

The last two frameworks for analysis on Lawrence's list figure prominently in this book. Ultimately, however, archaeologists and scholars working on vernacular housing interested in social explanations, in household structure, and in spatial images, draw their inspiration from the same sources, rather than from one another. And then architectural studies have sometimes been more reticent than archaeology in following new fashions. '*Anthropology*,' says Stea (1990, 25), 'while dealing with the developing world, has in the area of housing and settlement remained "the science of *man* . . ."' The gender framework has been taken up only slowly in architectural studies. To these external sources of social theory I shall turn in the final section of this introduction. But let me end this part of the discussion with one last thought on why archaeologists have paid so little attention to architectural theorists.

Books like *A Modern Theory of Architecture* (ALLSOPP 1977) mix a bit of an Italian Renaissance *palazzo*, two Corbusier houses, a cave at Lascaux, Stonehenge, and several thatched cottages into a domiciliary potage. The servings dished up are cross-cultural perspectives on oppositions of sacred *versus* profane, cross-cultural anecdotes on gender distinctions, or cross-cultural insights into public and private differentiations. This chapter begins with Rapoport's anecdotal evidence for the near universal importance of the corner as a sacred place. I am not arguing that this is bad. But it lacks the necessary coherence for widespread adoption as an analytical framework. Moreover, as Stea (1990, 22) notes, 'most Western scholars are still more comfortable with dichotomies than with dialectics', with the result that 'vernacular experts and architectural historians too often separate religious from domestic architecture . . . It is not always recognized that there is an element of the sacred in much mundane architecture or of much mundane in sacred architecture . . .'

Presumably the truth of the matter is simply that houses cannot generate theory for understanding the social world. The theories producing the best social archaeologies of houses seem to come from outside architectural studies. The only possible exception, the only true social theory that could come out of architectural studies would necessarily be closely related to the most important characteristic the built environment possess: its capacity to order space and organise human contact. Such a theory could only be developed from a method of describing and measuring the space of buildings.

Measuring space and describing buildings

Formal spatial or architectural analyses in this volume contrast with more intuitive architectural descriptions (these are ultimately Lawrence's frameworks 2 and 1). The former can be daunting to the uninitiated and Chapman's chapter will have to be read more than once by Chalcolithic experts who are novices at gamma or BUB analysis, if they want to comprehend it. Brown's comment on Chapman is in practice more a cautionary guide to the two spatial analyses most commonly used by archaeologists and is thus a valuable aid to such novices (I am myself one). A paper by Sally Foster (1989), cited by many in this volume, also offers the novice a good guide to access analysis. Formal analyses have a terrifyingly scientific appearance. Indeed, rectangular dissection of large houses is really only possible with a computer. However, much of the empirical measurement turns out to be fairly subjective: what constitutes a room or closed space within a building (think of something like an open plan office) and how does one compartmentalise space outdoors into quantifiable units? Some of the analyses are so narrowly physical or morphological that the results seem to convey little meaning *per se*. Thus an index of inter-house spacing tells us whether a settlement is more or less nucleated, but a formal index tells us much less than a plan because a formal index is simply a number. These spatial analyses, therefore, come into their own when different sites or different phases of the same site are compared. We can then see when sites became more nucleated or less open, when movement throughout the settlement was more 'ringy' (that is, had more alternative passages), when privacy within houses increased or decreased, or when the dwellings in a settlement tended to increase in size or the variation of complexity and size altered.

Different from indices that consist of nothing more than a number, justified maps of access analysis are extremely informative from just a glance. They graphically depict the relationship of rooms in a house in terms of possible movement from the outside to any room. Over a hundred houses have been so represented within this book. There are none for Romano-British villas, for although Eleanor Scott has wanted to do such analyses, the excavation record is generally too poor to allow all the doorways to be recognised. Likewise there are none for post-Reformation Scottish tower-houses. I have relied, as I most often do, on intuitive recognition. In access analysis jargon there was a move from tree-like patterns to those with more rings. In social historical terms there were more stairs and thus independent passages of movement to and fro became possible, with fewer rooms acting as passageways for other rooms. The question of independence of communicating paths through houses and social privacy or publicity is mentioned again without access maps in my comment on Eleanor Scott's paper.

By eschewing formal spatial analysis, I am able to recognise only very obvious changes in spatial patterning in tower-houses. This has the advantage of saving a lot of time in drawing justified access maps. It may also be that these broad changes are more real in social historical terms than the small fluctuations of the values of various indices between sample groups. But much detail is surely lost, and intuition is not always to be trusted, especially if an enquiring eye is searching for a pattern already predetermined by hypothesis. Much better, then, to use the method of Douglass Bailey, who has invented his own method of spatial analysis.

Bailey superimposes phases of buildings at Ovčarovo and analyses the amount of house continuity. The lazy or non-mathematically minded may look at the plans and decide for themselves how many newly-built houses of the later horizon count as 'successors' to previous houses and how many count as 'new'. Repetition of an early house is taken to have occurred formally when 75 per cent of the walls of the early house were reused in the new building. The numbers of 'repeated houses' are then turned into percentages and listed in a table to plot the fall, rise, and subsequent fall of such conscious architectural expression of continuity.

Traditional descriptive methods are used by Colin Richards. The measurable directional orientation of Neolithic hearths is striking. The more intuitively recognised contrast of left- and right-hand sides of houses and ease of access through them is perhaps less striking, but nonetheless significant. Richard Hingley similarly charts binary oppositions that can be empirically measured: movement, closeness to fire, quantity of debris. But in his case, Hingley piles one opposition on top of another when comparing 'public' and 'private' spaces. The public is characterised by open access, centrality, light, the 'cooked', and cleanliness. The private is characterised by constricted access, periphery, darkness, the 'raw', and uncleanliness. Some of these are physically measurable, some must be inferred, such as cooking from the hearth, and lack of cleanliness and the 'raw' were derived from phosphate analysis. Eleanor Scott charts increasing formalisation of villa plans. In my chapter on tower-houses I use an intuitive approach to a whole series of architectural features including room arrangement and function, prestigious elements such as grand front stairs and long portrait galleries, and external architectural arrangements and their ideological connotations, in order to suggest that conflicts created between the different elements led to the wholesale demise of tower-house architecture early in the seventeenth century. It could be said that Chapman and Richards stand at two extremes. Chapman carries out spatial analyses and seeks differences in the results that ask to be explained or used in historical synthesis. Richards only follows up distinctions already spotted and which, moreover, have already begun to be fitted into a meaningful interpretation.

No one in this volume used 'transformational grammar' in their study of buildings, a method favoured by several American ethnographers. Glassie acknowledges a debt to the great linguist, Noam Chomsky. He and many other symbolic anthropologists and archaeologists take the line that language and all material culture are socially produced to communicate information. Material culture, vernacular architecture included, thus has a vocabulary, grammar, and syntax, but these communicative rules and elements are understood and used by speakers and builders unconsciously. The archaeologist, like the linguist, can study the system and thereby perceive the rules governing the 'language'. Figure 1.1 reveals just how complicated the procedure can be; these are 'statements', with constructional rules grammatically depicted, of vernacular architecture in middle Virginia, as understood by Henry Glassie.

I make no pretence at having looked through the over one hundred subdivisions of his eleven rule sets: 1) forming the base structure; 2) extension; 3-4) massing and piercing the extended form; 5) expansion backward; 6-7) massing and piercing the backward expansion; 8-9) massing and piercing the upward expansion; 10) roofing; 11) subtypification. As the basic rules stand, however, they are fairly self-explanatory. They more or less represent

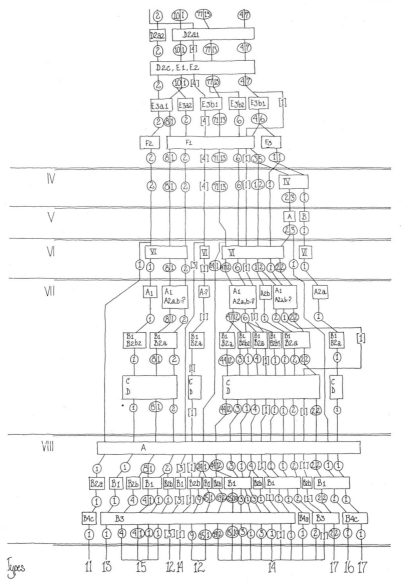

*Figure 1.1 Only part of Glassie's diagram of the transformation of the XY₃X base struc-
ture into types 11, 12, 13, 14, 15, 16, 17. The numbers in the rectangles refer to specific
rules in the architectural competence. The numbers in the circles are numbers of real
houses to which the rules in the rectangles apply. The numbers in brackets are those of
'ungrammatical' houses moved aside in order to avoid the rules that do not fit them.*

the steps taken by the builder, decisions made as the building progressed
from the ground up. I have used my own, and far less systematic, intuitive,
and rather inept version of a transformational grammar in my chapter on
tower-houses. I have isolated a number of elements in the vocabulary and
grammar such as decoration on the sky-line, unadorned exterior walls, iron
grills on windows, symmetry or non-symmetry of windows, open gunshot
windows on the ground floor, round stair towers, long galleries, and so on.
The introduction of some new architectural elements in the seventeenth
century produced 'grammatically' incorrect tower-houses. They syntax of
tower-houses was verticality; seventeenth-century innovations all spoke
horizontally. While the form and layout of houses changed little, and access
analysis would reveal only minor difference, the vocabulary and message of
sixteenth-century houses was fighting strength and determination to exercise force, that of seventeenth-century houses was good taste and legal
political authority.

Understanding the social

Social interpretation is what I had planned would form the core of my ses-
sion and, as already noted above, the various authors use varying frameworks. One is an attempt to derive social insights directly from spatial or
architectural analyses. This is something Hillier and Hanson have done, as
do most archaeologists who use their access analysis. There can be difficulties in this, for as Brown notes in his comment on Chapman, the methodology of space syntax 'is seen as the necessary and privileged route to social
interpretation.' Thus 'relational structure, as embodied in the access graph,
is equated directly with social structure: access relations are treated as
reified social relations.' This is a dubious proposition. To take one
example, late Norse houses in Greenland and Iceland contrast sharply with
early Norse houses. The greatly increased complexity and control of access
in 'deep' houses may indeed be related to increasing social stratification,
but two alternative explanations based on the increased warmth of the
complex houses are equally valid. One possibility is that a marked decline
in climatic conditions necessitated drastic measures to keep people warm
and alive; equally it could be that there was an increased need to produce
cheese for taxation, which was achieved by incorporating the byres into
complex long-houses in order to increase their warmth, thereby prolonging
lactation in the cattle.

Spatial analyses must be seen as no more than ways of measuring buildings and settlements, in the same way that polished stone axes can be
measured for length, weight, hardness, and brittleness. Converting these
measurements into social meanings needs to be made more explicit. It
seems fair to allow Chapman's recognition of changing house dimensions
as reflecting variation in lineage size. But does restriction and 'control' of
movement equal increased social control and power?

Sometimes it does. Tom Saunders suggests that the regularisation of tenement plot sizes was a formal arrangement indicative of lordly control, for it was made the basis of fiscal assessment on land held for feudal rent (and here it is worth noting that feudal rent extended to include labour services, renders in kind, and cash rent). The strict control of movement along a central road and the dominant position of feudal manors, allowing surveillance, helped lords keep track of peasant movements and the success of their agricultural production. Thus, knowledge was power. Similarly the 'tactical' positioning of tower-houses owed little to military considerations but quite a lot to the passage of cattle and knowledge of the movements of friends and enemies up and down the glen.

Saunders and I write from Marxist perspectives and are accustomed to thinking in terms of control, force, and coercion. Much of the work inspired by Hillier and Hanson is less specific about what is meant by control of access. Those who take this approach talk of the controlled meetings of inhabitants and strangers (this is found in the chapters by Chapman, Brown, Scott). This approach takes its cue from work done on twentieth-century society, which does not think in terms of power over the household, although parental control of children's movements is certainly relevant. Moreover, the inhabitant-'stranger' confrontation is surely anachronistic in most prehistoric contexts; meetings on tells between tell dwellers and others who lived elsewhere may have been common but would the latter not have most often been related lineage members, trading partners, allies, or dependants rather than 'strangers'?

But the amount of restriction and control of movement does not necessarily correspond to increased social control and power. Thus, in Scottish tower-houses the development is from an originally more tightly restricted, controlled line of movement (complete with lordly spy-holes!) through the house to later, less restricted passage with more stairways, 'vertical corridors' if you like. However, the social development was one from a more egalitarian household with higher ranking dependants as servants, to a less egalitarian household with more formal relationships between masters and increasingly lower ranking servants. The independent movement of unseen servants up and down the back stairs is an example of increasing formalisation and increasing control and exploitation, but in the terms of access maps the spatial configuration would be deemed less restricted, less controlled.

If we do not find the truth of the form and shape of society from simply reading the space of house, were do we find it?

The truth is in the details which are often provided by stringent methods of measurement and analysis. Frank Brown's chapter on the inter-war worker's cottage reveals that architects were explicitly conscious of how

rooms should be arranged to provide the greatest 'comfort', which included minimum room sizes, sunlighting of living rooms, and, to my mind
the most interesting, the seclusion of the living room by restricting access
to 'as few doors as practicable', preferring only one from the lobby. The
details, of which inter-war architects were apparently unaware, come out in
rectangular dissection: for a south-facing house there was only *one* plan that
fitted the requirements set out by the local government board's Housing
Manual governing room dimensions and the interconnection of rooms.

One can easily see that a wealth of social questions could be followed up
given the Walter Tudor's Report. Why was the parlour given so much
prominence, why was there emphasis on seclusion, what concepts of dirt
and pollution or social incongruity were present when the parlour was not
to open to the scullery? I was once amazed to discover that young newly
married friends disregarded a house they were at first keen to buy when it
was pointed out to them that to hang up washing in the back garden it
would have to be carried through the living room.

Brown restricts his study to examining the ideological implications of
one detail of spatial arrangement. The inter-war semi-detached house
shows a remarkable preference for a specific plan but not for its mirror
image. The reason, Brown argues, is that house entrances are placed far
away from each other, rather than next to each other, to increase the
impression of separation. The ideal of owning a fully detached house was
strong enough to result in plans that actually put parlours side-by-side,
separated only by a party wall, thus threatening to decrease privacy,
because from the outside the two halves appeared visually to be more
independent.

Not surprisingly ideology figures in several other contributions. My own
chapter discusses the relationship of martial architecture to feudal forms of
power and lordship. Colin Richards and Richard Hingley use the tried and
trusted anthropological approach of series of structural oppositions: left-
right, mid-winter-midsummer, cardinal compass points, and light-dark.
Connotations of life and death are clearly demonstrated for Orkney and
the probability of gendered meanings are discussed by Hingley. Such a
method might be applied one day to medieval long houses in Greenland
and Iceland, if I be permitted to return to that example. At Vallhagar in
Sweden early medieval long houses and dependent houses showed a
marked tendency for east-west and north-south orientations (Figure 1.2).
Dennis Doxtater (1990) presents a series of structural oppositions of a
cosmological nature, much as Richards and Hingley do (indeed, compare
Figure 1.2 with Richards' Figure 5.5). Doxtater argues that there was a
radical inversion of farmstead building orientations following the Reformation when the major rites of passage – marriage, birth, and death – were
staged in the church rather than the farm *stue*. The late Norse changes in
Iceland and Greenland were similarly accompanied by a radical re-

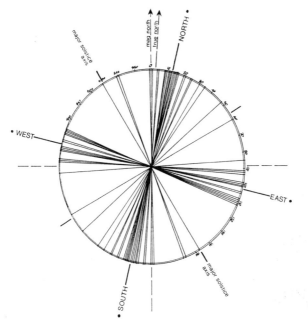

Figure 1.2 Ridge orientations of Viking longhouses excavated at Vallhagar, Sweden (after M. Stenberger).

orientation. Clearly there is more to be considered than just poor weather.

Cosmological parallels from anthropology are used to suggest meanings for the seemingly all-important Neolithic Orcadian hearth. The continued importance of the central hearth into the Roman period, as chartered by Hingley, reveals how we cannot depend overly on one component of space, or we shall end by postulating a four-thousand year continuity of not only social structures, but belief systems. And the striking similarity of the roll-call of oppositions used in most cosmological studies must make us pause for a moment and reflect: are these oppositions fundamental components of human thought, or are we continually reproducing a seductive anthropological exercise.

Ideology similarly figures largely in Eleanor Scott's chapter. Her inspiration for the explanation of why Romano-British villas became more formalised in plan and increasingly ordered comes ultimately from Henry Glassie's work on Georgian architecture in Virginia and Ireland. The symmetry and order of Georgian architecture obscured the earlier distinctions that allowed instant recognition of different rooms and their functions; it acted as a mask. Attempts to explain this as a denial or masking of social changes have been popular (e.g. LEONE 1984). Criticisms have, however, been forthcoming.

Creating a social archaeology of houses or a social theory of space is not at all easy. The seduction of equating the relational structure of space with reified social relations, as Brown sees implicit (if not explicit) in much of the work done in the wake of Hillier and Hanson, is understandable. Space and architecture could then be said to generate their own social theory. But, for the present, there have been no sustained attempts to do this. To endow space and architecture with theoretical meaning, archaeologists have had to turn to other bodies of social theory. Thus discussions of space and architecture in terms of social theory locate houses within any one of a number of -isms, such as feminism, Marxism, structuralism, or processualism.

These 'isms' will be too familiar to the reader to warrant discussion here, and if not there are now dozens of books, many of which are even readable, which deal with Marxism and with the theoretical schools built up since the 1960s. But there is one particular school which is, or should be, most influential. Saunders castigates most of the present archaeological debate for failing to assert the basic premise 'that spatial structures are simultaneously both the medium and the outcome of human action.' Space constricts, guides, channels, hinders, and stages various activities, social actions, and political struggles. But at the same time space is constructed by the activities, social actions, and political struggles that constitute society. 'There exists, therefore, a reflexive relationship between social and spatial structures, a link between the production of space and the reproduction of social relations.' Saunders is effectively outlining Bourdieu's theory of practice or Giddens' structuration theory.

That more is not made of Pierre Bourdieu by contributors is slightly surprising, given the popularity of his work on the Berber house and the fact that he was frequently cited in archaeological circles a few years ago. This school is clearly influential in Richards' chapter and figures in Scott's, Saunders', and Bailey's contributions. This social theory, which concentrates on the physical presence of actors in the constitution of social structures, is highly appropriate to a social archaeology of houses.

For Bourdieu it is through everyday practice that we learn about the world and recreate it. The *habitus*, or natural habitat, of the child undergoing socialisation is the physical surroundings of the parental house. It is here that gender roles are learned and ascribed, for example. I am reminded of Robin Evans's (1971, 337) observation:

> I am sure it has been noted by many that half the domiciliary public buildings of England erected in the 19th century are divided along their axes of bilateral symmetry by a solid and unpunctured wall, or some other suitable obstacle, in order to clarify the murky relationship between male and female. Infants' school was my own introduction to this distinctly architectural means of intellectual

clarification; and thus it is that ideas about the nature of things are built into the structure of our surroundings, creating a novel topos that reflects the patterns of its own, all too human, causes, and which becomes, in the end, self-justifying – if only because to ignore the existence of a wall is an act of the sheerest folly, leading inevitably to concussion and unsightly abrasions.

The reason, perhaps, that structuration theory has begun to languish slightly in the theoretical writings of archaeologists is that it does not provide simple answers. It is a theory about how society reproduces itself, how its members learn about the social order, and how human action actually creates institutions. But how does Bourdieu's theories on the *habitus* explain how or why round-houses, which served well over a hundred generations of inhabitants of the British Isles, should be replaced by rectangular houses? Structuration theory was not devised specifically to explain change, which is an obsession with archaeology. Exceptionally there is the simple idea that social reproduction is not perfect. Members of society learn how to go about their daily life, but either through stupidity or ulterior motives they introduce changes and novelties. The newly-recreated society is always different, be it ever so slightly different. But this hardly explains how anyone could go quite so far wrong as to build a Roman villa instead of an Iron Age round-house.

The result is that the theory of social praxis, how everyday practices and existence recreate society, is associated with historically specific contexts, events, and conditions, which are generally interpreted in traditional historical terms. And not surprisingly this is precisely what happens in every chapter in this volume that deals with the question of change. I see the end of tower-houses as the result of new forms of political authority, closely linked to government office and government tastes that were increasingly English (Johnson discusses diffusionism, graciously without citing my explanation of fashion spreading from London). Bailey explains the end of Bulgarian rebuilding of houses on top of the foundations of previous houses because it was no longer essential to prove rights of occupation and to control land; power had passed to those who controlled the production and trade of gold and other valuables. Chapman likewise relates the fall and rise or rise and fall of all sorts of IHS, BUB, gamma, and alpha analyses to the historical momentum of ever-increasing scale of successes and failures in the swings of lineage fortunes. There is clearly some 'processual' thinking underlying all these historical scenarios that are used to explain changes.

Structuration theory has never really broken free of its dependence on traditional historical explanations of social change. The only attempt has been the 'unintended consequences' theory. Although constrained by historical traditions and physical conditions, human actors act knowingly, with

purpose and intent, and almost always with an eye on improving their lot
('their' can be understood as any sort of factional interest). However,
because everyone is busy doing their own thing the result is always unexpected and almost invariably not what anyone wanted at all.

Here I am beginning to digress, but not nearly enough to give a real taste
of the muddle that is archaeological theory in Britain today. If I were to in-
sist we pursued structures to rupture, or that movement through a building
was like a striptease, I would be borrowing the inordinately pretentious
metaphors of Derrida and Barthes. This is the stage that present-day British
archaeological theory has reached: *philosophes français*, whose (apologies to
Mensonge) intellectualism is impressive but whose theoretical realism – the
author is dead; the reader creates the text; and Barthes will be autograph-
ing copies of his latest book at FNAC – never threatens to escape the cereb-
ral artifices of the Sorbonne or a good French bourgeois post-prandial
dinner table.

Architecture, it appears, cannot create its own social theory. A social
archaeology of houses adopts or follows the mainstream schools of social
theory. Few are likely to pick up Ricoeur, Derrida, Barthes, and Lacan and
fuse their theories into an analysis of domestic structures. The only possible exception is that deconstruction and post-deconstruction have fuelled
one aspect of social theory that has been around for a least as long as
people accepted that society was built on conflict and antagonisms (thus it
has been slowly emerging and battling with the systems theories or processualism of the New Archaeology). That aspect is so utterly prosaic that it
is almost painful for anyone to have to admit that it has been largely overlooked or undervalued; it is that meaning is not constant, it changes
through time, according to context, and with different perceivers: the text
is created by the reader.

Johnson notes at the end of his chapter that at the 'local, individual level
the meanings of "old houses" vary along lines of age, gender, and class',
and they carry 'diverse and often apparently contradictory social messages.'
Richards notes in passing that the meaning of houses depends on whether
they are seen from the inside or outside, here following Henrietta Moore.
It is Bailey, however, that takes this line to its fullest extent. He stresses that
meaning changes with seasons, activities, and time of day – in the morning
houses issue forth their occupants, in the evening receive them back again
– and with the age, gender, and social position of the perceivers.

This range and variety of meanings is something the social archaeology
of houses will have to explore more in the future. Most of the contributors
here ignore the phenomenon. Thus I make no mention of the views of
women or poor tenant farmers; the conception of tower-house imagery
held by the Church or children is left untouched. I could try to vindicate
myself by saying that I limited my discussion of tower-house meaning and
ideology to that related to forms of political authority because it was a

change that I believe broke tower-houses as a form of acceptable architecture. However, I have more probably taken the same approach to cosmology as Richards and most other anthropologists, assuming that one complex world view is shared by all. The cosmological interpretation of Richards and Hingley almost rest on the premise that there is largely a single coherent meaning or system of meanings.

It is surprising enough that the authors of these chapters have managed to use their chosen social theory so well, to have asked them to improve on the weaknesses inherent in any of those theories would have been quite unreasonable. If Lévi-Strauss himself left problems in structuralist theory, it is not for Richards to sort them out while digging up Neolithic houses in Orkney. Much of 'theoretical archaeology' written today is simply long-winded sociology or, worse, French philosophy with a feeble archaeological example tacked on at the end. On occasion that example undermines all that the author has said, for the interpretation falls short of the sophistication we were led to believe was forthcoming. The chapters in this book grapple first and foremost with archaeological problems. The social theory used was chosen because it inspired the writers in their study of houses and because they were enthusiastic about social archaeology.

Bibliography

Allsopp, Bruce 1977. *A Modern Theory of Architecture*. Routledge (London).

Bourdieu, Pierre 1973. 'The Berber house' in Mary Douglas (ed.) *Rules and Meanings*, 98-110. Penguin (Harmondsworth).

Bourdieu, Pierre 1977. *Outline of a Theory of Practice*. Cambridge University Press (Cambridge).

Doxtater, Dennis 1990. 'Socio-political change and symbolic space in Norwegian farm culture after the Reformation' in Turan (ed.), 183-218.

Duncan, J. (ed.) 1981. *Housing and Identity: cross-cultural perspectives*. Croomhelm (London).

Evans, Robin 1971. 'The rights of retreat and the rights of exclusion: notes toward the definition of wall' *Architectural Design* 41, 335-9.

Foster, Sally 1989. 'Analysis of spatial patterns in buildings (access analysis) as an insight into social structure: examples from the Scottish Iron Age' *Antiquity* 63, 40-50.

Glassie, Henry 1975. *Folk Housing in Middle Virginia: a structural analysis of historic artifacts*. University of Tennessee Press (Knoxville).

Graves, C. Pamela 1989. 'Social space in the English medieval parish church' *Economy and Society* 18, 297-322.

Hillier, Bob and Julienne Hanson 1984. *The Social Logic of Space*. Cambridge University Press (Cambridge).

Lawrence, Roderick J. 1990. 'Learning from colonial houses and lifestyles' in Turan (ed.), 219-257.

Leone, Mark 1984. 'Interpreting ideology in historical archaeology: the William Paca garden in Annapolis, Maryland' in D. Miller and C. Tilley (eds.) *Ideology, Power and Prehistory*. Cambridge University Press (Cambridge).

Rapoport, Amos 1969. *House Form and Culture*. Prentice-Hall (Englewood Cliffs, N.J.)

Stea, David 1990. 'The ten smudge pots of vernacular building: notes on explorations into architectural mythology' in Turan (ed.), 20-30.

Turan, Mete (ed.) 1990. *Vernacular Architecture*. Avebury (Aldershot).

Two

The Living House: Signifying Continuity

DOUGLASS W. BAILEY

Traditional archaeological analyses of spatial patterning have not examined the meaning of houses. In a social concept of the 'house', a single house is subject to a range of differing perspectives. The proposition that houses have many altern- ative meanings and usages in society is illustrated by tracing one such altern- ative perception of houses in a settlement from Bulgaria in the fourth millen- nium bc. The example presented is the tell Ovčarovo, a Chalcolithic settlement from the north-eastern part of the country. At Ovčarovo, the repetition of house floor-plans and the display of house-shaped artefacts were used to signify the con- tinuity of occupation through successive horizons of habitation.

Introduction

To write a social archaeology of the house is to write, and read, of many things. An archaeology of houses is an archaeology of space, of artefacts, and of people. Studies identifying, describing, mapping, and assigning function to the built environment were popular in the archaeologies of the 1970s and 1980s. I contend that a large portion of this research avoided an important direction of enquiry. Traditional spatial analyses failed to note the archaeological potential for a plurality of meanings of spatial organisa- tion. Although traditional lines of research have produced tools useful for the measurement of the physical dimensions of the built environment, they have failed to inform upon the social reality of the house.

I do not intend to present a review of the academic history of the study of artefact distributions or spatial unit analysis. However, in approaching the questions posed in a social archaeology of the house, it is useful to con-

sider in which direction recent work on the archaeology of space has
headed. Once these traditions have been illustrated, I shall redirect the
enquiry towards a more realistic understanding of the house as encountered in a social archaeology. I shall then present one example of how a
social archaeology would profit by considering houses as living participants
in prehistoric social action.

Spatial definition: mapping units

The methodologies developed to identify and map the relationship of
spatial units have enjoyed popular success in recent archaeological research
(e.g. FOSTER 1989; BOAST AND YIANNOULI 1986). With the advice and tools
of the architect, archaeologists have learned to define and identify spatial
cells in the material record. Maps are drawn, diagrams are constructed.
The sequences of cellular articulation and disarticulation are used to construct modern knowledges of the ancient built environment. Buildings are
thus defined in terms of their component cells. A closed space is taken to
equal a cell; the connection of one cell with another is measured in terms
of continuity and separation. Thus cellular mapping provides an explicit
method of quantifying spatial patterning.

Most influential of the cell mapping techniques have been the syntax and
grammar methodologies of Bill Hillier and Julienne Hanson (HILLIER AND
HANSON 1984; HILLIER et al. 1976; HILLIER et al. 1987; see also STINY AND
MITCHELL 1978; STINY 1980). The cell syntax and grammar approaches
have become popular tools in the social archaeologist's workshop. By mapping cells of space and quantifying their interrelationships, measures of
access, depth, or of spatial permeability are calculated and used to nourish
interpretations of the social meaning of space. Some houses can be defined
as defensive, deep, and out of bounds to the non-local public; others are
open, permeable, and public. This approach's emphasis on the social, its
methodological simplicity, and the minimal amount of information which
it requires, makes it attractive to the archaeologist.

The title of Hillier and Hanson's work, *The Social Logic of Space*, pro-
claims their main directive: that spatial organisation has a social logic. A
method of establishing and recovering the relationship of one space to
another is a significant advance in archaeological science. However, one
should not overlook the limitations of applying the cell-syntax methodology. From the raw material of two-dimensional floor-plans, space syntaxes
and grammars forge their results on an anvil of statistical evaluations. Critical suspicion is warranted where such methodologies are applied as singu-
lar cases of evidence in support of social conclusions. A space syntax is a
single piece of evidence, just as a pattern of artefact distributions is but one
of many other archaeological clues which must be studied in an assessment
of the built environment. With Hillier and Hanson (and their method as
applied in archaeology) the contention is that space has a single logic: in

this case a social one which is defined in terms of permeability, access, and the depth of spatial architecture. The application of space syntaxes, however, is most successful when it is combined with other methods and categories of information.

A positive component of the space syntax and grammar approaches is the emphasis which they place on the social importance of spatial organisation. Space is socially constructed; its description and analysis inform and determine human activity and belief. While a great deal of attention has been paid to this aspect of Hillier and Hanson's work, specifically in attempts to practise social archaeology, it must be remembered that attempts to connect the spatial to the social have formed a substantial and explicit part of archaeological and other social scientific research goals over the last thirty years.

Artefacts, activities, and function

The most mature tradition of the spatial definition focused on artefact distributions and associations (WHALLON 1973; 1974; 1984; HIETALA 1984a; NARELL 1962; BINFORD 1981a; 1981b; SPETH AND JOHNSON 1976; CLIFF *et al.* 1975; CARR 1984a; 1984b). These studies identify distributions and associations of artefacts as coherent groups of material culture reflecting the loci of human activity. Thus, associated artefact patterns are taken to identify areas of particular human activities. The patterns are verified by any of a number of statistical methods (e.g. nearest-neighbour; multivariate analysis; non-parametric testing; constrained and unconstrained cluster; dimensional analysis of variance; k-means distributions; contour-map grid-squares). In this sense spatially defined activity areas can be defined as houses, as workshops, as seasonal camps, or as other functionally defined spatial evidence of human activity. The artefacts chosen to identify different spaces suggest functional meaning to the interpreter of the place: flint debitage and tool blanks equal workshops or hunting camps; hearths and bone debris equal kitchens; anthropomorphic figurines equal sanctuaries and temples; large covered pots indicate storage rooms.

An important prerequisite for the correlation of spatial trends (defined by artefact distributions) with social relevance (for the occupation and use of that space) is the definition of space being investigated (e.g. houses, workshops, markets, temples, villages, among other things). In archaeological terms, therefore, the distribution of particular classes of artefacts defines space and suggests interpretations of that space. In many cases micro-level artefact distributions may be the only available evidence of spatial definition and use. Such is the case at temporary loci of activities (e.g. hunting camps) in earlier prehistory or other times when permanent buildings were not used or have not survived. In most other cases, however, artefacts are grouped by their inclusion in, or exclusion from, built structures.

The analysis of distributions of artefacts and spatial units has dominated archaeological concern over the *definition* of areas of space. Spatial relationships of rooms, houses, and villages are quantifiable and calculable, and thus they assume authoritative status, in the same manner as artefact distributions are defined and consecrated through statistical formulations. The difference between explaining the patterning of artefacts and explaining the patterns of spatial cells is slight. In both attempts similar assumptions of the relationship between spatial pattern and social behaviour are made. In the case of artefactually defined spaces, function is assumed and assigned to types and classes of artefacts. Thus the presence of stereotypic artefacts identifies the function of the space within which they are found. Thus, loomweights designate textile production and hearths identify kitchens. In the spatial-cell tradition the relationship of one cell to another, or group of cells, is identified and assigned a meaning by its interpreter: closed deep space is private, open shallow space public.

I contend that while these approaches to understanding the social meaning of space in prehistory have provided valuable tools with which spatial patterning may be addressed, they do little to inform us of the social meaning of the house.

The definition and meaning of houses

To recover the meaning of houses from the archaeological record, it is necessary to assess the terminology in use and, where appropriate, explicitly redefine the concepts to be used. One must ask therefore, what is the value of the term 'house' for the social archaeologist? One answer to this question is found in a consideration of its etymological definition.

The dictionary reveals that a house may be 'a building for human habitation; especially a building that is the ordinary dwelling place of a family'; or 'a building for human occupation, for some purpose other than that of an ordinary dwelling' (e.g. an almshouse, an ale house); or 'a place of worship'; or 'a building for the entertainment of the public generally; in a tavern; ale-house, or public house'; or 'a building for the keeping of cattle, birds, plants, goods, etc.' (e.g. cow-house; greenhouse; hen-house); or 'the place or abode of a religious fraternity; a religious house'; or 'a college or a university' (e.g. Peterhouse); or 'a boarding house attached to and forming a portion of a public school'; or 'a building in which a legislative or deliberative assembly meets' (e.g. Houses of Parliament or Representatives); or 'a place of business; business establishment or firm' (e.g House of Fraser); or 'a theatre' (e.g. a playhouse); or 'the audience at a theatre'; or 'the habitation of any animal; a den; a burrow; nest; the shell of a snail, tortoise; in which the animal lives or into which it returns'; or 'one-twelfth part of the heavens' (e.g. the houses of Aquarius).

Etymological definition provides a range of different perspectives on the generic term 'house'. 'House' denotes a place of worship, eating, drinking, dwelling, entertainment, farming, education, legislation, economic activity, or astral observation. Indeed the presence of numerous variations on the definition of the word inspires one contention of my argument: that any one thing, be it word, artefact, or component of the built environment, has a multitude of meanings dependent on social and material context.

In these definitions one finds a common theme which is useful in our search for an archaeologically applicable definition. The etymological background of 'house' focuses on the continuity of action over time in one location. Thus a house is a building which serves as 'the ordinary dwelling place of a family'. The family includes 'ancestors and dependants; a lineage, or a race; especially one having continuity of residence'. Similarly, to dwell is 'to abide or continue for a time, in a place, state, or condition; to remain as in a permanent residence, to reside; to occupy as a place of residence; to inhabit'. A dwelling is 'a continuous, especially habitual, residence'. To reside is 'to dwell permanently or for a considerable time, to have one's settled or usual abode, to live in or at a particular place; to remain or continue in a certain place or position'. Abode denotes 'the action of waiting; delay; a temporary remaining; a stay; a habitual residence or dwelling'. Settlement is 'the placing of persons or things in a fixed or permanent position'. To inhabit is 'to dwell in, occupy as an abode; to live permanently or habitually in, to reside in'.

The condition of permanent or repeated attendance or living is also an important part of the archaeological conception of 'house'. House and related concepts (domestic, dwelling, abode, habitation) share a concern with the location of human action not only in space but, equally importantly, in time.

For the social archaeologist, therefore, the concept 'house' has two important aspects. The first of these is that its meaning is contextually dependent. The meaning of the word 'house', and I suggest the interpretation of its archaeological correlate, is dependent on a particular context. The context, whether of social, material or other parameters, defines the meaning of a house. Thus the context is social in that it is what the occupants of a house perceive their house to be. The context is material in that it is what the house contains, what it is constructed from, how it is ordered in three dimensions and how that ordering relates to other houses.

The second important aspect of the concept 'house' is the continuity and repetition of action. To define the house outside the limits of three-dimensional space is to build a better understanding of the meaning of 'house'. To move beyond the third dimension is to confront the dimension of time. Much of spatial archaeology thrives on sub-units, grammatical formulations, and statistical calculations and thereby drives towards concrete definitions of space: measurements of depth and axiality (HILLIER AND HANSON 1984); built area to unbuilt area (CHAPMAN this volume); or door width and distance from door to hearth (FLETCHER 1984). Thus, while

traditional spatial archaeologies have focused on horizontal displacement
and description (cell mapping, depth studies, etc.), I suggest that a social
archaeology of the house must also consider space as a vertical construct.
By this I mean that the repetition and variation of spatial morphology over
time involves the vertical perspective. In this sense, a house is not a 'house'
if its identified usage cannot be attested through a succession of occupa-
tions and actions. It is this consideration of the element of time upon
which I wish to expand in the example presented below of fifth millennium
Bulgarian houses.

The general conception of 'house' (i.e. repeated action in one location in
a social context) which I have produced may appear vague and rather
loose. This may be especially the case when compared to the checklist definitions which have populated traditional archaeology and anthropology
until recently (e.g. civilisation, modern society, primitive cultures). In order
to move the debate beyond previous researchers' construction of methodologies for recognising and patterning space (and into realms where meaning can be recovered), I have chosen not to provide a step-by-step checklist
definition. Equally I do not wish to tie the archaeological conception of
'house' to predetermined and culturally limited definitions. Thus, although
I have drawn on modern western etymological dimensions of the word
'house', I have used these concepts to produce a definition dependent on
situation-specific contexts, both social and material.

I contend therefore that a productive manner of appreciating the social
archaeology of space, and more specifically of houses, does not start from a
single definition. The definition of a house, as well as the meaning of that
house, exists in many different dimensions. This is the case whether the
definition is archaeological (e.g. types and locations of tools, hearths, and
pots or closed cells) or etymological ('the living place of the family'). A
social definition, therefore, must begin by acknowledging that a single
space has a multitude of meanings to the people who create, use, abandon,
and study it.

Do not misunderstand. To call for a multiplicity of meanings for the built
environment is not to drift into hyper-relativism where anything goes and
where any meaning or definition can be justified. Contexts are the referents which anchor each separate social meaning of a house to reality.

Systems of activities and systems of settings

Amos Rapoport has introduced a related line of reasoning to the archaeological debate (RAPOPORT 1988; 1990). Rapoport's most recent contribution (1990) is a summary and update of his research of the past twenty
years in the field of environment-behaviour. The social archaeologist has
much to learn from Rapoport's work. In his article 'Systems of activities
and systems of settings', Rapoport helps to debunk the myth that built
space binds and contains single social meanings. To handle the built

environment, Rapoport uses the term 'setting' instead of house or architecture. A setting is 'a milieu which defines a situation, reminds the occupants of the appropriate rules and hence of the ongoing behaviour appropriate to the situation defined by the setting. . . . The setting frequently provides the appropriate props for these behaviours and activities' (RAPOPORT 1990, 12; see also RAPOPORT 1979; 1982; 1988).

Of particular relevance to the multiplicity of meanings for a house is Rapoport's contention that it is inaccurate to consider a 'setting' or an 'activity' as a single unit. Rather, one must think in terms of systems of activities occurring in systems of settings. Thus a specific building is linked through the activity systems of its occupants to a social context which exists beyond the limitations of its own physical boundaries. In this way, Rapoport introduces the multiplicity and changeability of meaning of the built environment.

Rapoport's environment-behaviour work is relatively new to archaeology despite its own disciplinary maturity. More frequently, in archaeological analysis of the house, citations are made of Pierre Bourdieu's writings on the Kabyle House (BOURDIEU 1962; 1973; 1977). As Bourdieu has raised some of the issues I am presenting here, it is useful to consider his work briefly. Bourdieu considers the house, like all spatial forms, to be a mnemonic aid for its occupants. Thus the relational form of house space provides a durable medium for imposing schemes of social organisation on human perceptions. Furthermore, the organisation of space not only reflects, but also generates, social structures and practices. Bourdieu details the house as the principal locus where generative social schemes are objectified: the Kabyle house is an example of the construction of social meaning within a built structure. The majority of Bourdieu's analysis rests on the author's claims of structural oppositions between interior areas of the house and their social, biological, or natural referents (e.g. nocturnal and dark = female; day and light = male).

I do not wish to draw attention to Bourdieu's use of the antagonistic principles which he sees embedded in the house. Rather, I wish to borrow from the Kabyle House analysis Bourdieu's insistence that for any one house-unit there exists a variety of perceptions. Just as Bourdieu relates a male:female perspective of the house, so also does he note the internal:external perspective. The house exists at one level of meaning when considered from one side of its threshold, another when considered from the opposite side.

While it may be argued that Bourdieu's selection of antagonistic principles are simplistic and structuralist reductions, a social archaeology of houses benefits from two conditions of his work. The first of these is the belief that one house exists on numerous levels of perception and thus may have a number of different meanings. The acceptance of multiple meanings for a single house broadens the scope for a social archaeology of the house. Thus, for example, it is acceptable to consider houses both in functional terms, as adaptations to environmental extremes, and in social terms as tokens in strategies of social competition. Just as one may argue that the origin of permanent habitation in the European Neolithic was an adaptation of people to climatic changes of environment which permitted settled agriculture, so also is it legitimate for the social archaeologist to relate the conspicuousness of house construction, occupation, and ownership to displays of wealth and resource control. It is a question of replacing mono-functional explanations of houses with multi-functional explanations.

The second useful contribution made by Bourdieu to the social archaeology of houses is the contention that the relationship between spatial organisation and social structure is discursive. That is to say, the built environment is as much an active generator of social behaviour as it is a reflection of it. The literature on the discursive nature of material culture, which includes the built environment, is well presented in other sources and need not delay us here (see, for example, SHANKS AND TILLEY 1987, MOORE 1982; 1986, etc.)

Thus, a satisfactory social archaeology of the house begins with the assumption that houses (like all social constructs in the past or present) are definable in numerous ways, from an equally numerous range of perspectives, in many different social and material contexts. In addition, houses not only *reflect* social structure and activity; they play an equal role in *determining* that structure and activity.

Multiple meanings of houses: different perspectives

My contention is that the meaning of a house is multi-dimensional and subject to repeated reorientations. The house therefore exists simultaneously within the dimensions of time, space, possession, wealth, protection, craftsmanship, access, permeability, weather patterns, technological ability, and so forth. Indeed it may prove impossible to exhaust the inventory of levels of perception. Each methodology, each society, and each individual will value the house differently by implementing different standards of measurement. Meanings of houses shift within temporal, spatial, and social parameters.

As an example of the multiplicity of house meanings, consider a house defined in terms of production and consumption. Thus, a house could be interpreted as the centre of food production, containing the hearth, the grinding stone, and other kitchen equipment as well as being the locus for biological production through physical acts of conception, gestation, and birth. Similarly it is possible to consider the house as a centre of consumption. The food is processed, prepared, eaten, and digested. Wood and other fuels are consumed at the hearth and in the oven; deceased inhabitants are interred beneath the floor.

On yet another level, the same house may be seen in terms of its location in seasonal events: as a centre for the preparation of seeds for sowing, for the repair and preparation of tools for reaping and processing agricultural produce, and as a place of storage for the processed crop. In the same context the house may serve as a focus for the birthing, milking, shearing, or breeding of animals.

Or one may alter the meaning by shifting, not the activities performed in the space, but the scale of time over which activities are performed. While a longer time-scale reveals production and consumption activities of farming and stockbreeding in a seasonal time-frame, other perspectives are highlighted by the framework of a single day. In the morning the house is a generator, issuing its occupants into the day's activities. In the afternoon it serves as a centre for domestic chores. In the evening it is a receptacle offering shelter for the night.

Rapoport has written of the unavoidable temporal component of space. This involves 'the differential sequencing of activities in time as well as in space, their tempos (numbers of activities over unit time) and rhythms (the periodicity of activities related to different cycles: life time, animal, seasonal, profane time, sacred time, festivals, work day vs. weekend, day and night etc.)' (RAPOPORT 1990, 15).

The perspectives on which I have based these examples are limited to perspectives on the internal elements of a house. An equally diverse selection of perceptions of the reality of a house can be generated from an external perspective (cf. Bourdieu and the threshold of the Kabyle house). In this way, one house may be considered in relation to a neighbouring house, or to the collectivity of houses within a neighbourhood, village, or region, or to each house in a distant village. In Rapoport's scheme, activities occur not in architecture but in 'systems of settings which include outdoor area, settlements and beyond – the whole cultural landscape' (RAPOPORT 1990, 15).

The existence of not only a multitude of meanings but also of types of boundaries to a house presents problems for the 'objective' methods developed to analyse houses in the archaeological record. If, as I argue, the relationship between rooms of one house to those of another or of houses to houses is not static but shifting, then how do existing methodologies for identifying and quantifying units of space handle the resulting fluctuations in meaning? I suggest that they do not handle it very well at all. [1]

---

[1] There exists considerable debate (e.g. between Kent and Adams) over the accuracy of limiting specific spaces to specific meanings (KENT 1984; 1990a; ADAMS 1987). In a review of Susan Kent's book, *Analyzing Activity Areas*, William Adams has quite correctly objected to Kent's willingness to define rooms in modern Euro-American houses (bedroom, kitchen, closet, bathroom, dining room, family room or den) in terms of single functions. Adams raises the point that a typical bedroom is used as a place 'to sleep, rest, get well, die, have sex, procreate, watch TV, read, nurse babies, wrap presents, lay coats', etc. (ADAMS 1987). Thus for Adams, and for the social archaeologist, it is important to recognise that meanings of rooms and houses shift with different users and perceivers and at different times.

Active material culture and durable artefacts

The determination of the meaning of a house in a social archaeology therefore is a multi-dimensional task: it is social, it is material, it is spatial, and it
is temporal. The goal for the archaeologist is to broaden one's perspective
on what a house meant as it was built, used, and abandoned in the past.
Previous research has presented the house as a fixed context for activity
and perception: the house is seen as a centre for production; as a shelter;
as a reflection of social structure; or as a goal of economic desires. As an
exercise in broadening our perspective, I shall present an analysis of housing from one settlement in Bulgaria during the fourth millennium bc. My
analysis suggests one useful perspective from which a social archaeology of
a house may be pursued.

I suggest that a profitable approach to houses begins by considering the
house as a living entity. In this way the house becomes active and mobile.
Certainly Bourdieu (1977), Hillier and Hanson (1984), Moore (1982; 1986),
and others have argued for an active role for the house in social constitutions of archaeological reality. The reflexive nature of material culture has
been a popular topic amongst theoretical archaeologists of the 1980s. It
appears to me, however, that this activeness has not been employed in the
archaeological perception of the house.

To inject some life into the apparently lifeless, passive, and material
requires the acknowledgement of two assumptions. First is the contention
that material culture plays an active role in the social construction of reality
(cf. HODDER 1982). Thus material culture is subject as well as object (cf.
SHANKS AND TILLEY 1987). It both creates, is created by, influences, and is
influenced by, the constitutions of social perception. As Bourdieu would
agree, the house is an active component of the material culture world.

The second assumption required in the enlivening of the house is that
the physical nature of material culture (especially terracotta and stone) in-
vests certain artefacts with the power to function successfully as determin-
ants of social behaviour and perception. Houses are constructed from a
range of durable physical materials. They are built of permanent (stone) or
semi-permanent (wattle and daub, mud-brick, pisé) materials; they occupy
fixed locations in space.

To best consider a house as living, I suggest that the actions of a house
are best read in terms of a biography. By this I mean that the house is an
active participant in society just as a human member of society is. The
house plays a variety of roles in the creation and maintenance of social
reality. The house therefore is to be addressed as an entity which lives
within a variety of social and material contexts. Thus, one may speak of the
life-cycle of a house: a house is born, it lives, it dies, it is buried or
cremated, and its spirit is remembered after its death. To illustrate the concept of a living house, let us consider an example from a Chalcolithic

settlement tell from north-east Bulgaria.

The living house in the Bulgarian Chalcolithic

The Bulgarian Chalcolithic has been relatively well studied both by Bulgarian (TODOROVA 1978; 1982; 1986) and foreign archaeologists (e.g. RENFREW 1969; 1986; CHAPMAN 1983; SHERRATT 1983) In broadest chronological terms it represents the fourth millennium BC. Popularity for investigating the remains from this period of eastern Bulgaria was assured by the publicity of the sensational discoveries of large quantities of gold at the Varna cemetery on the Black Sea coast (IVANOV 1983; CHAPMAN this volume; FOL AND LICHARDUS 1988; KATINCHAROV AND MOHEN 1989). Of equal attraction for a social archaeologist are the numerous settlement tells distributed across the country. From the excavation of these tells an increasingly accurate picture is being produced of the social reality of the Bulgarian Chalcolithic.

Professor-Doctor Henrietta Todorova of the Archaeological Institute of the Bulgarian Academy of Sciences has excavated several Chalcolithic tells in the north-eastern region of the country (Golyamo Delcevo, Polyanitsa, Ovčarovo). I shall use the results of her excavation at Ovčarovo as a basis for my investigations of the living house. The site of Ovčarovo is situated in the northern foothills of the Stara Plannina mountains. To the south of these mountains lie the better known sites of Karanovo and Azmak; 100 kilometers to the east is the coast of the Black Sea and the cemetery at Varna. Todorova excavated Ovčarovo *in toto* in 1971-74 (TODOROVA *et al.* 1983).

Before excavation Ovčarovo stood 4.5 metres high and consisted of thirteen vertically successive habitation horizons. Todorova defined the beginning of each horizon with the construction of a new level of houses. From fifteen radiocarbon dates we know that the tell was occupied for a period of at least 570 years.[2]

During the six centuries when the tell was occupied, at only one time were two succeeding horizons separated by an archaeologically detectable hiatus. This occurred between the tenth and eleventh horizons. The consequences of this break in occupation will be discussed in more detail below. This is not to say, however, that a series of local seasonal relocations and abandonments did not take place. As Todorova has noted, the site was located in a flood plain and thus was subject to low-scale seasonal flooding. In addition, there is geomorphological evidence that more substantial floods occurred at a more sporadic rate. Todorova reports that flooding occurs in these places in modern times every two to three years if not more

---

[2] Bln 1357 3470 ± 60; Bln 1358 3575 ± 60; Bln 1359 3690 ± 60; Bln 1360 3735 ± 60; Bln 1361 3775 ± 60; Bln 1545 3895 ± 40; Bln 1363 3670 ± 60; Bln 1362 3855 ± 60; Bln 1364 3666 ± 60; Bln 1365 3715 ± 60; Bln 1366 3795 ± 60; Bln 1367 3825 ± 60; Bln 1493 3990 ± 80; Bln 1368 3845 ± 60; Bln 1546 4040 ± 80.

frequently; several times excavations at the related site of Golyamo Delčevo
had to be delayed for this reason (TODOROVA *et al.* 1975, 6). Sherratt has
noted similar situations in Hungary (SHERRATT 1982, 313). The response to
the floods was the construction of 'emplekton' walls on the south-eastern
sides of the tell at Ovčarovo as well as at other tells in the region
(Polyanitsa, Radingrad, Targovište). While it has been argued that these
banks and ditches served a defensive function, it is more probable that they
were employed to divert and drain flood water away from the settlements
and into nearby rivers: in the case of Ovčarovo, the Oteki River. Indeed,
Sherratt has suggested that the construction of tells be considered as part
of flood defences (SHERRATT 1972, 522). The 'emplekton' dykes protected
the settlement against disruption caused by floods of low intensity. I
suggest however that floods of a more severe nature caused the occupants
to temporarily abandon the site.

While conclusive evidence for the movement of peoples to and from
Ovčarovo is difficult to recover, I contend that the patterns of house redecoration suggest patterns of abandonment and reoccupation. It is clear
that some if not all of the houses at Ovčarovo were redecorated on a regular basis. Evidence of redecoration is found in the multiple layers of
coloured plaster from the interiors of certain houses. In one house from
horizon IV the walls, floor, and oven had forty-seven layers of yellow, black,
red, pink, and white clay and an oven in the house had been rebuilt three
times (TODOROVA 1982, 121; TODOROVA *et al.* 1983, 45). The cycle of redecoration can be compared with calculations for the duration of this horizon (eighty-two years) and it is probable that replastering took place every
other year.[3] I suggest that redecoration was a maintenance activity performed at times of reoccupation from the time of a house's birth until its
destruction, abandonment, or rebuilding.

The evidence of seasonal floods, as well as of more severe episodes of
flooding, combine with the patterns of house redecoration to suggest that
Ovčarovo experienced short periods of site vacancy. Thus these series of
inescapable abandonments and reoccupations broke the continuity of settlement at Ovčarovo. Therefore there arose a need for a mechanism to ensure settlement continuity during these breaks in occupation. Continuity
had to be legitimated in the short term (e.g. between seasonal relocations)
as well as in the long term (e.g. between the rebuilding of subsequent hori-

---

[3] I have estimated the duration of each horizon using the radiocarbon dates. These estimations
are most accurate for those horizons from which multiple radiocarbon dates were taken, less
accurate for those horizons where only one date was produced, and least accurate for those
horizons with no dates. For the horizons with multiple dates, the difference between the earliest
and latest dates with the horizon equals the duration. At the crudest level (that is for the
horizons without dates: I, II, IV, V, XIII) therefore, I have calculated the duration as the
difference between the latest carbon date from the previous horizon and the earliest date from
the succeeding horizon. Thus for horizon IV, the duration of habitation is approximately eighty-
two years.

zons). As I shall argue below, the implementation of strategies based on house-shaped or, as I shall term it, tectomorphic imagery answered the threats to continuity created by seasonal or longer-term abandonments. [4]

Table 2.1 Longevity of houses, measured in the number of single, double, triple, and quadruple generation houses in each horizon at Ovčarovo.

| Horizon | Single | Longevity of Houses on Generations | | | Total |
		Double	Triple	Quadruple	
I	7	0	0	0	7
II	8	2	0	0	10
III	9	1	0	0	10
IV	7	2	0	0	9
V	9	0	0	0	0
VI	10	1	0	0	11
VII	13	0	0	0	13
VIII	6	3	0	0	9
IX	4	4	3	0	11
X	5	1	1	2	9
XI	7	0	0	0	7
XII	7	0	0	0	0
XIII	N/D	N/D	N/D	N/D	N/D

Note N/D: Horizon XIII had been disturbed by ploughing and thus no information regarding architectural organisation was available.

The houses at Ovčarovo

From twelve levels of settlement rebuilding at Ovčarovo Todorova recovered the remains of 113 houses (TODOROVA 1982, 119-43; TODOROVA *et al.* 1983, 27-42, Plates 13, 15, 17, 19-23, 26, 29-31). In an attempt to understand the biography of these houses, I traced the 'life-spans' of each house through the successive horizons. Some houses were short-lived, not surviving the horizons into which they were born (e.g. all the houses from horizons V and XI; see Figures 2.6 and 2.12). Indeed, this was the case with the majority of houses (see Table 2.1). Other houses were rebuilt through a series of successive horizons (three houses from horizon VII survived into horizon VIII; four houses from horizon VIII into IX; four houses from horizon IX into X). I based the determination of the survival of a house from one horizon to the next in the following manner. I compared the orientation and layout of house floor-plans in one horizon with the orientation and layout of floor-plans in the succeeding horizon (Figure 2.1). If the floor-plan of the preceding house was repeated at a significant level (i.e.

---

[4] Tectomorphic meaning 'building-shaped' from the Greek 'tektone' for carpenter or builder. Tectonic refers to building or construction in general, especially in connection with architecture.

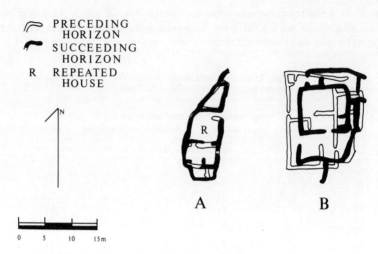

PRECEDING
HORIZON
SUCCEEDING
HORIZON
R   REPEATED
HOUSE

A   B

0   5   10   15m

Figure 2.1   Example of the identification of repeated houses from Ovčarovo.
A: repeated house; B: non-repeated house.

more than 75 per cent of walls in the preceding house were repeated in the succeeding house) then the succeeding house was termed a repeated house (see Figure 2.1a).[5] If on the other hand the floor-plans matched less than 75 per cent of their walls, then the house was considered an unrepeated house (Figure 2.1b). The results of these comparisons are listed in Table 2.1 and are illustrated in Figures 2.2–2.12.

Thus repeated houses are those which survived into the succeeding generation of buildings at Ovčarovo. While each house has an individual biography, each group of houses in use during particular horizons is a member in a generation of house ancestry. For example, in horizon I at Ovčarovo seven houses were built and in use and thus I would argue were born and lived in the first generation. Five of these houses did not survive the rebuilding into horizon II. The two that did survive into the second horizon thus are said to be second generation houses. Three new houses were born into the second generation at Ovčarovo, that is, were built in horizon II. Of the ten houses in horizon II one survived into the third generation in horizon III (see Figures 2.2–2.3). By noting the life span of each house within succeeding horizons, I identified those generations of houses which had high proportions of survivors from the previous generation. The frequency of houses of first, second, third, and fourth generation status is presented in Table 2.1 and the percentage of house repetitions from one horizon to the next is given in Table 2.2. For example horizon

---

[5] 75 per cent being the equivalent of three walls being repeated from a perfectly square house.

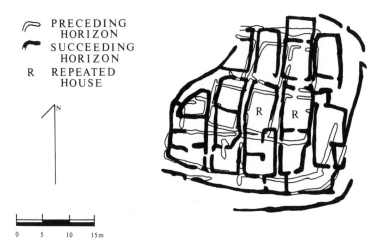

Figure 2.2 Superimposition of floor-plan from horizon II onto the floor-plan of horizon I from the settlement at Ovčarovo (after Todorova et al. 1983, plates 13 and 15).

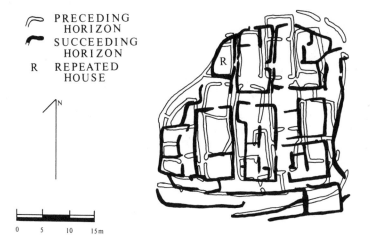

Figure 2.3 Superimposition of floor-plan from horizon III onto the floor-plan of horizon II from the settlement at Ovčarovo (after Todorova et al 1983, plates 15 and 17).

VIII, IX and X display high percentages of survival (33, 36, and 40 per cent respectively). In other generations of houses repetition of house floor-plans and thus percentage survival was considerably lower. For example, horizon III had one surviving house from the previous generation (thus 10 per

Table 2.2 Survival of houses at Ovčarovo in terms of repeated houses in each horizon and as a percentage of total houses in each horizon.

Horizon	Number of repeats from preceding horizon	Percentage of all houses in horizon
I	Not applicable	
II	2	20
III	1	10
IV	2	22
V	0	0
VI	1	9
VII	0	0
VIII	3	33
IX	4	36
X	4	40
XI	0	0
XII	0	0
XIII	N/D	N/D

Note N/D: Horizon XIII had been extensively disturbed by ploughing and thus no information regarding architectural organisation was recovered.

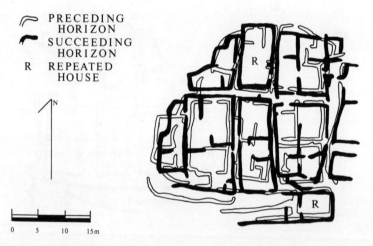

Figure 2.4 Superimposition of floor-plan from horizon IV onto the floor-plan of horizon III from the settlement at Ovčarovo (after Todorova et al. 1983, plates 17 and 19).

cent). Other horizons had no survivors at all: horizons V, VII, XI, and XII; thus 0 per cent).

I contend that repeating houses in successive horizons functioned to en-sure continuity of settlement. Continuity of occupation had come under

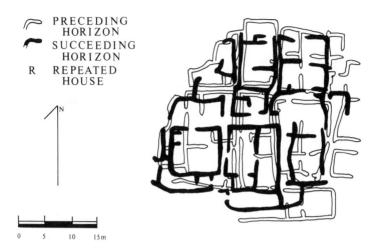

Figure 2.5 Superimposition of floor-plan from horizon V onto the floor-plan of horizon IV from the settlement at Ovčarovo (after Todorova et al. 1983, plates 19–20).

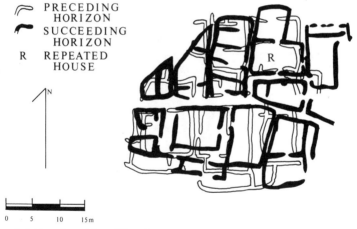

Figure 2.6 Superimposition of floor-plan from horizon VI onto the floor-plan of horizon V from the settlement at Ovčarovo (after Todorova et al. 1983, plates 20–1).

threat not only by breaks in occupation but also by increasing levels of competition for viable settlement space (SHERRATT 1972, 533). As Todorova has documented, it is during the later periods of the Chalcolithic, that the density of settlement increases (see Table 2.3; TODOROVA 1986, 85–9, table 32).

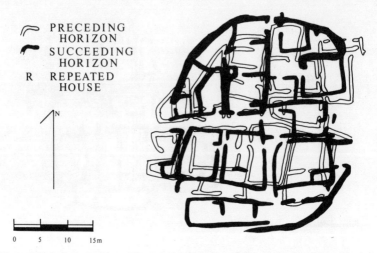

Figure 2.7 *Superimposition of floor-plan from horizon VII onto the floor-plan of horizon VI from the settlement at Ovčarovo (after Todorova et al. 1983, plates 21–2).*

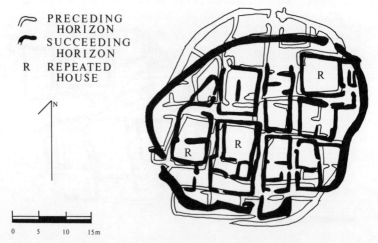

Figure 2.8 *Superimposition of floor-plan from horizon VIII onto the floor-plan of horizon VII from the settlement at Ovčarovo (after Todorova et al. 1983, plates 22–3).*

The period of significantly high percentages of house survival in horizons VIII through X is intriguing (Table 2.2; Figures 2.8–2.10). Why are house repetitions so common during these horizons and not in others? One part of the answer to this question is related to the increasing competition for settlement space. As detailed in Table 2.3 the number of settlements in the

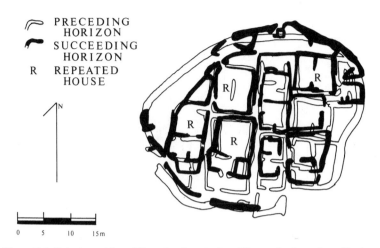

Figure 2.9 Superimposition of floor-plan from horizon IX onto the floor-plan of horizon VIII from the settlement at Ovčarovo (after Todorova et al. 1983, plates 23 and 26).

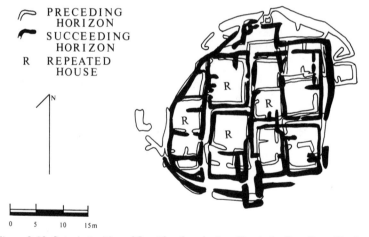

Figure 2.10 Superimposition of floor-plan from horizon X onto the floor-plan of horizon IX from the settlement at Ovčarovo (after Todorova et al. 1983, plates 26 and 29).

north-eastern region of the country increased dramatically from the middle Chalcolithic. As the number of sites increased, the number of settlers increased, so the density of settlement increased and the level of competition for land, as well as for other resources, intensified. Thus, during the earlier horizons at Ovčarovo, cycles of seasonal settlement relocation would

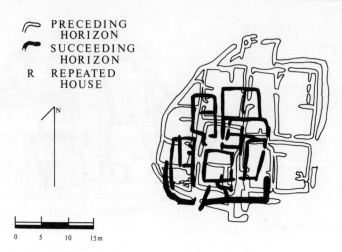

PRECEDING
HORIZON

SUCCEEDING
HORIZON

R   REPEATED
HOUSE

N

0   5   10   15m

Figure 2.11 Superimposition of floor-plan from horizon XI onto the floor-plan of horizon X from the settlement at Ovčarovo (after Todorova et al. 1983, plates 29–30).

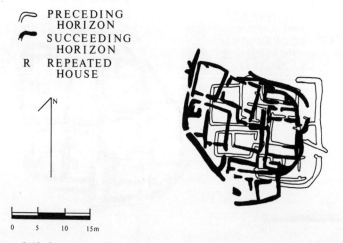

PRECEDING
HORIZON

SUCCEEDING
HORIZON

R   REPEATED
HOUSE

N

0   5   10   15m

Figure 2.12 Superimposition of floor-plan from horizon XII onto the floor-plan of horizon XI from the settlement at Ovčarovo (after Todorova et al. 1983, plates 30–1).

not have necessitated explicitly intense legitimation of settlement continuity. However, this is not to say that competition for settlement space (especially in terms of individual houses) did not occur.

House plan repetition was only one of a number of tools used to legitimate habitation and social continuity. The continuous creation of the tell it-

Table 2.3 Number of settlements occupied after Todorova's ceramic chronology. Numbers in brackets are percentages of regional total (after Todorova 1986, table 32).

Area	I	Early II	III[a]	Chalcolithic Middle I[b]	I[c]	Late II[d]	III	Total
North-east	6	9	5	19	14	15	12	80
	(8)	(11)	(6)	(23)	(18)	(19)	(15)	
North-west	7	6	8	3	1	6	8	39
	(18)	(15)	(20)	(8)	(3)	(15)	(21)	
Thrace	10	12	13	11	6	13	18	83
	(12)	(14)	(16)	(13)	(7)	(16)	(22)	
Total	23	27	26	33	21	34	38	202
	(11)	(13)	(13)	(16)	(10)	(17)	(19)	

Notes
a Ovčarovo horizons I-IV
b Ovčarovo horizons V-VII
c Ovčarovo horizons VIII-X
d Ovčarovo horizons XI-XIII

self, a visible landmark of occupation, would have served to suggest continuity of habitation to foreign visitors and warned off potential competitors from the right to occupy the site. I contend that an additional means of legitimating house continuity and personal rights was accomplished through the production and display of tectomorphic images, specifically miniature three-dimensional representations of houses (see Figure 2.13). I suggest that these tectomorphs were used to legitimate individual and group rights to reoccupation and overcome breaks in settlement continuity. Tectomorphs were used in this way to supplement the practice of house floor-plan repetition.

Tectomorphs at Ovčarovo

Todorova recovered ninety-eight tectomorphs during her excavations at Ovčarovo (Table 2.4). A more accurate frequency is calculated by weighting these gross totals against the size of each horizon to determine the frequencies of tectomorphs per 100 square metres (column 2 in Table 2.4). Next, by ranking the horizons by their tectomorph per 100 square metre score (column 3 in Table 2.4) and comparing these ranks with rankings calculated for all other classes of artefacts from Ovčarovo (column 5 in Table 2.4), a score of tectomorph rank difference was produced (column 6 in Table 2.4). The measure of rank difference reveals in which horizons abnormal frequencies of tectomorphs were produced. Thus in certain horizons (II-IV, XI-XIII) a smaller than expected number of tectomorphs were produced. In other horizons (I, VI–VIII) a larger than expected number were produced. In two horizons (V and X) the expected frequency was close or equal to that of the observed number.

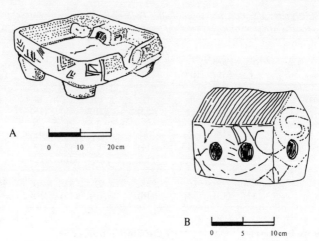

Figure 2.13 Miniature tectomorphic representations from north-eastern Bulgaria. A: Ovčarovo; B: Polyanitsa.

Table 2.4 Corrected frequency and ranking of tectomorphs.

	Tectomorphs			All artefacts[a]		
Horizon	Gross number	Per 100 sq. m.	Freq. rank[b]	Per 100 sq. m.	Freq. rank[c]	Rank difference[d]
I	3	.65	4th	3.46	10th	+6
II	2	.22	9th	6.02	5th	-4
III	3	.21	10th	4.34	8th	-2
IV	2	.18	11th	8.86	3rd	-8
V	54	5.02	1st	11.76	2nd	+1
VI	13	1.23	2nd	4.22	9th	+7
VII	9	.72	3rd	1.84	13th	+10
VIII	3	.33	8th	2.60	12th	+4
IX	4	.44	6th	2.64	11th	+5
X	3	.42	7th	5.18	7th	0
XI	2	.56	5th	15.02	1st	-4
XII	0	0.00	12.5th	6.46	4th	-8.5
XIII	0	0.00	12.5th	5.29	6th	-6.5

Notes

a Flint, stone, bone, antler, and complete pots.

b Frequency of tectomorphs per 100 sq. m. ranked from largest to smallest by horizon.

c Frequency of all artefacts per 100 sq. m. ranked from largest to smallest by horizon.

d Difference between ranking for all artefacts and ranking of tectomorphs. A positive value (+) indicates a horizon in which more tectomorphs were produced than would be expected in light of the frequencies of other artefacts. A negative value (-) indicates a horizon in which fewer tectomorphs were produced than would be expected.

I contend that in those horizons where traditions of settlement continuity were threatened, the need for an image representing stability and continuity inspired the production and display of miniature tectomorphs. Thus in horizon I the need to establish primary occupation rights was great and thus a relatively high number of tectomorphs were produced.

Once continuity had been established in horizon I, modest measures of tectomorph display and house repetition were employed in horizons II–IV. Horizon V had no surviving houses from the previous horizon yet had the largest number of tectomorphs (fifty-four). The number of tectomorphs is large only in gross terms. When considered in the context of the duration of this horizon and the large number of other artefacts produced during this horizon, the number is less surprising. Horizon V is the horizon at Ovčarovo with the longest duration and produced the second greatest number of artefacts (see column 4 in Table 2.4). I suggest that during this horizon a number of settlement relocations occurred. With each return to Ovčarovo, a new set of tectomorphs would have been produced. Horizons VI and VII combined an abundance of tectomorphic imagery (+7 and +10 in terms of rank difference) with an almost total absence of repeated houses (only one from horizon V into VI). As Todorova's survey showed (see Table 2.3) it is at this time, the middle Chalcolithic, that site density and competition for land increased dramatically. The abnormally high production of tectomorphs in these horizons is a response to these pressures.

Horizons VIII–IX saw both a large number of tectomorphs (+4 and +5 in rank difference) and the largest percentages of repeated houses (33, 36, and 40 per cent). In the final three horizons the only evidence of any strategy to legitimate continuity is the two tectomorphs from horizon XI; no houses were repeated in any of these last horizons. During occupation and reoccupation of horizons I through X a combination of strategies was employed to legitimate occupation and continuity of housing. I contend that the increase in the use of strategies to legitimate continuity in horizons VIII–X is a reflection of the increasing competition for arable and inhabitable land. The need to sustain occupation rights would have been highest during these horizons and thus the heavy use of both strategies of legitimation is to be expected.

However, as Table 2.5 confirms, neither strategy to legitimate continuity was practised in the final two periods of settlement at Ovčarovo (horizons XII and XIII). If competition for settlement space increased towards the end of the Chalcolithic, why do these final horizons exhibit no record of efforts to maintain continuity or ensure occupation? Indeed, in light of the absence of repeated houses in horizon XI and the low frequency of tectomorphic miniatures, I suggest that the strategies of continuity legitimation had failed by the end of horizon X. It is clear that neither strategy of legitimating continuity retained its effectiveness after the end of horizon XI.

The end of effectiveness for the continuity strategies is the product of

Table 2.5 Comparison of tectomorph frequency and house
repetition by horizon at Ovčarovo.

Horizon	Number of houses surviving from preceding horizon		Gross number of tectomorphs	Rank difference of tectomorphs
I	Not applicable		3	+6
II	2	(20%)	2	-4
III	1	(10%)	3	-2
IV	2	(22%)	2	-8
V	0	(0%)	54	+1
VI	1	(9%)	13	+7
VII	0	(0%)	9	+10
VIII	3	(33%)	3	+4
IX	4	(36%)	4	+5
X	4	(40%)	3	0
XI	0	(0%)	2	-4
XII	0	(0%)	0	-8.5
XIII	N/A	(N/A)	0	-6.5

Note N/D: Horizon XIII had been extensively disturbed by
ploughing and thus no information regarding architectural
organisation was recovered.

the complete destruction of horizon X by fire; the occupational hiatus
between horizon X and XI; and the broader changes in social organisation
taking place in south-eastern Europe at this time. Horizon X was destroyed
by fire and marks the end of continuous settlement at Ovčarovo. After a
50–60–year hiatus Ovčarovo was reoccupied in horizon XI (TODOROVA et al.
1983, 46). This final reoccupation of the site is distinguished from that of
the previous ten horizons, not only by the layer of sterile soil between horizons X and XI and the absence of strategies to legitimate continuity, but
also by a significant change in settlement organisation. This change is manifest in a reorientation of the settlement axes and a severe reduction in
settlement size (Figures 2.11–2.12).

  The tradition of settlement continuity established and maintained during
the first ten horizons had been broken; the site had been terminally abandoned at the end of horizon X. When reoccupied fifty years later, neither
means of legitimating continuity and settlement occupation were required.
I suggest that with the destruction of horizon X Ovčarovo had lost its value
as settlement space. This is due in part to the gradual decrease in area
available for occupation; as the tell had grown vertically horizon by horizon, so it had shrunk horizontally. Indeed, only a fraction of the habitation
area available in the early horizons (1,300 square metres in horizons III or
IV) was available for horizon XII (456 square metres). Furthermore, I
suggest that the lack of interest in ensuring continuity and legitimating

occupation is a factor of the wider socio-cultural changes taking place at this time in Bulgaria.

The social formula of the early, middle, and the beginning of the later portions of the Chalcolithic period was characterised by the importance of resource and land control. The production and trade of copper and gold from Bulgarian sources, as well as the distribution of the marine mollusc *Spondylus gaederopus* from the Aegean (RENFREW AND SHACKLETON 1979), were important variables in the prestige networks and social structures in Chalcolithic south-eastern Europe on the whole. The importance of metal sources, the process of ore extraction, and the control of established resource areas for the distribution of prestige goods favoured a settled life-style which ensured control of resources, land, and trade: hence the popularity of the tells in north-eastern Bulgaria. When these broad social strategies began to shift during the later phases of the Chalcolithic (SHERRATT 1982; 1983) and when different systems of goods and abilities came to be valued (e.g. mobility, movement of goods), the value of settlement continuity dropped.

Thus in the final phase of occupation at Ovčarovo (horizons XI–XIII), it was not necessary, or desirable for that matter, for the occupants of the settlement to prove their rights to settle, occupy, and control the territory associated with the site. Indeed, continuity of settlement occupation was no longer an important bargaining variable. The bases of social interaction had shifted from continuity to more transient criteria. A foreshadowing of the increasing role of the individual is seen during the earlier phases of the Chalcolithic in the production and use of artefacts related to personal adornment (e.g. gold and copper jewellery, *Spondylus* bracelets). At the end of the Chalcolithic individual wealth and status became variables of social importance more greatly admired and manipulated than were settlement history and the legitimation of social position in the Chalcolithic present with reference to the Chalcolithic past. Settlement continuity had become less valuable than individual mobility and resource transport (SHERRATT 1983, 195). Thus the disappearance of strategies to ensure continuity of settlement can be explained. The large number of tell settlements dwindled and then disappeared; tectomorphic miniature representations were no longer produced.

Conclusion

The official publication of Todorova's excavations of Ovčarovo offers one perspective of the role of houses in the lives of the settlement's inhabitants. Houses were the centres of living, sleeping, cooking, eating, pottery production, and grain storage. Todorova outlined the prehistoric meaning of Ovčarovo houses in traditional terms by describing their component features; estimating the man-hours of labour which would have been required for their construction, and calculating the population of the site

(TODOROVA *et al.* 1983, 27–47).

I contend that while there is nothing incorrect with Todorova's treatment of housing at Ovčarovo, or with her conclusions with respect to house size and population, additional insight into the social reality of life at Ovčarovo is gained from a different perspective on the house. As much as providing shelter from the elements and a locus for sleeping and eating, the houses at Ovčarovo were living beings: they were born, they lived, grew, died, and were remembered after their death in miniature representations. The houses at Ovčarovo, through their position as symbols of occupational continuity, participated in maintaining social continuity. Either by the repetition of floor-plans or their representations in miniature form, houses were active components of a complex strategy to maintain stability through time.

At Ovčarovo the sequence of house rebuilding and the changing perspective of continuity and its legitimation during times of competition for settlement space is an example of the results available from alternative perceptions of houses recovered in the archaeological record. I chose to envisage the houses at Ovčarovo from a biographical standpoint. The biographical analogy and the legitimation of continuity are by no means the only correct interpretations of the Ovčarovo house sequence. Doubtless investigations based on other dimensions (e.g. house contents, house size, the house as storage facility, the house as wealth) would provide additional information which could be added to the continuity aspect as outlined in this chapter, as well as to Todorova's original conclusions. By considering an increasing number of diverse perspectives (social, material, and otherwise), the social archaeologist can produce an increasingly accurate reconstruction of the social reality of houses recovered from prehistory.

Bibliography

Adams, William H. 1987. 'Review of Susan Kent, Analyzing activity areas: an ethnoarchaeological study of the use of space' *Historical Archaeology* 21:1, 105–7.

Binford, Lewis R. 1981a. 'Behavioural archaeology and the "Pompeii premise"' *Journal of Anthropological Research* 37, 195–208.

Binford, Lewis R. 1981b. *Bones: Ancient Men and Modern Myths.* Academic Press (London).

Boast, Robin and Yiannouli, Eugenia (eds) 1986. 'Creating space' *Archaeological Review from Cambridge* 5:2, 136–205.

Bourdieu, Pierre 1962. *The Algerians*, translated by A. Ross. Beacon Press (Boston).

Bourdieu, Pierre 1973. 'The Berber house' in M. Douglas (ed.) *Rules and Meanings*, 98–110. Penguin (Harmondsworth).

Bourdieu, Pierre 1977. *Outline of a Theory of Practice*. Cambridge University Press (Cambridge).

Carr, Christopher (ed.) 1984a. *Statistical Analysis of Architectural Data Structure*. Academic Press (New York).

Carr, Christopher 1984b. 'The nature of organization of intrasite archaeological records and spatial analytic approaches to their investigations' in M. Schiffer (ed.) *Advances in Archaeological Method and Theory* 6, 103–222.

Chapman, John 1983. 'Meaning and illusion in the study of burial in Balkan prehistory' in A. Poulter (ed.) *Ancient Bulgaria*, 1–42. Department of Archaeology (Nottingham).

Cliff, A. D., P. Haggett, J. K. Ord, K. Bassett, and R. B. Davies 1975. *Elements of Spatial Structure: a Quantitative Approach*. Cambridge University Press (Cambridge).

Donley, Linda W. 1982. 'House power: Swahili space and symbolic markers' in I. Hodder (ed.) *Symbolic and Structural Archaeology*, 63–73. Cambridge University Press (Cambridge).

Fletcher, Roland 1984. 'Identifying spatial disorder: a case study of a Mogol fort' in H. J. Hietala (ed.) *Intrasite Spatial Analysis in Archaeology*, 196–223. Cambridge University Press (Cambridge).

Fol, Alexander and Jan Lichardus 1988. *Macht, Herrschaft und Gold*. Moderne Galerie des Saarland-Museum (Saarbruchen).

Foster, Sally M. 1989. 'Analysis of spatial patterns in buildings (access analysis) as an insight into social structure: examples from the Scottish Iron Age' *Antiquity* 63, 40–50.

Fritz, John 1978. 'Paleopsychology today: ideational systems and human adaptation in prehistory' in C. Redman *et al.* (eds.) *Social Archaeology: Beyond Dating and Subsistence*. Academic Press (New York).

Glassie, Henry 1975. *Folk Housing in Middle Virginia: A Structural Analysis of Historic Artifacts*. University of Tennessee Press (Knoxville).

Hietala, Harold J. (ed.) 1984a. *Intrasite Spatial Analysis*. Cambridge University Press (Cambridge).

Hietala, Harold J. 1984b. 'Intrasite spatial analysis: a brief introduction' in H. J. Hietala (ed.) *Intrasite Spatial Analysis*, 1–3. Cambridge University Press (Cambridge).

Hietala, Harold J. 1984c. 'Intrasite spatial analysis: further directions' in H. J. Hietala (ed.) *Intrasite Spatial Analysis*, 278–80. Cambridge University Press (Cambridge).

Hillier, Bob and Julienne Hanson 1984. *The Social Logic of Space*. Cambridge University Press (Cambridge).

Hillier, Bob, Julienne Hanson, and H. Graham 1987. 'Ideas are in things: an application of the space syntax method to discovering house genotypes' *Environment and Planning B: Planning and Design* 14, 363–85.

46 DOUGLASS W. BAILEY

Hillier, Bob, A. Leaman, P. Stansall, and M. Bedford 1976. 'Space syntax' *Environment and Planning B* 3, 147–85.

Hodder, Ian 1982. *Symbols in Action.* Cambridge University Press (Cambridge).

Ivanov, Ivan 1983. 'Le Chalcolithic en Bulgarie et dans la necropole de Varna' in A. Poulter (ed.), 154–63.

Katincharov, Roumen and Jean-Pierre Mohen (eds.) 1989 *Le Premier Or de L'humanité en Bulgarie 5ᵉ Millenaire.* Museé Nationaux de Paris (Paris).

Kent, Susan 1984. *Analyzing Activity Areas.* University of New Mexico Press (Albuquerque).

Kent, Susan (ed.) 1990a. *Domestic Architecture and the Use of Space.* Cambridge University Press (Cambridge).

Kent, Susan 1990b. 'Activity areas and architecture: an interdisciplinary view of the relationship between use of space and domestic built environments' in S. Kent (ed.), *Domestic Architecture and the Use of Space,* 1–8. Cambridge University Press (Cambridge).

Kramer, Carol 1979. 'An archaeological view of a contemporary Kurdish village: domestic architecture, household size and wealth' in C. Kramer (ed.) *Ethnoarchaeology: Implications of Ethnography for Archaeology,* 139–63. Columbia University Press (New York).

Markus, Tom A. 1987. 'Buildings as classifying devices' *Environment and Planning B: Planning and Design* 14:4, 467–84.

Moore, Henrietta 1982. 'The interpretation of spatial patterning in settlement residues' in I. Hodder (ed.) *Structural and Symbolic Archaeology,* 74–9. Cambridge University Press (Cambridge).

Moore, Henrietta 1986. *Space, Text and Gender: an Anthropological Study of the Marakwet of Kenya.* Cambridge University Press (Cambridge).

Naroll, R. 1962. 'Floor area and settlement population' *American Antiquity* 27, 587–9.

Poulter, Andrew (ed.) 1983. *Ancient Bulgaria.* Department of Archaeology (Nottingham).

Rapoport, Amos (ed.) 1976. *The Mutual Interaction of People and Their Built Environment.* Mouton (The Hague).

Rapoport, Amos 1979. 'On the environment and the definition of the situation' *International Architect* 1:1, 26–8.

Rapoport, Amos 1982. *The Meaning of the Built Environment: a non-verbal communication approach.* Sage (Beverly Hills, Calif.).

Rapoport, Amos 1988. 'Levels of meaning in the built environment' in F. Poyatis (ed.) *Cross-cultural Perspectives in Non-verbal Communication,* 317–36. C. J. Hogrefe (Toronto).

Rapoport, Amos 1990. 'Systems of activities and systems of settings' in S. Kent (ed.) *Domestic Architecture and the Use of Space,* 9–20. Cambridge University Press (Cambridge).

Rathje, William L. 1983. 'To the salt of the earth: some comments on household archaeology among the Maya' in E. Z. Vogt and R. M. Leventhal (eds.) *Prehistoric Settlement Patterns: essays in honor of Gorden R. Willey*, 23–34. University of New Mexico (Albuquerque).

Renfrew, A. Colin 1969. 'The autonomy of the South-East European Copper Age' *Proceedings of the Prehistoric Society* 35, 12–47.

Renfrew, A. Colin 1986. 'Varna and the emergence of wealth in prehistoric Europe' in A. Appadurai (ed.) *The Social Life of Things*, 141–68. Cambridge University Press (Cambridge).

Renfrew, A. Colin and N. Shackleton 1979. 'Neolithic trade routes realigned by Oxygen Isotope Analyses' in A. C. Renfrew (ed.) *Problems in European Prehistory*, 183–9. Edinburgh University Press (Edinburgh).

Shanks, Michael and Tilley, Christopher 1987. *Social Theory and Archaeology*. Polity Press (Cambridge).

Sherratt, Andrew 1972. 'Socio-economic and demographic models for the Neolithic and Bronze Ages of Europe' in D. Clarke (ed.) *Models in Archaeology*, 477–541. Methuen (London).

Sherratt, Andrew 1982. 'The development of neolithic and copper age settlement in the great hungarian plain, part 1: the regional setting' *Oxford Journal of Archaeology* 1:3, 287–316.

Sherratt, Andrew 1983. 'The eneolithic period in Bulgaria and its European context' in A. Poulter (ed.) *Ancient Bulgaria*, 188–98. Department of Archaeology (Nottingham).

Speth, J. D. and G. A. Johnson 1976. 'Problems in the use of correlation for investigation of tool kits and activity areas' in C. Cleland (ed.) *Cultural Change and Continuity*, 35–75. Academic Press (New York).

Stiny, G. 1980. 'Introduction to shape and shape grammars' *Environment and Planning B* 7, 343–51.

Stiny, G. and W. J. Mitchell 1978. 'The Palladian grammar' *Environment and Planning B* 5, 5–18.

Todorova, Henrietta 1978. *The Eneolithic Period in Bulgaria*. British Archaeological Reports S49 (Oxford).

Todorova, Henrietta (ed.) 1982. *Kupferzeitliche Siedlungen in Nordostbulgarien*. (Materialien zur Allgemeinen und Vergleichenden Archäologie 13) (München).

Todorova, Henrietta 1986. *Kameno-mednata Epocha v Bulgaria*. Izdatelstvo Nauka i Izkystvo (Sofia).

Todorova, Henrietta, St. Ivanov, V. Vasilev, M. Hopf, X. Quitta, and G. Kohl (eds.) 1975. *Selishnata mogila pri Golyamo Delčevo*. (Raskopki i Proučvania 5) Archaeological Institute of the Bulgarian Academy of Sciences (Sofia).

Todorova, Henrietta, Vasil Vasilev, I. Ianusecic, M. Koraceva, and P. Valev (eds.) 1983. *Ovčarovo*. (Raskopki i Proučvania 8) Archaeological Institute of the Bulgarian Academy of Sciences (Sofia).

Whallon, Robert Jr. 1973. 'Spatial analysis of occupation floors. I. Application of dimensional analysis of variance' *American Antiquity* 38, 266–78.

Whallon, Robert Jr. 1974. 'Spatial analysis of occupation floors. II. The application of nearest neighbour analysis' *American Antiquity* 39, 16–34.

Whallon, Robert Jr. 1984. 'Unconstrained clustering for the analysis of spatial distribution in archaeology' in H. J. Hietala (ed.) *Intrasite Spatial Analysis*, 242–77. Cambridge University Press (Cambridge).

Wilk, R. R. 1983. 'Little house in the jungle: the causes of variation in house size among modern Kekchi Maya' *Journal of Anthropological Archaeology* 2:2, 99–116.

Three

Social Inequality on Bulgarian Tells
and the Varna Problem

JOHN CHAPMAN

Regularities in the construction of settlement space are the norm for human communities, but the symbolic significance of the size of the deviations permissible from agreed spatial norms have received diametrically opposed interpretations. The dialectic between spatial regularities and variations is explored in the context of completely excavated village plans of tell settlements in Bulgaria. Directional trends are discerned in superimposed occupation horizons, with the aid of analytical techniques such as built/unbuilt space ratio, minimum interbuilding distance, and access analyses.

The complexity of differentiation of house attributes and control over space is seen as a result of differential reproductive success, which led to the emergence of more successful lineages. The Varna cemetery – a unique display of corporate wealth in the eastern Balkans – reveals comparable trends in increasing formalisation in mortuary space. It is suggested that this was the result of competition over the social reproduction of alliances, a competition related to the social inequalities created on tell settlements.

Introduction

In 1972, agricultural operations led to the discovery of a prehistoric cemetery on the outskirts of the Black Sea resort of Varna, in Bulgaria (IVANOV 1973). The excavations which ensued revealed the earliest concentration of goldwork in the world, dating to *c.* 5000 CAL BC. A plethora of publications and museum catalogues have ensued over the last seventeen years (BEST 1984; DEMOULE AND LICHARDUS-ITTEN 1989; GEORGIEV 1978; 1988; GIMBUTAS 1977a; b; GOLDSCHATZE 1975; IVANOV, I. 1975; 1978a; 1987b; 1983; 1984; 1988; 1989; LICHARDUS 1984; 1988; RADUNČEVA 1989; REN-

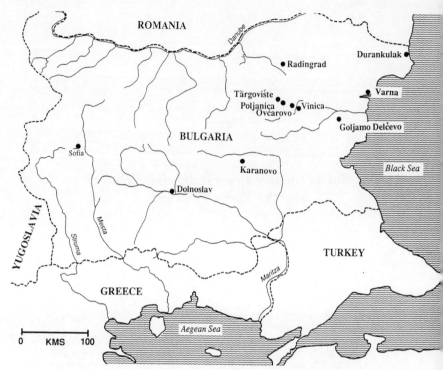

Figure 3.1 Map of Bulgaria with sites mentioned in the text.

FREW 1978; 1986; TODOROVA 1978a; b; c; 1989a; b), of which the most
complete are the Saarland Museum and the Paris catalogues (FOL AND
LICHARDUS 1988; LE PREMIER OR 1989). Most commentators accept that the
differential wealth deposited in a small number of the Varna graves was
commensurate with Renfrew's (1982, 4) third criterion of social ranking –
personal ranking by way of wealth accumulation. The evidence for social
ranking at Varna was no less spectacular for being unexpected – no other
sites at the time in Eastern Europe provided unequivocal evidence for such
social inequalities (Figure 3.1).

Despite commentaries and analyses of the Varna finds for almost two
decades, there are three problematical questions which stubbornly remain
unanswered and which, together, constitute the 'Varna problem': 1) the
uniqueness in the Bulgarian Chalcolithic of the social inequality found at
Varna; 2) the social and settlement context of those buried at Varna; 3) the
origins of such social inequality. In this chapter, I attempt to provide
answers to each of these questions, while recognising the limitations of my

approach for the second query.

If we reject the claim (IVANOV, I. 1978b; 1983; 1988) that Varna represents a 'civilisation' or the cemetery of a 'state', we can define the social context of the problem of lower-level social inequalities more clearly. Renfrew (1982, 1–8) has defined three possible classes of evidence which would indicate social ranking: central place settlements, large-scale public monuments and major personal wealth accumulation. A fourth criterion may be added to this list, which is partly implicit in criteria one and two; this is the control of social space, by which social leaders exert so much ritual power as to assert the rules, constraints and principles by which spatial meaning is developed in a settlement or monument. Foucault (in RABINOW 1984, 252) states that 'space is fundamental in any exercise of social power', and it is social power that determines the degree of inequality in any given society. In the Chalcolithic of north-east Bulgaria, there are signs of very significant control over social space on some of the long-lived tell settlements which were dispersed evenly over the Bulgarian landscape. In this chapter, I explore the ideological dimensions of social power in tell settlements, which betray considerable formalisation of planning, comparable to the formalisation of burial space and customs in the late Neolithic and Chalcolithic of Bulgaria (cf. CHAPMAN 1983).

Tells

While almost ubiquitous in the settlement patterns of the Near East and Anatolia (MELLAART 1975), tells are limited in their European distribution to Greece, Bulgaria, Romania, Yugoslavia, and Hungary. In the Neolithic and Chalcolithic, the densest distributions lay in Greece, Bulgaria and Macedonia, from the earliest Neolithic (c. 6000 CAL BC) to the end of the Chalcolithic (c. 4000 CAL BC). Living on tells began on a minority of sites in the middle or late Neolithic in southern Romania, in northern Yugoslavia, and in eastern Hungary (CHAPMAN 1989).

In form and associated behaviour, tells can be distinguished from the flat sites which are predominant in the north and west Balkans (CHAPMAN 1989). Sherratt (1983) has identified three important elements in tell formation – the intensive use of mud for building, a high degree of locational stability, and the concentration of houses into a coherent unit. Yet there are even more fundamental distinctions between tells and flat sites which relate to their symbolic as much as their functional properties, both diachronic and spatial.

Temporality

The development of a settlement mound is a temporal process, beginning with a flat site which is consistently reoccupied in such a way as to produce a recognisable accumulation of deposit. The question, 'When does a tell become a tell?' can be answered only etically; an archaeological answer may be after a minimum of three generations have built their homes on the same space. Thereafter, even when not occupied, the tell is a social landmark expressing during initial use a clearly defined place-value, or nexus of stored meaning in the landscape, as well as a place-value through long-term community participation. A tell is also a constant reference point, a *habitus* of stability in a possibly changing world, an active contributor to contemporary social identity (CHAPMAN 1988). In any descent-based group, where relations with ancestors are critical for social reproduction, tells are a physical and social expression of continuity with the ancestors, who once lived in the same place. In cases of dispute over relations with the ancestors, those living on the higher tell have visual proof of more direct descent from the forefathers, whether or not settlement continuity actually existed. Of course, physical continuity of tell occupation is not necessarily a sign of social continuity: tradition and place can be used to foster the illusion of social continuity when it is non-existent. But in many cases there is empirical support for the notion of long continuity in the occupation of tells. Here, the ideological security provided by the conviction that the inhabitants are treading where their ancestors once trod is a strong reason for continued residence, perhaps just as important as the quality of local arable and pasture land (cf. DENNELL AND WEBLEY 1975).

Spatiality

While central to the community's strategy for maintaining direct relations with the ancestors, the tell is also actively used for creating and maintaining social space for the living. Many of the facets of social space will be explored later; at this juncture, it is important to discuss only one measure of spatial structure in order to draw some behavioural distinctions between tells and flat sites. These two classes of settlement can be clearly differentiated on the basis of varying ratios of built:unbuilt space (BUB ratios) (Figure 3.2: cf. CHAPMAN 1989, 35). In flat sites, BUB ratios higher than 1:5 are extremely rare; consequently, there is abundant space between houses, whether for loose, organic settlement growth or for horticulture, the creation of open air ceremonial spaces, or high-temperature pyrotechnical activities. On the tell, by contrast, BUB ratios rarely fall lower than 1:2 and there is consequently very little unbuilt space for outdoor ritual, dancing, group meetings, pyrotechnology, horticulture, or animal keeping. There is little published evidence for outdoor food preparation or consumption on most tells. The main spatial features are the structures themselves and all communal activities would have to take place within the structures or off the tell. Indeed, the proliferation of activities off the tell complements the division of land for arable and pasture, with the likelihood of complex arrangements to balance household holdings with communal land use, perhaps related to focal points of social interaction.

Another contrast between tells and flat sites lies in the degree of poten-

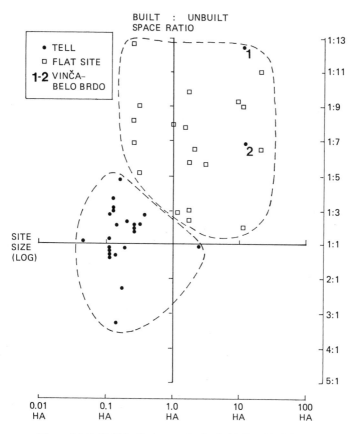

Figure 3.2 Built:Unbuilt space ratios for the Balkan Neolithic.

tial for growth in the two forms. If every settlement is dynamic, whether in the turnover of people, artefacts, or structures (DOXIADES 1968, chapter 2), some settlements are more dynamic than others. The difference lies in the growth of the total texture of settlement, a process inhibited by the initial organised tell plan but stimulated by sites where growth could be absorbed into the existing texture. On tells, there is so little 'negative' space (*pace* KEMP 1977–78) that expansion is strongly constrained by the initial settlement layout; by contrast, flat sites are full of both positive and negative space and internal growth is largely unchecked.

It can be readily appreciated that the social costs of having a direct relationship with the ancestors would have been strong conformity to patterns

of spatial behaviour within and outside the tell. Such behavioural constraints are not simply given, but are part of social action, the construction
of *habitus*. The role of planning in such highly-organised settlements as the
tells of north-east Bulgaria will need no further emphasis; it will be interesting to discover which social actors were foremost in the process of establishing and maintaining social norms and constraints for communities living on tells.

Table 3.1 Social power in the archaeological record.

Type of power	Control over	Dimensions of archaeological record
I	Ritual knowledge	Differential distributions of figurines, symbols, temples
	Practical knowledge	Differential spread of innovations (pottery, metal)
	Structuring knowledge	Cognitive data
E	Land	Type and extent of land division
	Labour	Location of production
	Tools and facilities	Extent of spread of innovations
	Raw materials	Type of exploitation of mines and quarries
	Exchange products	Differential artefact
	'Surplus' resources	Discard (hoards, houses, graves)
M	Others' territory	Extent and differentiation of offensive-defensive capabilities
	Others' possessions	
	Others' manpower	Evidence for slavery
P	Labour	Form of urban settlement plan
	Residence	
	Landscapes	Formalisation of landscape

Note I – ideological; E – economic; M – military; P – political

Social power, social space, and dimensional order

The theoretical underpinning for this treatment of the tell communities of
north-east Bulgaria is drawn from developments of Michael Mann's (1986)
model of social power. Mann theorises human communities not as 'culture
systems' comprising reified sub-systems, not as 'societies', bounded, totalis-
ing and holistic, not as horizontally divided into 'base' and 'superstructure',
but rather as 'social networks', unbounded, overlapping and often concentric. Through these networks, individual and institutional actors
mobilise social power to effect their control over people and resources.
Four overlapping, interdependent sources of social power are defined: 1)
ideological, 2) economic, 3) military, and 4) political. The principal areas of
behaviour controlled by these four classes of power are defined (Table 3.1),

FORMALISATION AS AN ASPECT OF
IDEOLOGICAL POWER

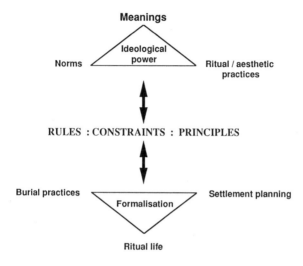

Figure 3.3 Ideological power and formalisation.

together with those dimensions of the archaeological record most sensitive to their recognition.

In this chapter, my main interest is in ideological power, divisible into three areas of social practice: norms, beliefs, and ritual/aesthetic practice. Norms are what structure or limit a community's social environment so as to make certain actions or beliefs unthinkable or impossible. Beliefs are the positive counterpart to norms, the developmental structure which provides a cognitive framework for social reproduction. Ritual practices concern the performances, seen or unseen, which embody important ritual knowledge or practical information vital to the group. Aesthetic practices encode the meanings of the group's cognitive framework and power structure in such a way as to conceal or reveal critical group information. Those with the power to frame the rules, principles and constraints upon which group ideology rests do so largely through the process of 'formalisation'. This operates to distinguish ideological practice from other kinds of practice and to create or reinforce structures of signification in order to consolidate ideological power. The relationship between ideological power and formalisation is illustrated above (Figure 3.3).

Two aspects of ideological power will be explored here in respect of social space. The first is the concept of dimensional order owing to

Fletcher (1977; 1984); the second is the principles of space syntax developed into a wide range of socio-spatial models by Hillier and Hanson (1984; cf. HILLIER *et al.* 1978).

Dimensional order

In two influential papers, Fletcher (1977; 1984) contends that, just as humans use consistent interpersonal spacing in their everyday behaviour (HALL 1962), so humans can be expected to arrange their material spatial context in like manner. Fletcher (1984, 197) views settlement remains in the context of information theory, with the structures in a settlement acting as communication devices transmitting messages about the organisation of space. He (1984, 200) defines two factors contributing to spatial order, viz. coherence in the absolute dimensions of the dimensional messages in a settlement, and the consistent variation found within these dimensions. Nevertheless, the decay of older structures and their replacement by new buildings introduce a long-term decay of the original spatial message with time, a loss of focus prevented only by the construction of a new spatial order elsewhere, or the removal of much of the older spatial format.

A problem with Fletcher's approach lies in the contradiction between his two interpretations of variations in spatial coherence. His earlier view (1977, 146–7) was that tolerance of a high level of dimensional variability is probably adaptive, since the maintenance of close conformity to an ideal type requires considerable effort. Later, however (1984, 220), he argued that the decline of spatial coherence can be a cause of settlement abandonment just as severe as attack or the loss of subsistence resources. The reliance on notions of biological adaptation at group, rather than at individual, level is dubious (CHAPMAN 1986); instead, it may be more productive to consider variations in the forms of ideological power necessary to maintain tight spatial coherence against the pressures of household nonconformity.

Space syntax

The theoretical aims of Hillier and Hanson (1984) are to develop a general theory of socio-spatial relations based on formal principles of analysis. The authors (1984, x-xii) castigate those sociologists who model a-spatial society and those architects who design a-social space. By defining buildings as 'transformations of space through objects', Hillier and Hanson (1984, 1) lay the basis for their study of buildings: the ordering of space in buildings concerns the ordering of relations between people. Access within settlements and inside buildings for inhabitants, visitors, and strangers lies at the heart of their model. A wide range of examples illustrate the continuum of architectural patterns from a level of minimum control over access in foraging societies to highly structured patterns of control over access in

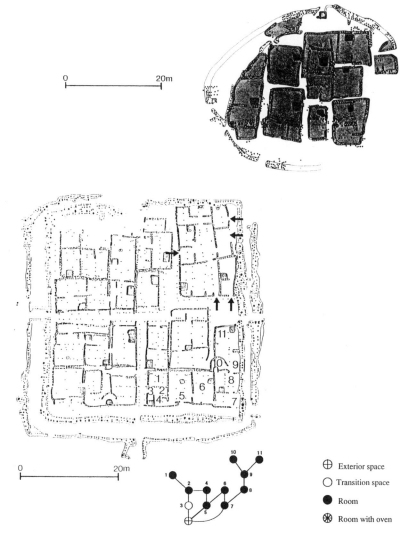

*Figures 3.4 and 3.5 Plan of Ovčarovo phase IX
and plan of Poljanica, phase III with justified access map.*

recent buildings (cf. MARKUS 1982; for an archaeological example, see
FOSTER 1989a and b). The model which Hillier and Hanson (1984, 33–42)
develop to explain the origins of complex plans takes as its starting point a

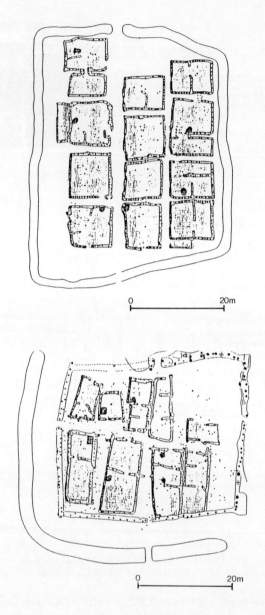

Figures 3.6 and 3.7 Plan of Tărgovište phase I and plan of Radingrad phase II.

random spatial configuration and the subsequent application of rules and constraints on the random process. In this sense, the Hillier and Hanson model is compatible with the concept of ideological power, applied through the conceptualisation of rules and constraints and putting them into operation.

The data set

The data used here to explore the multi-dimensional meanings of the settlement plan and the domestic house is a set of four totally excavated Chalcolithic tells from north-east Bulgaria.

Ovčarovo (Figure 3.4), a thirteen-level tell near the town of Tărgovište, dates from *c.* 4650–4050 CAL BC (TODOROVA *et al.* 1983). Phases I–IV date from the early Copper Age, phases V–VII to the middle Copper Age and phases VIII–XII to the late Copper Age. Phase XIII is post-Copper Age. There is a stratigraphic hiatus between phases X and XI and also possibly between phases IV and V. (All ^{14}C dates have been calibrated according to Pearson *et al.* 1986).

Poljanica (Figure 3.5), an eight-level tell near Tărgovište, dates to *c.* 4750–4350 CAL BC (TODOROVA 1982). Phases I–III are dated to the early Copper Age, phase IV to the middle Copper Age and phases V–VIII to the late Copper Age (TODOROVA 1988, 88). There are no apparent breaks in occupation.

Tărgovište (Figure 3.6), a four-level tell near the town of the same name, dates to *c.* 4550–4350 CAL BC (TODOROVA 1982). Phases I–III are dated to the middle Copper Age and phase IV is dated to the late Copper Age (TODOROVA 1988, 88). There is an apparently unbroken occupation sequence.

Radingrad (Figure 3.7), a five-level tell near the town of Razgrad, is dated to *c.* 4750–4350 CAL BC (IVANOV, T. 1982). Phase I is dated to the early Copper Age, phases II–III to the middle Copper Age and the final two phases (IV-V) to the late Copper Age (TODOROVA 1988, 88). No breaks are recorded in the sequence of occupation.

Five general observations may be made about these sites:

1. Each settlement is enclosed and defended, whether by banks and ditches or by palisades, thereby heightening the boundedness of the social groups. Opposed entrances, whether two or four, are the norm, adding to the geometric order of the settlement forms.

2. Each settlement is planned, so that the foundation of the settlement was a deliberate act of colonisation. From the morphology of the phase plans, it seems highly probable that each phase was built as a single phase of construction, in an operation whose scale was not unlike that of building a megalith. Using Startin's (1978) *Linearbandkeramik* house data as a basis for calculation, it may be estimated that the construction of the fifteen houses in Poljanica III would require

over 20,000 worker-hours, as compared to the 10,000 worker-hours necessary for the construction of a southern British long barrow (STARTIN AND BRADLEY 1981).

3. In many instances, houses very similar in plan are found super-imposed in two or three building phases. This suggests that, in many cases, we are dealing with, literally, 'ancestral homes' (for more details from Ovčarovo, see BAILEY this volume).

4. Some of the houses in the data set are remarkably complex by the standards of houses known from prehistoric Europe (for a general survey based on house variability, see PIGGOTT 1965). This complexity takes, in the main, four forms: two-storey structures (Radingrad), multiple rooms (up to eleven rooms at Poljanica), multiple entrances (up to seven at Poljanica) and rooms full of furniture, redolent of comfort and domesticity. In a general sense, therefore, the complexity of the settlement plans is partially reflected in the complexity of some of the individual houses. But the relationship between settlement level and house level of analysis is never as simple and as clear-cut as in Sahlins' (1974) reflectionist hypothesis based on the domestic mode of production.

5. Some of the houses are remarkably large, by the standards of most European prehistoric houses. House size varies between and within sites but houses with floor area of over 100 square metres are not uncommon, especially at Poljanica.

The essential task before us, then, is to capture in all its variety the social structures of the communities who built these houses. The approach is to use three measures of dimensional space, ultimately derived from Fletcher's (1977) approach, and both alpha- and gamma-analysis, as developed by Hillier and Hanson (1984).

The architectural analyses

The dimensional analyses

Three measures are used here to assess the degree of continuity between settlement levels at the four tells. These are: the ratio of built to unbuilt space (or BUB ratios); house dimensions (or HD) ; and inter-house spacing analysis (or IHSA).

The two preconditions for these analyses are the complete excavation of a settlement and the presence of a unambiguous settlement boundary. These conditions are rarely satisfied in European prehistory, a fact that increases the value of the Bulgarian data. The analyses also rely on the clear definition of houses, both conceptual and spatial. 'Houses' can be defined as ensembles of rooms either (a) interconnected by doorways or (b) with a wall or walls common to only that suite of rooms.

This definition includes free-standing structures, seemingly separate buildings which are actually connected by doorways, and extra rooms built on to existing structures but with no common doors. In practical terms, the analyses rely on the recognition of external house limits and, in particular, the identification of doorways and/or entrances to rooms. In the Bulgarian tells, doorways have been identified through the presence of regularly wider spacings between vertical posts and, in some cases, special floor treatment.

BUB ratios. The BUB ratio represents a primary definition of the built environment. While Fletcher (1984, 218) has demonstrated the utility of dimensional analysis of rooms, the co-occurrence of multi-roomed and single-roomed structures renders room size analysis less valuable. In this analysis, spatial coherence is defined by the clustering of house length or width around a mean value, with little overlap between the standard deviations. For external dimensions, the size along the outside of the walls or the outside edges of post-holes is used. Overlap in the standard deviations of length and width is seen as a blurring of the spatial pattern which defines the concept of a 'rectangular house'. This measure is a reflection of the size and importance of rival and related households, whether more or less successful. Because of the tell residents' emphasis on housing, much of the social competition between households is expressed through the medium of house morphology, whether size or decoration. The development of larger houses as expressed through HD analysis is, of course, related to the magnitude of BUB ratios.

IHSA. While BUB gives an overall picture of built space and its limits, IHSA offers a clearer idea of on-site dimensional order. This measure relates to the density of site housing and thus the intensity of personal interaction; tolerance of problems arising from both inter-audibility and inter-visibility are implicated. The inter-house space is the shortest distance between any point on the external walls of a building and the wall of its nearest neighbour. On tell sites, IHSA also has implications for access. To the extent that inter-household competition is expressed through larger, more complex houses, IHSA values are also an indication of such competition.

Formal analyses

The two analyses considered here are related to the interior space of buildings (gamma, or access, analysis) and to the continuous open space within a settlement (alpha analysis) (HILLIER AND HANSON 1984).

Access analysis. Access analysis treats the relationships between each partition of interior space in terms of permeability, viz. the ability to move between and through spaces. All the details of a space (size, furnishings, and fittings, etc.) are ignored except for its doors and boundaries. Access maps are produced which show the configurations of movement from one or more entrances to the furthest interior space of each building (see Figure 3.5). In such maps, the concept of 'depth' is significant: the deeper the building, the greater the degree of control over access to encounters, resources, and space. Comparison of access maps of all the buildings of an occupation phase can provide information about the generative principles used to 'produce' individual structures, or what has been termed, by biological analogy, the 'genotype' (HILLIER AND HANSON 1984; HILLIER *et al.* 1987).

On tells, the constraints on outdoor activities imply either a range of activities away from the tell or an increased range of indoor activities, or both. In relatively undifferentiated one- or two-room structures, it is doubtful if there is a special space set aside for visitors, whether close kin or non-kin. Non-residents would be received in the general living area, however it may have been symbolically patterned (see RICHARDS this volume). Increased 'depth' signifies greater building complexity as well as functional and stylistic differentiation and may well include the creation of encounter spaces for guests, with implications for hospitality, eating and drinking. 'Deep' houses provide greater opportunities for production and storage of food and artefacts, as well as the coding and display of ideological information, whether in interior layouts or furniture and fittings. If an increase in the number of rooms in a building is balanced by an increase in the number of entrances, there is less emphasis on control of domestic space. But where 'deeper' houses have few entrances, household control of domestic space is stressed, especially in relation to visitors.

For the access analysis of the tells, it has been found useful to distinguish 'shallow' buildings (those with one or two access levels) from 'deeper' buildings (those with three or more access levels). Similarly, the houses can be divided into 'open' structures (those with three or more doors) and 'closed' houses (those with one or two doors).

Alpha analysis. Hillier and Hanson (1984, 90–7) define the two principal properties of open continuous space within a settlement as axiality and convexity:

> Insofar as axiality refers to the maximum global extension of the system of spaces defined linearly, whereas convexity refers to the maximum global extension of the system of spaces unified two-dimensionally, the sociological referents of axiality and convexity follow naturally. Axiality refers to the global organisation of the system and therefore its organisation with respect to . . . movement in and through the system; whereas convexity refers to the more local organisation of the system and therefore to its organisation . . . from the point of view of those who are already statically present in the system.

In this way, the settlement plan can be analysed in relation to the way it structures encounters between inhabitants (with their concern for convex spaces) and strangers (with their concern for axial access).

The relationship between visitors and residents begins with the visitors' approach to a settlement. The dominant height of a tell, often enhanced by boundary markers such as banks and palisades, creates an impression on visitors matched by the number and complexity of entrances into the bounded settlement space. The symbolic significance of site entrances aligned on the cardinal points may be related to prohibitions on the use of certain entrances by certain people. Over the threshold, visitor movement and encounters are related to the nature of outdoor space. The more spaces are axial rather than convex, the more they are concerned with access only; this reduces the quality of encounters, whether involving talk, play, discussion, or more formal events. The more convex the outdoor spaces, the more encounter places there are where even a medium-sized group of people can meet without going off site or indoors. There is thus a tension between two principles on tell settlements: the desire of households for larger and more complex houses, often with special provision for visitor space, and the community's desire for more unbuilt encounter space, more 'neutral' than the domestic space of any particular household for meeting and social action. In summary, an important socio-spatial principle of tell living is that, as households become more expansionist and competitive, the quantity and quality of outdoor encounter space declines.

The properties of axiality and convexity can be analysed using, as a basis, two types of map. An axiality map summarises properties of straight-line access in open settlement space by drawing the smallest possible number of straight lines which form a grid passing around and between all free-standing structures (e.g. Figure 3.8a). A convexity map is produced by drawing the minimum number of convex spaces (a space which cannot be crossed by the extension of any of its boundary lines) which would cover all of the open settlement space (e.g. Figure 3.8b). On the basis of axiality and convexity maps, it is possible to calculate measures to define levels of settlement plan integration, axial articulation and grid convexity. A commentary on the methods used to calculate these measures is provided in Hillier and Hanson (1984, 98–123); however, the interpretation of many of the measures discussed is not made explicit.

Eight measures were felt to be useful for the alpha analysis of the tells, which represents the first attempt at this form of analysis for prehistoric sites.

Convex articulation. This measures the degree of integration of convex spaces in a settlement. The measure is calculated by dividing the number of buildings into the number of convex spaces. Lower values indicate less

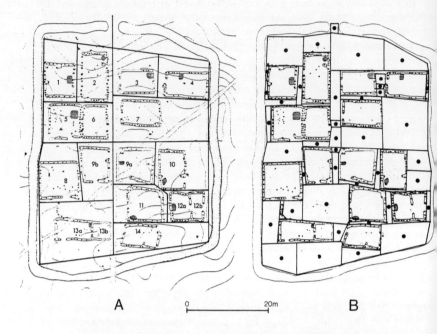

A   0   20m   B

Figure 3.8 Axiality map (a) and convexity map (b) of Tărgovište phase II.

This parameter is a surrogate measure of the ratio of outdoor to indoor encounter spaces; higher values may indicate more outdoor meeting areas. However, the tendency for the formation of 'untidy' spaces, too small for any encounters, to accompany the building of larger houses or 'islands' (i.e. groups of abutting houses not separated by a pathway) can distort this value on densely-built sites.

Grid convexity. This measures the extent of permitted deviation from an 'ideal' orthogonal grid by comparing the number of convex spaces with the minimum that could exist for a regular grid with the same number of 'islands' (HILLIER AND HANSON 1984, 98–9), according to the formula:

$$\text{grid convexity} = \frac{(\sqrt{I} + 1)^2}{C}$$

where I is the number of 'islands' of free-standing structures and C is the number of convex spaces. The results are plotted on a scale from 0 to 1, with high values indicating little deformation from an 'ideal' grid pattern.

This parameter measures the 'griddiness' of a village plan. The advantage of a 'griddy' system is that, through the layout of geometrically regular space, it is possible to increase the number of buildings on site. However, the use of islands rather than individual houses complicates the analysis of griddiness, since the clumping of houses into islands is itself a measure of household expansion. On sites where islands mostly comprise single houses, convex space is generally both simpler and larger than on sites with complex islands, with their untidy, less usable space. Hence, this parameter reflects the importance of two variables simultaneously: the degree of household expansion and the extent to which outdoor space is regular ('tidy') or untidy.

Axial articulation. This measures the degree of integration for circulation in open settlement space. Calculated by dividing the number of axial lines by the number of buildings, the measure indicates high integration of routes by low values and vice versa. Low values indicate a settlement with a rather grid-like, regular pattern, with many long pathways. High values indicate it is harder to move around the outdoor space, generally because of the expansion of some of the buildings.

Grid axiality. This measures the extent of axial deformity from an 'ideal' orthogonal grid by the use of the formula (HILLIER AND HANSON 1984, 99–100):

$$\text{grid axiality} = \frac{(\sqrt{I} \times 2) + 2}{L}$$

where I is the number of islands and L is the number of axial lines. A low value (less than 0.15) in a range from 0 to 1 indicates a high degree of axial deformity and vice versa.

Depending on the degree of clumping of houses into islands, this parameter is close to being the inverse of the axial articulation value. To the extent that houses are not clumped into islands, there is less axial deformity because there is less untidy space. Insofar as the community manages to develop grid axiality, it helps to control household expansion, in turn reflected in high values for this parameter.

Convex ringiness. This measures how distributed the system is (i.e. the degree of alternative available routes between convex spaces). The measure is the number of rings in the system as a proportion of the maximum number of possible planar rings for that number of spaces. It is calculated by the formula (HILLIER AND HANSON 1984, 102):

$$\text{convex ringiness} = \frac{I}{2C - 5}$$

where I is the number of islands and C is the number of convex spaces.

The results can be interpreted as a measure of the flexibility of access around open settlement space, with high values (greater than 0.1) on a scale of 0 to 1 indicating flexible movement and therefore more community control over household expansion.

Axial ringiness. This measures the distributedness of the system with respect to axial lines of access. The value is calculated by the formula (HILLIER AND HANSON 1984, 104):

$$\text{axial ringiness} = \frac{2L - 5}{I}$$

where L is the number of axial lines and I is the number of islands.

Values will be higher than for the convex, often exceeding 1, for two reasons: the axial map is non-planar and the position of the axial lines in the equation has been inverted, as compared to the convex ringiness parameter. In the case of the tells, all axial ringiness values appear to be very high, indicating the relative ease of access routes on these sites.

Building space index. This measures the proportion of convex spaces with no entrance to any buildings. This parameter is expressed as a simple percentage. This measure appears to be based on two opposing principles: 1) an increase in the number, size and/or density of houses requires more entrances, leading to a lower BSI value, and 2) an increase in the number of multi-house islands leads to more convex spaces that could never be used, thereby increasing the BSI value. The relative weight of each variable must be determined in individual applications of this parameter.

Real relative asymmetry (measure of integration). This measures the depth of open settlement space from the entrance(s) to the settlement by calculating the mean number of convex spaces from each building to the entrance space (minus 1, = the entrance space) and calibrating the result for the number of convex spaces in the whole settlement. Two formulae are required for this calculation (HILLIER AND HANSON 1984, 108–13):

$$\text{relative asymmetry} = \frac{2(MD - 1)}{k - 2}$$

where MD is the mean depth for all buildings and k is the number of convex spaces in the system.

$$\text{real relative asymmetry} = \frac{RA}{D_k}$$

where RA is relative asymmetry and the D-value is the correction factor for the number of convex spaces in the system (D-values are given in HILLIER AND HANSON 1984, table 3).

In the case of the tells, each site has a varied number of entrances. The RA value is calculated for each separate entrance and the result is averaged. This important measure indicates the degree of settlement integration in respect of the entrance(s); values of 0.4–0.6 are considered as indicating strongly integrated sites, while values of 0.8 or more indicate more segregated sites (HILLIER AND HANSON 1984, 113).

The RRA parameter is an important measure of the possibilities of access to a settlement by a visitor. Because the measure is standardised for both the number of entrances and the number of convex spaces, it provides a useful comparative tool for assessing the ease of movement around outdoor space. Flexible, easy access is generally related to the extent to which community priorities for outdoor meeting space take precedence over the expansion of individual households.

The formal analysis of building and settlement plans gives an added precision and objectivity to the analysis of social space. Although sacrifices are made in the removal of building 'content' from the analyses, it is maintained that the comparison of results produced independently by formal and contextual analyses will yield more interesting results.

Table 3.2 Summary of analyses.

	Tărgovište		Radingrad					Poljanica				Ovčarovo		
	I	II	I	II	III	IV	V	I	III	IV	VII	VIII	IX	X
Convex articulation	4.00	3.00	2.00	3.00	2.62	2.64	2.615	2.00	1.73	2.53	3.125	4.125	4.00	4.00
Grid convexity	0.494	0.52	0.60	0.61	0.59	0.73	0.92	0.50	0.667	0.675	0.715	0.64	0.44	0.415
Axial articulation	1.25	1.33	0.75	1.375	0.92	1.18	1.15	0.75	0.80	1.20	2.00	2.125	1.89	1.625
Grid axiality	0.65	0.487	0.667	0.66	0.67	0.615	0.575	0.64	0.75	0.27	0.478	0.47	0.45	0.53
Convex ringiness	0.16	0.176	0.16	0.116	0.14	0.17	0.19	0.085	0.149	0.197	0.155	0.131	0.09	0.05
Axial ringiness	1.60	2.33	1.90	3.40	2.11	2.33	2.08	3.80	2.71	0.86	3.86	3.625	4.83	7.00
Building space index	73.50	75.50	63.50	62.50	61.80	65.50	73.50	59.40	46.10	57.80	45.40	58.00	80.50	78.10
RRA	0.365	0.535	0.696	0.44	0.91	0.49	0.50	0.78	1.14	0.77	0.74	0.57	X	X

The analysis of four Chalcolithic tells

The full range of analyses will be discussed site by site before a general discussion of the utility of each of the measures. The results are presented below as follows: BUB ratios (Figure 3.9); house dimensions (Figure 3.10); inter-house spacing analysis (Figure 3.11); gamma analyses (Figures 3.12–3.16); alpha analyses (Table 3.2).

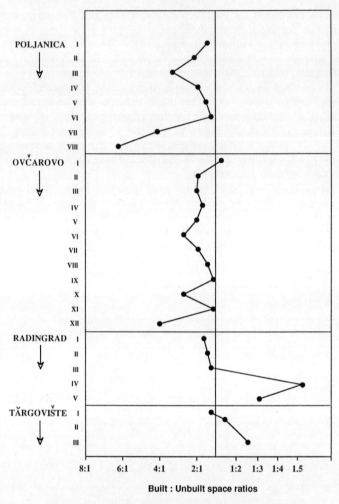

Figure 3.9 Built:Unbuilt space ratios for four Bulgarian tells.

Tărgovište

The BUB analysis indicates a unidirectional trend towards lower BUB ratios, and thus more internal unbuilt settlement space, the later the occupational phase. It should be noted that the absence of a clear village boundary in phase III made the calculation of BUB ratio impossible.

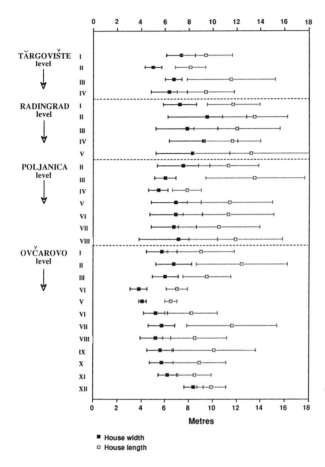

Figure 3.10 House dimensional analysis of four Bulgarian tells.

In the house dimension analysis, consistent values for house width throughout the sequence may be contrasted with two trends in house length: a trend towards longer houses with time and a trend towards increased dimensional variability in house length through time.

The variability in house dimensions is belied by a stable set of IHS indices through phases I–III; this stability betokens very uniform planning, despite a trend towards slightly lower values with time. But the values for phase IV indicate a major change in settlement layout, with larger and more varied IHS values for the first time in the settlement's history.

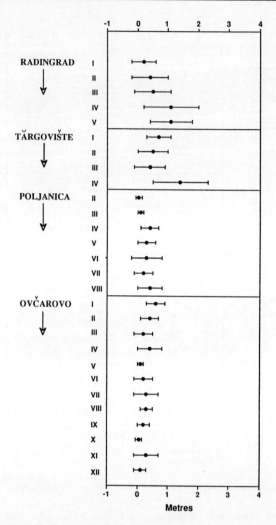

Figure 3.11 Inter-house spacing analysis of four Bulgarian tells.

The buildings at Tărgovište are almost all of the 'shallow', 'closed' type, with more one-level than two-level justified access maps and only one house with 3 access levels (Figures 3.12, 3.15). Similarly, one-entrance buildings predominate over those with two entrances, with no three- or four-entrances structures at all. In general, the Tărgovište houses are well integrated, simple in plan and lacking in strong spatial controls over permeability.

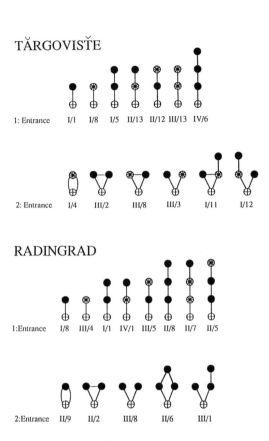

Figure 3.12 Access maps, Tărgovište and Radingrad.

Only phases I and II were amenable to alpha analysis, because of the ambiguity of the site entrances and boundaries (Table 3.2). In these phases, easy access for both residents and visitors is the result less of a regular, geometric layout than of a relative abundance of outdoor space. No measures are indicative of the development of strong competition between households as expressed in increased building size.

The site of Tărgovište comprises simple buildings within a strongly integrated settlement structure, regulated by a constrained IHS index until the major site reorientation in the final phase (IV). This change coincides with the ceramic change associated with the change from the middle to the late Copper Age. The plan change was facilitated by a slow but steady upward trend in the proportion of unbuilt space within the site boundaries. Combined with the expansion in unbuilt space, the increasing variability in house lengths betokens a smaller number of larger houses each with more outdoor space, at least from phase III to phase IV. In general, there is a lack of inter-household competition at the expense of community control.

Radingrad

The BUB ratios at Radingrad show one of the largest swings in the entire group. After a relatively stable set of high ratios in phases I–III, there is a sudden major shift to a site plan full of outdoor space.

In the last phase (V), the BUB ratio returns towards the higher ratios of the early phases, without reaching an even 1:1 ratio.

In comparison with the stable BUB ratios of phases I–III, there is marked variability in house dimensions, with shorter houses in phases I and III, but much longer houses in phase II. At the same time as the BUB ratio change in phase IV, house sizes are the most regular and smallest in the whole stratigraphy. Only slightly more variability in house lengths is found in phase V.

In contrast to the stability of the IHS index as found on other tells, the IHSA at Radingrad shows a trend towards larger and more diverse inter-house spacing through time. The most varied IHS values occur in phase IV, coeval with the major shift in site planning.

The buildings at Radingrad betray very little variation in their access maps; an overwhelming proportion of houses have one entrance and one or two access levels (Figures 3.12, 3.15). There is only one structure with a three-level access map, indicating the simplicity of formal planning for individual houses.

All phases at Radingrad comprise 'griddy' systems, with little axial or convex deformation (Table 3.2). Four out of the five phases allow ready access for visitors with respect to the site entrances: the exception is phase III. In three measures (grid convexity, grid axiality, and building space index), there is evidence for some inter-household competition: more so than at Tărgovište but not as much as at Ovčarovo and Poljanica. The relative ease of movement around the site is a function of the moderate quantity and quality of outdoor encounter space.

It is interesting to note the relationships between the various dimensional and formal measures with respect to village planning and the creation of social space. At Radingrad, the stability of building plans contrasts with variations in open settlement space and the uses to which it is put. The increasing constraints on outdoor circulation in phase III are hypothesised to have prompted the realignment of the settlement plan in phase IV, a plan change coeval with small and regular houses but greater variation in inter-house spacing. This pattern is rather different from the Tărgovište data, where smaller numbers of larger houses are built at a time

OVČAROVO

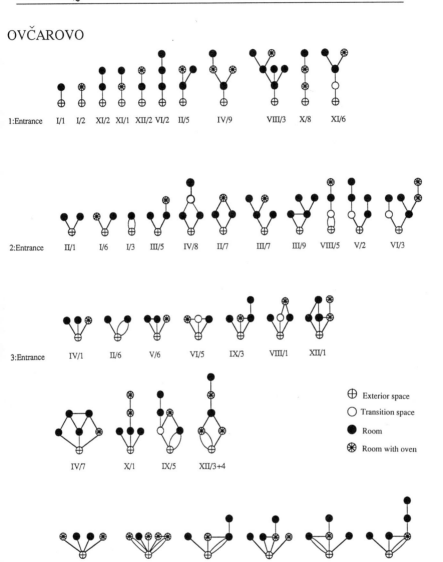

Figure 3.13 Access maps, Ovčarovo.

of increased open space. But, as at Tărgovište, the main change in the
Radingrad sequence is associated with the ceramic change from the middle
to the late Copper Age.

Ovčarovo

There are strong, possibly cyclical, trends through time in the BUB ratios
at Ovčarovo. BUB values increase in phases I–III, V–VI, X, and XII, while
declining values are noted in phases IV, VII–IX, and XI. The possible cyclical
nature of the patterning may well relate to inter-generational changes in
the creation and use of social space on the tell. In all levels but the first,
there was more built than unbuilt space on the tell.

The house dimension measures provide evidence of the greatest variability in the entire data set. Unlike at Tărgovište and Radingrad, this variation occurs in both house length and width. The overlap between house
length and width indicates such variation as to cast doubts over the 'ideal'
type of the rectangular house. Once again, cyclical patterning in this variability can plausibly be recognised: the greatest variations occur in phases
II, IV, VII and x. Whether such house size variations betoken lineage or
household competition and rivalry, there is good evidence for more successful and less successful households. In larger houses, it is an index of
lineage or household success, whether the household is larger or whether
each household member has more household space. It should be noted,
however, that any cyclical patterning in IHSA does not match the possible
cyclical changes in the BUB ratios.

In strong contrast to the fluctuations in BUB ratios and IHS indices, the
values for inter-house spacing are remarkably stable throughout the
sequence, with minimal variability except in phases IV, VII, and XI. The conformity to a well-established communal norm provides architectural stability in periods of major change in house size and quantity of outdoor space.

The Ovčarovo houses include, for the first time in this analysis, some
large, complex buildings with more tightly controlled patterns of permeability (Figures 3.13, 3.15). One-entrance houses are commoner than those
with two entrances, than those with three doors, with four-door houses the
rarest. The existence of multi-entranced buildings is in itself significant.

A single house (No. 10, phase VI) has as many as six entrances. The
occurrence of up to four levels of access in justified maps is a second sign
of complexity. When the ratios of shallow:deep houses and open:closed
houses are compared (Figure 3.16), there is a tendency for an inverse
relationship between the ratio of deeper houses and the ratio of open
houses. At Ovčarovo, the houses with the greatest number of entrances are
not the deeper houses; rather, as the ratio of one- or two-door houses rises,
so the ratio of deep:shallow houses increases. This represents at once a
more diversified domestic space and the possibility of closer control with
respect to entry.

The phases at Ovčarovo (VII–X) exposed to alpha-analysis (Table 3.2) cut across the cyclical patterning observed in BUB values and HD analysis. Two chronological trends are apparent: an increase in inter-household competition and expansion (grid axiality, building space index), and a decline in the ease of access (convex ringiness, axial articulation, RRA). The high frequency of multi-house islands and the decrease in the number of houses fit both trends.

Despite the overall stability in settlement plan provided by low, static IHS values and a moderately strong to strong overall integration of outdoor space, the Ovčarovo site exhibits major variation in house size, BUB ratios and access levels. In a plot of median house lengths against BUB ratios (Figure 3.17), three groups emerge with an additional outlier – the last phase (XII). Group 1 represents those small houses set in more outdoor space; group 2 includes larger houses with rather less outdoor space; and group 3 comprises the largest houses with if anything slightly more outdoor space. The important point is that, with one exception (phases V and VI), no two successive phases belong to the same group. Major inter-generational changes are the norm for Ovčarovo, with the likelihood of household or lineage competition being responsible for at least some of the fluctuations in household fortune. But these median values for house sizes should not camouflage the real within-phase variations in household size – a pattern which is reinforced by the combination of constraints over both access into buildings and permeability through houses. There is no evidence for a correlation between plan changes and major ceramic changes, whether from early to middle Copper Age or from middle to late Copper Age.

Poljanica

In every phase, there is more built than unbuilt space in the village. These high BUB ratios do, however, still vary, possibly cyclically: increasing ratios in phases I–III and VI to VIII alternate with a sharp fall in phases IV–VI.

The house dimension statistic shows considerable variation in house length throughout the sequence and some variation in house widths in phases V–VIII. Variations in house size appear to be cyclical, with larger median values in phases III, V, and VII and smaller values in II, IV, VI, and VIII. Cyclical patterning in house size appears not to be related to the longer cycles in BUB ratios.

In contrast to the variations in BUB ratios and house dimensions, IHS indices remain low with little variation throughout the sequence. If there is a directional trend, it is towards a small increase in IHS variability through time.

The buildings at Poljanica are some of the largest, most complex houses yet to be found in prehistoric Europe. Up to 25 per cent of all houses cover a floor area of more than 100 square metres, many are large, multi-roomed

A

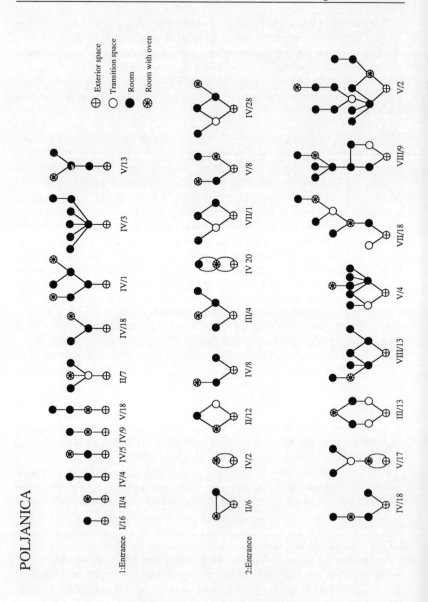

Figure 3.14a Access maps, Poljanica.

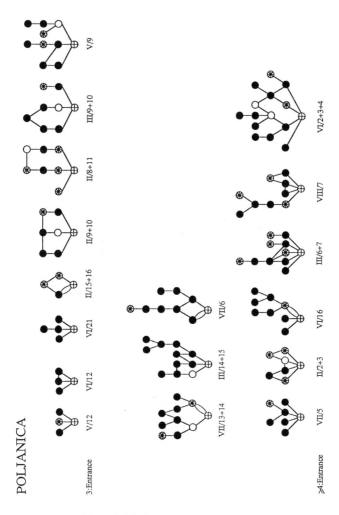

Figure 3.14b Access maps, Poljanica.

houses and some have multiple entrances (Figure 3.15). Although one-entrance houses are the commonest, and two-door houses are more frequent than three-, four-, or five-door houses, the buildings exemplify the widest range of entrance values in the data set. Similarly, justified access maps (Figure 3.14) indicate up to seven levels of 'depth', the most constrained domestic space among the sites studied here. Comparison of the

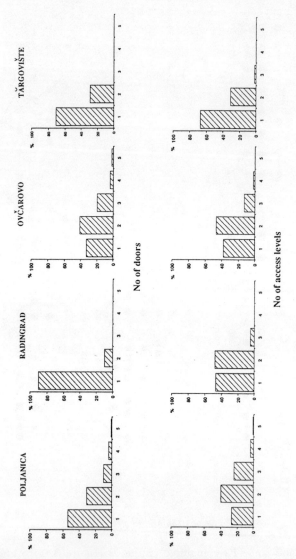

Figure 3.15 Summary diagram of access levels and number of entrances.

ratios of open:closed houses and shallow:deep houses by building phase at Poljanica (Figure 3.16) indicates almost a mirror image. From phase IV on-ward, there is an inverse relationship between the number of access levels and the number of entrances. In phases III and V the number of deep houses exceeds that of shallow houses – for the only time in the data set. A cyclical pattern can be observed in the varying ratios of access levels, with a relative increase in shallow houses in phases II, IV, and VI. It is also in these phases that median house dimensions fall. Hence, there appears to be a relationship between smaller houses and houses with fewer access levels and fewer entrances.

A second correlation is found for phases VI–VIII. At a time of increasing proportions of built space, to the highest values in this study, there is a clear tendency for deeper houses with more entrances. It seems likely that richer or more successful households or lineages are expanding their household space at the expense of what little unbuilt space survives within the village perimeter. This expansionist tendency continues to the end of the occupation and may be one factor prompting the abandonment of the site.

A sub-set of phases from Poljanica – phases II–IV – has been subjected to alpha-analysis (Table 3.2). These phases show some of the highest RRA values for the whole data set, indicating that outdoor movement was relatively constrained, more by the regular, geometric layout than by expansion in house sizes. The extent of inter-household competition varies with time: phase IV shows far more expansion than phases I and III (grid axiality). This expansion in phase IV is matched by access constraints (axial ringiness) because of the large number of single houses (and very few multi-house islands) and a not particularly geometric layout.

In summary, Poljanica compares well with Ovčarovo in its possession of a wide range of access levels and entrance possibilities, rather constrained open settlement space and a tendency to very high BUB ratios. The amount of social control exerted by those owning the Poljanica and Ovčarovo houses appears to differ in degree from that exercised at the other tell sites. This extension of social power is matched by the perhaps excessively large palisades erected around the site – as much for prestige purposes as for defensive capabilities. While the cyclical changes in settlement plan do not fit easily with the apparently linear progression of ceramic styles, there are two areas where architectural variation and ceramic change may be related. Changes in the BUB ratios are closely related to the changes from early to middle Copper Age and from middle to late Copper Age. It is only in the late Copper Age that we find the deepest houses with more entrances than before.

Discussion of measures

Most of the dimensional analyses used in this study are clearly defined, easy to apply, and fairly robust. Given the large sample sizes on most tell building phases, the measures are not readily distorted by one extreme value and the statistical basis of their interpretation is not in doubt. While

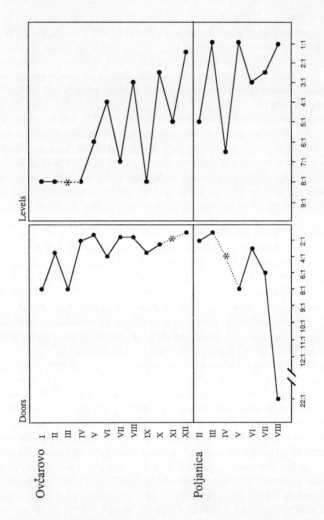

Figure 3.16 Ratio of open:closed and deep:shallow houses, Ovčarovo and Poljanica.

there can be little doubt that the prehistoric occupants of the tells did not conceive of their living space in such terms, the parameters selected can provide comparative measures of behavioural strategies developed at both the community and household levels.

As regards the measures calculated in alpha-analysis, the single most useful measure was the real relative asymmetry measure, since it provides an

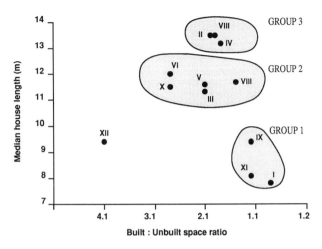

Figure 3.17 Median house lengths vs BUB ratios, Ovčarovo.

indication of the total integration of the site plan with respect to site entrances. RRA shows up considerable variation in what are clearly varied plans and has a robustness proportionate to sample size. Two common problems were encountered in alpha-analysis, relating to the interpretation of the values. First, the measures often related to two or more variables, whose implications sometimes (as with the building space index) acted in contrary directions. Hence, the apparent simplicity of the equations masked a lack of theoretical clarity about the underlying meaning of the parameters. Undoubtedly, more research is needed to elucidate the signifi-cance of some alpha-analytical techniques. Secondly, for the Chalcolithic tells in the sample, the parameters were measuring simultaneously two categories of information: the extent of regular, geometric space, and the extent of untidy, barely usable convex space. This problem may well be in-herent in an approach which ignores the quality and size of a block of space.

In the same vein, Hillier and Hanson's (1984) gamma-analysis has been criticised because it omits meaningful detail to capture essential structure (BOAST AND STEADMAN 1987). The clear answer is to carry out complement-ary analyses rather than eschew access analysis. In this study, gamma-ana-lysis has proved most useful at the inter-site level, in comparisons between complex and simple house designs. The full potential of access analysis at the intra-site level has not yet been exhausted for this data set. The simplic-ity of plan of most prehistoric European houses (e.g. Iron Age round-houses) renders access analysis unhelpful; it is a measure of the complexity of the Bulgarian tells that makes access analysis valuable in this study.

Discussion of results

The results of the dimensional and formal analyses of the four tells of Tărgovište, Radingrad, Ovčarovo, and Poljanica present some intriguing possibilities for interpretation. In general, there are two contrasting patterns which define two pairs of sites.

Pattern A – Tărgovište and Radingrad: 1) relative ease of movement around the settlement with respect to site entrances; 2) relatively little inter-household competition as expressed in the expansion of house size; 3) a tendency towards an increase in unbuilt space through time; 4) a tendency for larger, and more varied, inter-house spacing through time; 5) considerable if non-cyclical, variation in house dimensions through time, usually with a linear tendency to increased dimensional variability; 6) almost all houses have one or two access levels and there is a clear pre-dominance of one- and two-entrance buildings.

Pattern B – Ovčarovo and Poljanica: 1) relatively constrained access around the settlement with respect to site entrances; 2) moderate to high levels of inter-household competition, expressed through increases in household size and complexity; 3) a tendency to higher BUB ratios than in pattern A, combined with a tendency to higher BUB ratios through time; 4) a strong conformity to low, regular inter-house spacing values through-out the sequence; 5) markedly cyclical variations in house dimensions; 6) a wider range of rooms (up to eleven), entrances (up to six) and access levels (up to seven) than in pattern A, with higher ratios of deep:shallow and open:closed houses; 7) a tendency for inverse relationships between the ratios of deep:open houses and closed:open houses.

The differences between the two patterns are not such as to suggest a derivation from two polarised, incompatible ranges of behaviour. Rather, these patterns were the result of the different trajectories along a similar path towards social inequalities. In both cases, we are dealing with house-hold competition and rivalry within the limits set by tightly-organised communities.

In pattern A, it is possible to distinguish more stable 'genotypes', recur-rent patterns of house organisation defined by low access levels and few entrances. But superimposed upon that is the manifestation of competition for social power and prestige within the village. That this competition does not provide the dominant motor for social change is clear from the absence of major household differentiation; communal norms and values perhaps provide a successful check on social rivalries. This would suggest that formalisation of the village plan was implemented by common consent and that the changing, sometimes fragmenting, dimensional order would lead to increasing spatial chaos. It is perhaps no coincidence that there is a shorter occupation time on tells which exemplify pattern A.

In the pattern B cases, the cycles of competition are more visible, especially in house dimensions and changes in the use of vertically-inherited social space. Hence the 'genotype' for Pattern B tells is not so clearly defined. In these sites, control over domestic space is maintained in two ways: through constraints on access (both ingress and interiors of structures) and through less integrated axial plans with less unbuilt space. It can be seen that the less the unbuilt space, the more the constraints on outdoor movement. In settlements with high BUB ratios, regular, geometric order acts as a form of communal control over excessive expansion of individual houses. Such spatial control would have been in the hands of household or lineage heads, who would have held the power to formalise village plans and expand personal households.

As Coudart (unpublished conference paper) expresses it, variations in that culturally stable object, the house, correspond to a fundamental transformation of an egalitarian group. Here, there is a strong tendency to social inequalities on tells of the Pattern B variety. Insofar as those tells were longer-lasting, this partial transformation appears to have been successful.

The 'Varna problem'

We are now able to return to the three central questions comprising the 'Varna problem'. It is clear from the two pattern B tells in our sample, Poljanica and Ovčarovo, that the social inequality found in mortuary contexts at several east Bulgarian Chalcolithic sites has a domestic analogue. While it is clear that social differentiation can be inferred from many sites, it remains hard to relate the degree of social inequality inferred from settlement analysis to that interpreted from mortuary analysis.

The Varna cemetery is unique in the mortuary record of the Balkan Chalcolithic in its conspicuous consumption of prestige goods. So far, all the published interpretations of this display have made the 'reflectionist' assumption that the wealth of the grave goods mirrors the wealth and status of the living – presumably therefore priests or chiefs or both (IVANOV, I. 1978b; RENFREW 1978; GIMBUTAS 1977a; TODOROVA 1978b; RADUNČEVA 1989; DEMOULE AND LICHARDUS-ITTEN 1989; LICHARDUS 1988). This assumption has been challenged by many mortuary studies of the 1980s, in which it has been demonstrated that the living use the material remains buried or not buried at the time of death to construct and often manipulate their own social world (KRISTIANSEN 1987; O'SHEA 1984; SHENNAN 1986; TILLEY 1984; THOMAS AND WHITTLE 1986). An alternative to the reflectionist view of Varna is contained in Childe's (1945) dictum that, in a stable society, the grave goods tend to grow relatively and absolutely poorer and fewer as time goes on but wealthy graves may appear suddenly in times of social instability, as part of a strategy for the consolidation of emergent statuses. In this sense, Varna is comparable to the royal graves of Ur, the royal grave of Alaca Hüyük, the shaft-graves of

Mycenae, and the princely graves of Hallstatt D in the structural sense of a marker of status differentiation and social instability. The evidence for increasing social inequality has been noted in both tells and cemeteries; the tensions implicit in competitive emulation are most clearly demonstrated at Varna. It is in this sense that the Varna cemetery is unique in the level of competition and rivalry in late fifth millennium CAL BC society. Thus the problem of Varna is redefined: why are such tensions revealed at Varna and nowhere else? For a possible answer, we must turn to the question of the social and settlement context of the Varna cemetery.

Most of our Bulgarian colleagues have painted a picture, if not of a prehistoric state with 'cites' on the Varna Lake (IVANOV 1978; 1988), then of a grand inter-tribal union run on federal principles by a council of priests and chiefs with an administrative centre at the pile-dwellings on the Varna Lake (TODOROVA 1978c; RADUNČEVA 1989; TODOROVA AND TONČEVA 1975; for a contrary view of the relations between the cemetery and the pile-dwellings, see MARGOS 1978). While few of the Varna pile-dwellings have been sufficiently explored, it has to be said that the likelihood of a proto-urban centre boasting the complexity of an administrative centre for a large territory is low. These structural features are more properly associated with Renfrew's early state module – an urban centre at the peak of a three-level settlement hierarchy, with a temple and written records (RENFREW 1975). The postulation of such features in eastern Bulgaria in the fifth MBC bears within it a germ of truth about extensive alliances but pitches the level of logistic and administrative control excessively high.

An alternative to a state-based federation of tells and temples is no less impressive for being a pre-state social structure more closely in tune with the prehistoric realities of the period. It is the expansion of socio-political alliances rooted in lineage power, with its ideological power dispersed through a number of ritual centres and based on economic power gained through intensified surplus production channelled into far-flung exchange networks. There can be little doubt from Varna alone, but also from many other sites, of the wide range of exotic raw materials and goods in circulation in Chalcolithic Eastern Europe (GIMBUTAS 1977a; TODOROVA 1988). Similarly, the ritual evidence marshalled by Radunceva (1989) for close links between the finds from the Dolnoslav shrines and the grave goods of the Varna cemetery indicates the extensive nature of ideological symbolism, an attitude to communal identity reinforced by the widespread adoption of the same fine ware styles in the Karanovo VI – Kodjadermen – Krivodol – Varna group (RADUNČEVA 1989; cf. SHERRATT'S (1972) 'network linkage' idea).

Within the changing social world of the fifth millennium CAL BC, the trend toward social inequality was accompanied by three sources of community tension: 1) tensions between more successful and less successful households and lineages, manifested as a struggle between the traditional egalitarian ideology and a more competitive, individualistic ideology; 2) tensions between use and/or ownership of surplus resources by households, lineages, or the whole community (these tensions would be exacerbated by competition over craft production and the resultant prestige goods); 3) the competition between lineage heads within the wider alliance structures, as balanced against the degree of co-operation essential to the maintenance of an exchange network.

In past accounts, authors such as Renfrew (1978) and Todorova (1978b) have stressed the similarities between houses on tells. Whittle (1985, 160–5) went further to interpret the similarities in vernacular architecture as a concealment of the tensions or rivalries endemic to the Chalcolithic societies. The analysis of Chalcolithic tells has demonstrated, however, that social power as manifested in control over access to exterior and interior space varied widely both between and within settlements. However, the centrality of the ancestor cult to tell living made it impossible to resolve these economic and ideological contradictions, which contained an element of inter-regional rivalries. The impossibility of successful resolution of these conflicts in a domestic space which was at the same time place-centred and resonant with local ancestral tradition led to the emergence of an 'alternative' formal place, outside the domestic domain of tell-and-local-cemetery, in which representatives of households or lineage heads could attempt to resolve the social issues dividing past from present. The principal contradiction was the possibility of the emergence of further social inequality – not merely the development of stronger lineages beside weaker ones, but the increased hierarchisation implicit in the leadership of an inter-regional alliance – perhaps a regional paramount. How was this struggle conducted in the context of the Varna cemetery?

By 1988, the total number of graves identified at Varna had risen to 281 (IVANOV, I. 1988). Both Ivanov (1988) and Lichardus (1988, *Abb.* 51) have identified a core area of symbolic and/or particularly wealthy graves. It is proposed that the vast majority of the cemetery functioned as a mortuary space for the pile-dwellings on the Varna Lake; it was in the core of the cemetery where the most significant social action took place. In Lichardus's (1988) classification of Chalcolithic graves by wealth and diversity of grave goods, the first and second categories of wealth are represented only in the Varna cemetery. All seven category A burials are found in the core of the cemetery. The concentration of wealth, especially in gold, deposited in these graves marks an attempt made by competing lineages to prove their fitness to the status role of alliance paramount by the deposition of corporate prestige in the grave of their dead leader. This hypothesis explains the symbolic graves, with their missing bodies, as burials of lineage leaders who died far from the cemetery, whose lineage deposited rich finds if there were a plausible candidate for paramount from amongst their own numbers (e.g. Grave 36) and who deposited scanty funeral offerings if no such successor were available (e.g. Grave 27). In this sense, the astonishing wealth concentrated in a few graves is explained by the accumulation of lineage wealth, utilised in such a way as to support the ambitions of successful lineage leaders or to conserve lineage wealth until future candidates for paramountcy emerge. It is against the picture of competitive elites jockeying for immediate social power that Varna reveals its hidden social meaning, a meaning well masked beneath a panoply of golden treasure. It is in the tells of eastern Bulgaria that the first signs are shown of these emergent elites and the origins of their social power.

Throughout the Neolithic and much of the Chalcolithic periods in Bulgaria, tell settlements are known in which the range of house size and differentiation is indeed limited (TODOROVA 1978b; GEORGIEV 1988). It is only in the later Chalcolithic that social differentiation becomes visible in vernacular architecture, as a symbol of the breakdown of the egalitarian social *mores*. The hypothesis offered to explain such differentiation is one of differential reproductive success, tied to the emergence of successful lineage/household heads whose social power is based on intensification of production, increasing diversion of surplus into craft production and ritual, and the management of increasingly far-flung exchange networks. In this sense there is a fundamental disagreement with authors such as Todorova (1978b), Ivanov (1978a), and Radunčeva (1989), who see a rigid separation between commerce and craft production on the one hand and agriculture and pastoralism on the other. In this model the production of larger surpluses from mixed farming by larger lineages is converted into ever-increasing ceremonial offerings, marriage gifts to increase still further the size of the kinship network, and feasting to ensure the expansion of the labour pool. In this model the differential reproductive success which can be generated for one or two, perhaps more, generations is developed into a wider range of social power by the increased productive possibilities of the large, successful corporate group (CHAGNON 1979a; 1979b). The inherent instability of such kin-based groups, which rely as much on the existence of a strong leader as on other structural conditions intrinsic to the social order, means there is a tendency to cyclic rises and falls in the fortunes of particular households and/or lineages. It is just such tendencies which characterise the changes in house dimensions and access patterns in the tells of our data set from north-east Bulgaria.

Conclusions

There can now be no doubt that, in the Bulgarian Chalcolithic, social inequality is manifested not only in the mortuary domain of cemeteries but also in the domestic arena of tell settlements. The analysis of the social space of four tells in north-east Bulgaria, Poljanica, Ovčarovo, Tărgovište, and Radingrad, has revealed undoubted evidence of social differentials in two main ways. There is differentiation in positive aspects of house attributes such as size, number of rooms or storeys, and style of decoration; inequalities are also found in control over space, whether access within the house or movement in exterior space. Of the four tells in the sample, Poljanica and Ovčarovo show evidence of a more complex spatial order than is found at Tărgovište and Radingrad. Such complexity is seen as a result of differential reproductive success leading to the emergence of more successful lineages, whose greater productive potential is transformed into a larger labour pool, a broader range of craft products and wider access into regional and inter-regional exchange networks, and whose greater success was exhibited in their domestic structures.

Vis-à-vis the three aspects of the 'Varna problem', it is now possible to identify trends in the increasing formalisation of both settlement and mortuary space in the period preceding, and coeval with, the Varna cemetery. While it is difficult to relate the degrees of social inequality attested on tells and at Varna, there can be little doubt that Varna is a display of corporate wealth so far unique in east Balkan prehistory. The context of the Varna riches is not so much an urban state based on a tribal federation of priests and chiefs, but rather a series of overlapping and extensive networks of ritual, exchange, and alliance, in which regional lineages are competing for greater access to, and control over, the alliances. The Varna cemetery is the locus of competition over the social reproduction of the alliance – competition for the position of paramount, the individual with a leading role to play in the alliance. The seed of the Varna phenomenon can be identified in the rivalries between lineages living on the tells, whose attempts to control and use larger proportions of productive surplus led to a spectrum of more and less successful social groups, none of whom was able to achieve lasting domination over any other lineage. The success of these groups in utilising productive surpluses is indicated by the rapid expansion of exchange networks in the fifth millennium CAL BC, both in areal extent and in quantity and range of items exchanged. The most successful of these corporate groups was able to accumulate such quantities of gold treasure as were deposited in the richest of the Varna graves. But the alliance structures collapsed as rapidly as they had expanded. The relationship of their disintegration to the demise of the highly structured social space of the tells is a fascinating topic, but one which merits a separate study.

———————————

Acknowledgements

Ross Samson, Doug Bailey, Chris Evans, and Frank Brown made helpful comments on earlier drafts. My main debt of gratitude is to Roland Fletcher, Bill Hillier, and Julienne Hanson for making me think about other ways of perceiving social space, and to John Nandris, who suggested that living on tells was somehow different. It has taken this far to work out part of what he meant.

Bibliography

Appadurai, A. (ed.) 1986. *The Social Life of Things*. Cambridge University Press (Cambridge).

Best, Jan G. P. 1984. 'The Varna necropolis: its historical significance' in A. Fol *et al*. 1984, 150–3.

Bintliff, John and Christopher F. Gaffney (eds.) 1986. *Archaeology at the Interface: studies in archaeology's relations with history, geography, biology and physical science*. BAR I–300 (Oxford).

Boast, Robin and Philip Steadman 1987. 'Editorial' *Environment and Planning* B 14/4, 359–61.

Brumfiel, E. M. and Timothy Earle (eds.) 1987. *Specialisation, Exchange and Complex Societies*. Cambridge University Press (Cambridge).

Burgess, Colin, Peter Topping, Claude Mordant, and Margaret Maddison (eds.) 1988. *Enclosures and Defences in the Neolithic of Western Europe*. BAR I–403 (Oxford).

Chagnon, Napoleon A. 1979a. 'Mate competition favouring close kin and village fissioning among the Yanomamo Indians' in N. A. Chagnon and W. Irons 1979, 86–132.

Chagnon, Napoleon A. 1979b. 'Is reproductive success equal in egalitarian societies?' in N. A. Chagnon and W. Irons 1979, 374–401.

Chagnon, Napoleon A. and William Irons (eds.) 1979. *Evolutionary Biology and Human Social Behavior: an Anthropological Perspective*. Duxbury, (North Sciutate, Mass).

Chapman, John 1983. 'Meaning and illusion in the study of burial in Balkan prehistory' in A. G. Poulter 1983, 1–45.

Chapman, John 1986. 'Human socio-biology and archaeology' in J. Bintliff and C. F. Gaffney (eds.) 1986, 94–109.

Chapman, John 1988. 'From "Space" to "Place": a model of dispersed settlement and Neolithic society' in C. Burgess *et al*. 1988, 21–46.

Chapman, John 1989. 'The early Balkan village' *Varia Archaeologica Hungarica II*, 33–53.

Childe, Vere Gordon 1945. 'Directional change in funerary practices during 50,000 years' *Man* 4, 13–9.

Clarke, David L. (ed.) 1972. *Models in Archaeology*. Methuen (London).

Clarke, David L. (ed.) 1977. *Spatial Archaeology*. Academic Press (London).

Demoule, Jean-Paul and Marion Lichardus-Itten 1989. 'Invention du métal et premières inégalités: la nécropole de Varna dans son contexte européen' in Le Premier Or 1989, 38–44.

Dennell, Robin and Derek Webley 1975. 'Prehistoric settlement and land use in southern Bulgaria' in E. S. Higgs 1975, 97–109.

Doxiadis, Christos A. 1968. *Ekistics: an introduction to the science of human settlements.* (London).

Fletcher, Roland 1977. 'Settlement studies (micro and semi-micro) in D. L. Clarke 1977, 47–162.

Fletcher, Roland 1984. 'Identifying spatial disorder: a case study of a Mongol fort' in H. Hietala 1984, 196–223.

Fol, Alexander, Edmund Buchner and Christo Danov (eds.) 1984. *Dritter Internationaler Thrakologischer Kongress zu Ehren W. Tomascheks, 2–6. Juni 1980.* Staatlicher Verlag Swjat (Sofia).

Fol, Alexander and Jan Lichardus 1988. *Macht, Herrschaft und Gold. Das Graberfeld von Varna (Bulgarien) und die Anfänge einer neuen europaischen Zivilisation.* Moderne Galerie des Saarland-Museums (Saarbrucken).

Foster, Sally M. 1989a. 'Analysis of spatial patterns in buildings (access analysis) as an insight into social structure: examples from the Scottish Iron Age' *Antiquity* 63, 40–50.

Foster, Sally M. 1989b. 'Transformation of social space: the Iron Age of Orkney and Caithness' *Scottish Archaeological Review* 6, 34–55.

Georgiev, Georgi I. 1978. 'Das Spätchalkolithikum in Bulgarien im Lichte der neuesten ärchaologischen Untersuchungen' *Studia Praehistorica* 1–2, 68–78.

Georgiev, Georgi I. 1988. 'Die Kupferzeit (Karanovo V und Karanovo VI) in Bulgarien' in A. Fol and J. Lichardus 1988, 27–49.

Gimbutas, Marija 1977a. 'Varna: A sensationally rich cemetery of the Karanovo civilisation' *Expedition* 19/4, 39–47.

Gimbutas, Marija 1977b. 'Gold treasure at Varna' *Archaeology* 30, 44–51.

Goldschatze 1975. *Goldschatze der Thraker. Thrakische Kultur und Kunst auf bulgarischem Boden.* Österreischisches Museum für Angewandte Kunst (Wien).

Green, David R., Colin Haselgrove, and Matthew Spriggs (eds.) 1978. *Social Organisation and Settlement.* BAR S-47 (Oxford).

Hall, Edward T. 1962. *The Hidden Dimension.* Doubleday, (New York).

Hietala, Harold (ed.) 1984. *Intra-Site Spatial Analysis in Archaeology.* Cambridge University Press (Cambridge).

Higgs, Eric S. (ed.) 1975. *Palaeoeconomy.* Cambridge University Press (Cambridge).

Hillier, Bill and Julienne Hanson 1984. *The Social Logic of Space.* Cambridge University Press (Cambridge).

Hillier, Bill, Julienne Hanson, and H. Graham 1987. 'Ideas are in things: an application of the space syntax method to discovering house genotypes' *Environment and Planning* B 14/4, 363–85.

Hillier, Bill, A. Leaman, P. Stansall, and M. Bedford 1978. 'Space syntax' in

D. R. Green *et al.* 1978, 343–81.

Ivanov, Ivan 1973. Newspaper article in *Polet*, 15 January 1973. (Varna).

Ivanov, Ivan 1975. 'Raskopki na Varnenskija eneoliten nekropol prez 1972 g.' *Izvestia na Narodnija Muzeji Varna XI*, 1–16.

Ivanov, Ivan 1978a. *Sukovishtata na Varnenskiya Chalkoliten Nekropol.* September (Sofia).

Ivanov, Ivan 1978b. 'Les fouilles archéologiques de la necropole chalcolithique à Varna' *Studia Praehistorica* 1–2, 13–26.

Ivanov, Ivan 1983. 'Le chalcolithique en Bulgarie et dans la necropole de Varna' in A. G. Poulter (ed.) 1983, 154–63.

Ivanov, Ivan 1984. 'Le développement sociale et économique dans les terres bulgares à l'époque chalcolithique à la lumière des fouilles de la necropole de Varna' in A. Fol *et al.* (eds.) 1984, 147–9.

Ivanov, Ivan 1988. 'Die Ausgrabungen des Gräberfeldes von Varna' in A. Fol and J. Lichardus (eds.) 1988, 49–66.

Ivanov, Ivan 1989. 'La necropole chalcolithique de Varna et les cités lacustres voisines' in Le Premier Or 1989, 49–56.

Ivanov, Totju 1982. *Radingrad. Tell et necropole des Vᵉ et IVᵉ millénaires avant J-C.* (Razgrad).

Kemp, B. 1977–78. 'The city of El-Amarna as a source for the study of urban society in ancient Egypt' *World Archaeology* 9/2, 123–39.

Kristiansen, Kristian 1987. 'From stone to bronze: the evolution of social complexity in northern Europe' in E. M. Brumfiel and T. Earle (eds.) 1987, 30–51.

Le premier or 1989. *Le Premier Or de l'Humanité en Bulgarie 5ᵉ Millénaire.* Réunion des musées nationaux (Paris).

Lichardus, Jan 1984. 'Zum frühkupferzeitlichen Totenritual im westlichen Schwartzmeergebiet' in A. Fol *et al.* (eds.) 1984, 137–46.

Lichardus, Jan 1988. 'Der Westpontische Raum und die Anfänge der kupferzeitlichen Zivilisation' in A. Fol and J. Lichardus (eds.) 1988, 79–130.

Mann, Michael 1986. *The Sources of Social Power*, vol. 1. Cambridge University Press (Cambridge).

Margos, A. 1978. 'Les sites lacustres dans les lacs de Varna et la necropole de Varna' *Studia Praehistorica* 1–2, 146–8.

Markus, Tom (ed.) 1982. *Order in Space and Society*. Mainstream Publishing Co. (Edinburgh).

Mellaart, James 1975. *The Neolithic of the Near East*. Thames and Hudson (London).

Miller, Daniel and Christopher Tilley (eds.) 1984. *Ideology, Power and Prehistory*. Cambridge University Press (Cambridge).

O'Shea, John 1984. *Mortuary Variability: an archaeological investigation.* Academic Press (Orlando).

Pearson, Gordon W., J. R. Pilcher, M. G. L. Baillie, D. M. Corbett, and F. Qua 1986. '14C measurement of Irish oaks to show the natural 14C variations from AD 1840–5210 BC' *Radiocarbon* 28/2B, 911–34.

Piggott, Stuart 1965. *Ancient Europe*. Edinburgh University Press (Edinburgh).

Poulter, Andrew G. (ed.) 1983. *Ancient Bulgaria*. Part 1. University of Nottingham Department of Archaeology (Nottingham).

Rabinow, P. (ed.) 1984. *The Foucault Reader*. Penguin (London).

Radunčeva, Ana 1989. 'La société dans les Balkans à l'age du cuivre' *Dossiers Historie et Archéologie* 137, 46–55.

Renfrew, Colin 1975. 'Trade as action at a distance' in Jeremy Sabloff and C. C. Lamberg-Karlovsky (eds.) 1975, 3–59.

Renfrew, Colin 1978. 'Varna and the social context of early metallurgy' *Antiquity* 52, 199–203.

Renfrew, Colin 1982. 'Socio-economic change in ranked societies' in C. Renfrew and S. Shennan (eds.) 1982, 1–8.

Renfrew, Colin 1986. 'Varna and the emergence of wealth in prehistoric Europe' in A. Appadurai (ed.) 1986, 141–68.

Renfrew, Colin and Stephen Shennan (eds.) 1982. *Ranking, Resources and Exchange*. Cambridge University Press (Cambridge).

Ruggles, Clive and Alasdair Whittle (eds.) 1981. *Astronomy and Society in Britain during the Period 4000 to 1500 BC*. BAR B-88 (Oxford).

Sabloff, Jeremy and C. C. Lamberg-Karlovsky (eds.) 1975. *Ancient Civilisation and Trade*. University of New Mexico Press (Albuquerque).

Sahlins, Marshall 1974. *Stone Age Economics*. Aldine (Chicago).

Shennan, Stephen 1986. 'Central Europe in the 3rd millennium BC: an evolutionary trajectory for the beginning of the European Bronze Age' *Journal of Anthropological Archaeology* 5, 115–46.

Sherratt, Andrew 1972. 'Socio-economic and demographic models for the Neolithic And Bronze Age of Europe' in David L. Clarke (ed.) 1972, 477–542.

Sherratt, Andrew 1983. 'The Eneolithic period in Bulgaria in its European context' in A. G. Poulter (ed.) 1983, 188–98.

Startin, William 1978. 'Linear pottery houses: reconstruction and man-power' *Proceedings of the Prehistoric Society* 44, 143–59.

Startin, William and Richard Bradley 1981. 'Some notes on work organisation and society in prehistoric Wessex' in C. Ruggles and A. Whittle (eds.) 1981, 289–96.

Tilley, Christopher 1984. 'Ideology and the legitimisation of power in the middle Neolithic of southern Sweden' in Daniel Miller and C. Tilley (eds.) 1984, 111–46.

Thomas, Julian and Alasdair Whittle 1986. 'Anatomy of a tomb – West Kennet revisited' *Oxford Journal of Archaeology* 5, 29–51.

92   JOHN CHAPMAN

Todorova, Henrieta 1978a. *The Eneolithic in Bulgaria*. BAR I-49 (Oxford).

Todorova, Henrieta 1978b. 'Das Spätäneolithikum an der westliche Schwarzmeerkuste' *Studia Praehistorica* 1-2, 136-45.

Todorova, Henrieta 1978c. 'Die Nekropole bei Varna und die sozialökonomischen Probleme am Ende des Äneolithikums Bulgariens' *Zeitschrift für Archäologie* 12, 87-97. .

Todorova, Henrieta 1982. Kupferzeitliche Siedlungen in Nordostbulgarien. *MAVA* 14 (München).

Todorova, Henrieta 1988. *Kamenno-metalna epoha*. Bulgarskata Akademia na Naukite (Sofia).

Todorova, Henrieta 1989a. 'La période chalcolithique en Bulgarie: une civilisation préurbaine' in Le Premier Or 1989, 30-2.

Todorova, Henrieta 1989b. 'Les débuts de l'urbanisme' *Dossiers Histoire et Archéologie* 137, 56-63.

Todorova, Henrieta and Goranka Tončeva 1975. 'Die äneolitische Pfahlbausiedlung bei Ezerovo im Varnasee' *Germania* 53, 30-46.

Todorova, Henrieta, V. Vassilev, Z. Januševic, M. Kovačeva and P. Valev 1983. *Ovčarovo*. Bulgarskata Akademia na Naukite (Sofia).

Whittle, Alasdair 1985. *Neolithic Europe: a survey*. Cambridge University Press (Cambridge).

Four

Comment on Chapman: some cautionary notes on the application of spatial measures to prehistoric settlements

FRANK E. BROWN

In the foregoing chapter, 'Social inequality on Bulgarian tells and the Varna problem', Chapman draws on a range of spatial measures as a way of eliciting information on social structure from the remains of four Chalco-lithic settlements in Bulgaria. Whilst applauding the general direction of this work, I feel that such an approach highlights the need for a clear understanding of the strengths and limitations of the formal methods that are employed.

At the most basic level, care must clearly be exercised in the handling of the system of formal representation itself. As well as ensuring that a mode of representation is applied rigorously and consistently across the sample, it is essential to be aware of the distortions that can arise simply through the *way* it is applied. Some measures are highly sensitive to subtle differ-ences in the technique of representation: one has to be careful that results are not an artefact of the particular formalism. Where supplementary (i.e. contextual) evidence is available, any anomalies should be quickly spotted. In the case of prehistoric archaeology, however, the scope for error is obviously magnified by the sparseness and ambiguity of the material remains and the customary absence of suitable non-archaeological material which might otherwise help to fill lacunae, test hypotheses, and check con-clusions.

Beyond these very practical considerations, it is crucial also to be clear about the theoretical underpinnings of the techniques that are used, how far these have been tested (or are testable), and to what extent one can treat spatial organisation as an independent variable with universal social 'meaning'.

This chapter discusses two of the analytical techniques used by Chapman. The aim is to assess the value and the limitations of the measures used and to look at some of the practical problems that might arise (and seem to have arisen) in applying them. The issues addressed here, being of a theoretical and methodological nature, naturally have implications beyond this specific analysis of Bulgarian tells.

Gamma analysis

The term 'gamma analysis', though no longer current in space syntax, was used by Hillier to refer essentially to the analysis of space within the building shell. Like all modes of representation and analysis developed by Hillier and Hanson as part of space syntax, it focuses on relational structure. Hence, the emphasis is placed on *topology*, above all on the relationship of access (termed permeability) both between rooms and between the inside and the outside of building. This is examined to the exclusion of other formal properties, such as shape and size, as well as of the physical material from which the building is constructed. To characterise the internal plan, Hillier and Hanson employ what is essentially a form of graph-theoretic representation.

The 'justified' access graph. Architectural applications of graph theory are by no means new (see, for example, MARCH AND STEADMAN 1970, chapters 10, 11, and STEADMAN 1973 on the graph representation of building plans). The important and original contribution of Hillier and Hanson was to develop the 'justified' access graph – the form in which one space (usually the exterior) is chosen as the 'root' and the other spaces arranged vertically above this according to their topological distance (the shortest number of access steps) they are away from the root. This is the formalism adopted by Chapman here.

One of the great virtues of the access graph is its visual clarity: it translates the topological structure of the building plan into a simple and highly legible diagram. When drawn in justified format, with the exterior as root, it becomes especially easy to determine the number of alternative routes there are into and out of the building, and the consequent relationship that each internal space has with the outside: tree-like patterns may be distinguished at a glance from those with cycles or rings. The advantage of this is more than merely a pragmatic one, since, as Hillier and Hanson have shown, these characteristics are intimately associated with questions of social interaction and social control, shedding light especially on the interface between strangers and inhabitants. While there is no one-to-one

mapping between functional organisation and access graph, certain graphs
have emerged as highly characteristic of certain building-types.

It is unnecessary to go further into the methodology of access analysis,
since this is well described elsewhere and the technique has already been
taken up in archaeological circles (e.g. FOSTER 1989 on Iron Age brochs).
The 'justified' form of access graph is certainly sufficiently instructive to be
a standard analytical tool, and it is appropriate that Chapman should make
use of it to elucidate the internal layout of tell dwellings. Some comments
are in order, however, on the social 'reading' of the access graph.

By expressing a spatial layout as a topological 'skeleton', we are able to
see, and measure, properties of a building which might otherwise be far
from obvious: a major gain. The price paid for such simplification, however, is a massive loss of information, much of which may be highly relevant to an understanding of the internal systematics of the dwelling. This
does not matter too much providing the limitations are borne in mind; one
can always reassemble the picture later. In the methodology of space syntax, however, this stripping away of information is more than a matter of
analytical convenience: it is seen as the necessary and privileged route to
social interpretation. The access pattern is interpreted as the underlying
generative mechanism of building form (hence the term 'genotype'), a fact
that gives the graph unique explanatory status. And the relational structure, as embodied in the access graph (and 'gamma' analysis more generally), is equated directly with social structure; access relations are treated as
reified social relations. Chapman's analysis, which likewise isolates the
access graph and establishes an equivalence between the dimension of
spatial control and that of ideological control, is founded on these
premises.

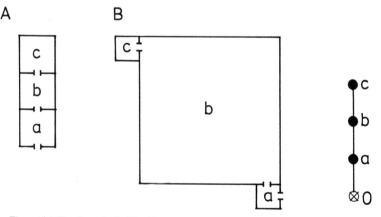

*Figure 4.1 Two hypothetical building plans with an identical pattern of access. The
access graph is drawn in 'justified' form.*

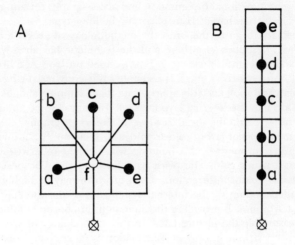

Figure 4.2 The 'shallowest' form of access graph (A) and the 'deepest' (B). While the linear sequence may be realised in both plan configurations, the radial pattern is only possible in the closely-packed arrangement.

Geometry and topology. The dangers of such an approach are manifest: at the crudest level A and B in Figure 4.1 would both have the same access graph, even though they are vastly different as buildings. Both the size of the individual rooms and the actual physical form of the building have profound implications as regards the use of space.

More importantly, from the point of view of social inference, syntactic analysis overlooks the crucial fact that the different geometric properties – shape, size, topology – do not operate independently, but *interact*. Dimensional constraints, on the overall plan or on its component spaces, can at times be critical in determining layout. Thus, Figure 4.2A illustrates one of the most common of all access patterns for dwellings, both ancient and modern – the star pattern. In this configuration all the rooms are accessible from a single space: in many cultures this may be a courtyard; in contemporary western society it is most likely to be a lobby or a hall. But as the figure shows, such an arrangement requires a site or plot which is spacious enough to allow rooms to be packed together in an appropriate fashion, i.e. so a, b, c, d, and e are all adjacent to f. On a long, narrow-frontage site – the kind that is characteristic of major thoroughfares – the star graph may be impossible to achieve within the constraints of the building envelope. Where two rooms cannot be placed side-by-side within the allotted frontage dimensions, it becomes obligatory to place them one behind the other, extending back from the street, or, where the plot is of insufficient depth to allow even this possibility, to stack them one on top of the other.

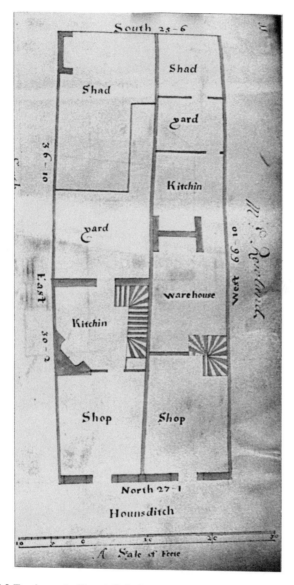

Figure 4.3 Two houses in Houndsditch, City of London (from the City Lands and Bridge House Properties, 1680-1720, Corporation of London Record Office).

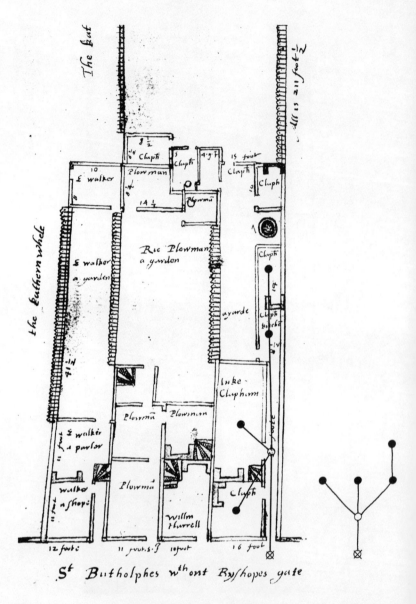

Figure 4.4 A radial access pattern in the ground-floor plan of a home near Bishopsgate,
London, c. 1612 (Christ's Hospital Evidence Book).

In the extreme case, each room becomes a through-route, giving rise to the linear access graph, see Figure 4.2B. Such linear sequences were not uncommon along the main streets of seventeenth- and eighteenth-century London, for example (Figure 4.3, and BROWN 1986). The point is that the dramatic degree of access restriction exhibited by these graphs crystallised not so much from social requirements as from humdrum physical constraints. To interpret the graphs purely as vectors of political or ideological control could lead to some very strange conclusions indeed.

Configurational vs. social explanation. Such mundane influences on building form may, of course, be dismissed by appeal to the wide range of strategies open to the builder to achieve a desired spatial pattern. The star pattern, or something approaching it, can be realised on the narrowest of sites by the simple expedient of inserting a corridor or passage along one side of the house (Figure 4.4). This will reduce the width of the main rooms somewhat, but the sacrifice might be considered worthwhile in the interests of privacy or separation of functions. How far such an arrangement is judged acceptable will depend on the historical circumstances and the prevailing social climate. To use, once again, a modern example, Muthesius (1982, 86) records a nineteenth-century terraced house in Bristol which included a hallway, even though the frontage width amounted to no more than 2.9 metres. Although the front parlour in this house must as a consequence have been minuscule by normal standards, the provision of a visitors' room, at the front of the house but with separate access, was clearly so important in social terms that it outweighed considerations of actual size.

But while it is clearly misconceived to treat spatial form as simply a product of physical constraints, independent of society, it is equally fallacious to regard it as an autonomous social language or a simple reflection of social structure. Space is not infinitely malleable, and social demands can achieve spatial expression only within the limits set by the laws of geometry. If we are to have any hope of 'reading off' social meaning from a building plan or other spatial artefact, therefore, we must, at the very least, take full account of the different physical parameters involved.

The above example of the terraced house, elementary though it is, well illustrates the point. Here it is not the fact that the house has a radial access pattern that is significant – this was common enough up and down the country – but that this pattern was realised in a plan of such tiny dimensions. In a bigger building, it would be relatively easy to achieve separate access to each room, and no special significance may attach to such an arrangement (this will obviously depend on its frequency of occurrence). But for the same thing to be repeated in a house of less than 3 metre frontage (and the house in Bristol is merely an example, albeit an extreme one, of a pattern repeated throughout the south of England), suggests a

great deal of social investment in privacy and separation. It is the interplay
of variables – topology, shape, size – not the access graph *per se* that is
telling.

Depth. It follows from what has been said that differences in 'depth', i.e. in
the number of levels, from one building to another, need not, in themselves, be expressive of differences in the pattern of domestic life. This is
not to deny the value of Chapman's inter-site comparisons, which are very
suggestive, but in view of the huge variation in house size (i.e. number of
rooms) across the sample, generalisations on the levels of 'access restriction' are not straightforward: a closer look is clearly required at the range
of access graphs among houses of a common size.

Room location. Individual rooms (i.e. rooms of a particular function) may
likewise change position for reasons other than social or ideological ones.
In some circumstances a move from one level to another may be highly
significant in social terms, indicating a possible change of status within the
household (see, for example, HANSON AND HILLIER 1979; also BROWN
1986). But accessibility may again be restricted by the basic room configuration. This is an important point to bear in mind when numerical
measures are applied to the graphs, e.g. the relative asymmetry (measure
RA) of Hillier and Hanson, which is used precisely to capture variability in
room 'depths' in a global sense. Although such a measure helps to give a
precise, numerical form to the differences in 'depth' among spaces, it by
no means follows that the figures can be taken as indices of social ordering
or social solidarity.

Effects of representation: internal space. Numerical analysis may also yield misleading results for other, very practical reasons, such as the way one
chooses to represent the layout as a graph. Graph representation, whatever
it may seem, is never a mechanical procedure. Where architectural plans
are concerned, it almost invariably involves some degree of qualitative
judgement. This is especially so where we are faced with curved spaces (e.g.
in Zulu kraals) or ones with several changes of direction, as is common
with corridors in large complexes. The question arises: when and how do
we cease to regard such a space as a single unit and divide it into separate
compartments? While the cellular layouts of Poljanica and elsewhere
present slightly less of a problem, one suspects that some interpretation
has also been required where the boundary walls of a space are ill defined
(see the examples illustrated in Figure 3.5 of Chapman's chapter).

Figure 4.5 of the present paper shows three hypothetical graphs, each representing two rooms, accessed from a common circulation space (e.g. a
hall). In the first the hall is treated as one compartment (hence represented
by a single vertex), in the second as two compartments (two vertices), in the

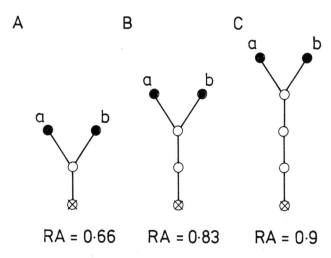

Figure 4.5 Variation in the 'Relative Asymmetry' of the system
according to the number of 'steps' from the exterior.

third as three (three vertices). Plans may well occur which are susceptible
to all of these interpretations (especially where the archaeological evidence
is unclear or incomplete). Measuring the RA of these systems, however,
with respect to the outside space, or what Hillier would term the carrier,
we find that the first graph gives a figure of 0.66, the second 0.83, and the
third 0.9. Hence, a striking increase in 'segregation' is found to occur as
additional circulation spaces are included (values range from 0 to 1, and
the higher the value, the greater is the segregation). Small decisions can
have large consequences. If formal measures are to be used as the basis for
comparative analysis, it is clearly necessary to be aware of such effects from
the outset.

Effects of representation: external space. Another example of the same phenomenon, and perhaps a more significant one as far as Chapman's analysis
is concerned, is the way that one chooses to represent space external to the
building. In Hillier and Hanson's work, external space is always regarded as
continuous and uniform for the purpose of graph representation. But external space, like that within the building, can also be highly differentiated:
there is a great deal of difference, for example, between a walled garden
and a street. In some circumstances, therefore, it might be more realistic to
designate the space as a series of units or compartments rather than as a
continuum. If this course is followed, however, the character of the access
graph may alter very significantly. Figure 4.6 gives a simple example of a
hypothetical three-room plan with entrances at the front and rear. Let us

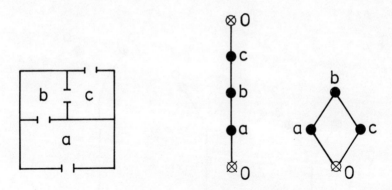

*Figure 4.6 Alternative representations of the access pattern
in a hypothetical building plan.*

assume, for the sake of argument, that the front access (at the bottom) is
from the street, while the latter opens on to a private garden. We therefore
have the choice of representing the front and back by a single vertex or by
two vertices, according to our priorities or our interpretation of the
available evidence. Essentially, only one link or edge in the graph is
affected by this decision, but when translated into the form of a 'justified'
graph (i.e. 'justified' with respect to the street), the differences are
dramatic. Where the external space is differentiated, we have a linear
sequence, four levels 'deep'; where it is undifferentiated, the graph is
reduced to a two-level 'depth', and acquires a cycle passing through the
outside space (it becomes what Hillier and Hanson term a 'distributed'
system). Not only is the 'depth' of individual spaces affected, but the
'permeability' characteristics of the whole graph are changed. It is easy to
see the distortions that may arise if numerical measures are attached to one
or other of these graphs.

In his study, Chapman appears to have opted in all cases to regard exterior space as a single entity, and thus to link all entrances to a common
base vertex. This has the virtue of consistency and seems consonant with
the archaeological evidence. His findings, however, are confusing and contradictory. From his discussion of measures (pp. 79–81) and the histograms
in Figure 3.15, it appears that the settlements resolve, somewhat strikingly,
into two distinct pairs: Targovište and Radingrad on the one hand, and
Ovcarovo and Poljanica on the other. The first pair are characterised, *inter
alia*, by the predominance of one- or two-entrance buildings; the second
include buildings with up to seven entrances. What is more interesting and
puzzling, however, is the fact that the second set tend to have 'deeper'
rather than 'shallower' access patterns than the first. As will be evident
from the above example, as long as the external space is assimilated into a

single vertex (the base vertex), an increase in the number of entrances will tend to make the 'justified' graph shallower, not deeper. But here, Chapman notes specifically that there is a tendency at Ovcarovo and Poljanica 'for inverse relationships between the ratios of deep:shallow houses and closed: open houses'.

If this is correct, the first question to ask is whether this is purely a function of size, i.e. are the most permeable houses the deepest simply because they have many more rooms than the others? If not, one then needs to question the accuracy of the access graphs themselves. Should it be true that depth is inversely related to openness, this makes for some fascinating possibilities regarding social control of the interior. However, one must suspect that some errors have crept into either the graph representation or the commentary, especially as, in his earlier remarks on Ovcarovo, Chapman observes that 'as the ratio of one- or two-door houses rises, so the ratio of deep:shallow houses increases' (p. 74), i.e. the very *opposite* of what he says in the conclusions, and exactly what we would predict on purely formal grounds.

Space and meaning. The final point is of a more general and theoretical nature, but is too important to be glossed over. Aside from the problems, both formal and empirical, of disentangling social from morphological parameters, how far is it justifiable to treat the relationship between social structure and spatial structure as intrinsically law-like? To what extent does consistency in spatial patterning, topological or otherwise, denote consistency in social patterning, and thus in social 'meaning'? Clearly, there is no one-to-one relationship between, for example, topological 'depth' (or, for that matter, RA) and social function. In many cases, 'depth' is found to correlate well with social hierarchy, the 'deepest' space within the complex being accorded to the most privileged person or sacred area of the building, e.g. the throne room, royal apartments, or a holy shrine. (In large, modern buildings, it may well be reserved, significantly enough, for the computer suite!) But 'depth' may also equate with 'profanity': in medieval houses, in London and elsewhere, the 'deepest' room was, more often than not, the privy at the end of the yard. In other cases still, the spaces most removed from the outside are reserved for storage or ancillary functions. For any individual building, the exact interpretation will depend on consideration of other attributes of the space(s) concerned, e.g. size, shape, physical (as distinct from topological) location, and, of course, furniture and fittings.

The underlying epistemological issue, however, is broader than this. Boast (1987, 453–4), following Giddens, has pointed, quite correctly, to the dangers of treating meaning as something fixed and unchanging, and has argued further that the built environment, as a meaningful object or form, only exists by virtue of our interaction with it. In her study of the Endo people of Kenya, Moore (1986) shows forcefully the way that space may act a medium for different and shifting discourses between men and women, while Graves (1989), in a discussion of the English parish church, likewise illustrates the ability of a particular spatial structure to sustain different meanings, the exact role being determined by context and invoked in practice. These are powerful arguments and would apparently do much to undermine the notion of space as an independent variable in a social sense. At the very least they suggest that 'retrodiction' of past social patterns is only likely to be possible on a very broad and strategic level.

These conclusions, however, are a double-edged sword in that they depend upon, and point towards, a shift away from the analysis of archaeological data as such: Moore's observations are based on detailed ethnographic study, whilst Graves's are drawn primarily from the study of documentary evidence. Given that the archaeologist must work primarily from the evidence of the artefact itself, it is still legitimate to stress the value of spatial analysis as an approach in its own right. Whatever its limitations for information retrieval, it may be the best tool that the archaeologist possesses – a fact that once again underlines the need for analytical rigour.

Alpha analysis

The other area where Chapman employs spatial analysis is at the level of the settlement itself, his intention being to clarify the pattern of space between dwellings and, as with the dwelling plan, to gain some understanding of what the differences from one tell to another actually 'mean' in social terms.

As before, one of the principal tools he uses – 'alpha analysis' – derives from Hillier and Hanson. Like gamma analysis this is a somewhat obsolescent term, but embraces a series of techniques and measures, all of which attempt to do for settlement analysis what the access graph does for the building plan, i.e. elucidate its relational structure. A relational analysis of the open space network of a settlement is inherently problematic in that, while the interiors of buildings are normally composed of well-defined, bounded elements (the rooms), settlement space has no such elements but is, by its very nature, continuous. To overcome this problem, Hillier and Hanson developed two distinct but complementary systems of representation: the axial map and the convex map. This is a wholly original technique and is well summarised by Chapman. Axiality is essentially one-dimensional, representing the maximum global linear extension of the system. It is intended to express, visually and numerically, the propensity for movement into and within the system, and especially the openness of the public space network to the penetration of strangers or outsiders. Convexity, its counterpart, records the two-dimensional extension of space (i.e. its 'fatness'). It aims to capture the interface between strangers and inhabitants. The former is a dynamic measure, the latter a static one.

As far as one can tell from the illustrations, Chapman's application of the techniques is fairly orthodox, although the axial map he illustrates (his Figure 3.8) appears rather more orthogonal than one would expect. The aim of the axial map is to represent the spatial system in terms of the fewest, longest lines of sight and access: an axial line is a continuous 'string' running through a series of convex 'beads'. In many cases the greatest length of line is achieved by cutting diagonally across a series of convex spaces rather than following the 'axis' (i.e. the centre-line) of a route in the strict sense. It may be that certain axes could be both longer and more richly interconnected than Chapman has shown – a factor that may well affect the measure of 'integration'.

This point of detail aside, various questions arise concerning the mode of analysis itself. Chapman draws on a whole battery of measures (eight in all), ranging from 'convex articulation' to 'axial ringiness', in an attempt to extract meaningful information from the open space network of the tells. As it stands, this 'grapeshot' approach is somewhat doubtful for the simple reason that the significance of the measures is, for the most part, highly indeterminate: there are no predefined rules of interpretation, and no sure way of assigning priority to one measure over another without the benefit of additional information, i.e. contextual evidence. In general terms, the measures have to be seen as part of a process of theoretical exposition and exploration rather than of empirical generalisation.

Measure of integration. The great exception to this is the integration measure, real relative asymmetry (RRA), whose implications have been extensively corroborated in practice. As Chapman has indicated, this is a global measure, based on calculation of mean 'depth' of all spaces in a system with respect to a particular 'root': it measures how near or far is the rest of the system from that space in terms of axial lines. In his analysis of the tells Chapman uses the site entrances as his root. A study of some seventy-five different urban areas (UNIT FOR ARCHITECTURAL STUDIES 1986) has shown a consistently strong correlation between RRA and space use and movement. Across a wide range of settlements, the most integrated routes (axes) were found to be the places where pedestrian movement was most intense, while segregated areas were where movement was sparse or non-existent. This empirical correlation has made it the single most useful and reliable measure in the space syntax armoury.

The importance of the integration measure for architecture is its potential for predicting patterns of movement and thus averting the kinds of dead spaces, 'urban deserts', that have become so familiar in modern developments, along with the undesirable social consequences (e.g. vandalism) that flow from them. For the archaeologist, there is the possibility that it may likewise point to the areas of greatest accessibility in ancient settlements, and thus of occupancy, social contact, and interaction. It would

then offer itself as an objective way to delineate social space and compare
the social control of space across settlements, as Chapman seeks to do here.

Since Chapman himself uses the integration measure to suggest possibilities rather than as a definitive tool, I shall confine myself to a few
general points about the method.

Movement and space-use: axial analysis vs. node-map analysis. Axial analysis
differs from conventional node-map analysis, as used in planning and
transportation modelling, by virtue of the fact that it asserts the importance
of alignment or linear extension in spatial systems in the prediction of
movement. In the latter, by contrast, it is considered sufficient to characterise the system on a purely topological basis (each street or distinct segment of the network being represented by an edge, and each junction by a
node, in similar fashion to the access graph). Axial representation thus
preserves something of the geometry of the open space network – a property lost in node-map analysis – but without going so far as to render the
system in all its detail. Although, as far as I am aware, no direct comparison
of axial and node-map analysis has ever been undertaken, extensive empirical tests, in the form of systematic observations of space-use, suggest that
the axial map will perform better in most, if not all, contemporary situations.

The corollary of this is that vision – the ability to see one's way through a
system – plays a far more important role in the apprehension and cogni-
tion of urban space than previously thought. It is this, rather than actual
physical distance, that emerges as the prime determinant of movement
through the system. This is an intuitively plausible conclusion (or hypothesis) with respect to strangers, i.e. people who are trying to navigate the
system for the first time, but is less convincing with respect to inhabitants
and others who are familiar with the layout. Once people know their way
around, we should expect them to depend far less on visual clues, and
make greater use of shortcuts, even if these are not very axial. Hence, variation in the pattern of movement is to be expected across settlements
according to the balance of inhabitants and strangers. Although Hillier has
developed various 'second-order' measures ('intelligibility', 'predictability')
to clarify the relationship between the local and global characteristics of
settlement space and, by extension, to predict what he calls the 'interface
potential' between strangers and inhabitants within a spatial system, these
measures are conjectural only, and their social correlates must remain
open to doubt.

The magnet effect. Axial mapping effectively excludes information on land-
uses, which can have an important influence on the patterns of movement.
Since people do not merely walk through a system but make for known
destinations within it, we should expect 'natural movement' to be distorted

by the 'magnet effect' of social attractants such as shops and places of work. The draw that is exercised by these centres may greatly outweigh the background level of movement generated 'naturally' by the spatial system. At present there is no way of assigning weight to these different factors, so that, for the archaeologist, it seems unsafe to infer too much from the global axial measure alone.

Problem of causality. A further complicating factor is the difficulty of distinguishing between cause and effect. For Hillier and Hanson, shops, market places, etc. will tend to occur in highly integrated locations because these are the points where people will naturally meet or congregate within the system. In other words, the main facilities arise in response to the pattern of natural movement, which in turn is generated by the morphology of the system, as characterised by the axial map.

It is equally possible, however, that the converse is true, i.e. that spaces which, through historical accident or special circumstance, become centres of activity are progressively altered to improve circulation and access. As the routes are widened and straightened to facilitate movement, the more likely they are to become 'integrated' in an axial map of the settlement. This may well have been the path followed in many medieval cities, where market-places were only rarely established *ab initio*. Encroachment was widespread during the later medieval period, and it is clear that projections and intrusions into public open space could make thoroughfares increasingly tortuous rather than increasingly axial. But the forces of individual expansion and colonisation were opposed by collective pressure and the strength of tradition, and there is no doubt that these countervailing influences were more likely to be effective in market-places and other busy 'public' areas than elsewhere. This is as true of ancient Mesopotamia (see FRANKFORT 1950, 109) as of medieval Europe (see the example of Tübingen in SAALMAN 1968, 32ff.). Hence, there is every reason to expect differences in status to be emphasised over time, with major thoroughfares becoming increasingly 'integrated' in the axial sense.

In practice, of course, the two factors – morphology and function – are so inextricably intertwined as to make it virtually impossible in most circumstances to say which set the whole process in train. This *evolutionary* aspect of social space, however, is important. Among ancient settlements, or settlements at an early stage of their development, it is quite conceivable that social contact flourished in spaces that had yet to develop the beneficial characteristics of convexity and axial integration, in which case RRA will not prove a very helpful pointer. And although Hillier postulates a 'globalising tendency' – a dynamic that preserves spatial order and intelligibility with growth – it is not inconceivable that the balance between local and global spatial characteristics should fluctuate over time in response to political and economic shifts, rather than remain constant.

Social and cultural traits. Patterns of activity are also strongly tied up with social and cultural traits: although physical movement can be seen as a material prerequisite of social patterning, the latter in turn serves to define and prescribe patterns of movement. It is axiomatic that a key distinction in many cultures is that of gender, men and women having distinct spatial domains. Home is characteristically the domain of women in many societies (ancient Greece, modern Arab countries of the Near East and North Africa). This home-centredness may be complemented by restrictions on movement outside the dwelling: in some Saharan towns women move about the settlement by an independent network of routes at rooftop level. Again it is difficult or impossible to identify such characteristics *a priori*: in all probability they can be extracted only by observation or from the historical record.

Axial representation. On a purely formal note, the system of axial representation itself has certain characteristics which may weaken or limit its predictive power. Most notably, the use of the axial line as a basis both of numerical measurement and of observation on the ground assumes homogeneity within and along that line. In practice, considerable variation may occur along the length of a major axis, in land-use, occupancy, and, one would infer, in the pattern of movement itself. There may also be marked qualitative differences from one space (axis) to another, as Chapman himself observes for Chalcolithic tells. In this respect, conventional node-map analysis would seem to have certain advantages, in that it ensures that every segment of space – the portion of space between junctions – is represented separately, allowing greater differentiation within the system. It seems highly likely that the performance of axial analysis could be considerably enhanced if the mode of description were modified to permit a similar level of differentiation. I understand that such a refinement is currently being explored by Hillier *et al.*

––––––––––––––

Bibliography

Boast, Robin B. 1987. 'Rites of passage: topological and formal representation' *Environment and Planning B: Planning and Design* 14:4, 451–66.

Brown, Frank E. 1986. 'Continuity and change in the urban house: developments in domestic space organisation in seventeenth-century London' *Comparative Studies in Society and History* 28:3, 558–90.

Foster, Sally M. 1989. 'Analysis of spatial patterns in buildings (access analysis) as an insight into social structure: examples from the Scottish Iron Age' *Antiquity* 63, 40–50.

Frankfort, H. 1950. 'Town planning in ancient Mesopotamia' *Town Planning Review* 21, 99–114.

Graves, C. Pamela 1989. 'Social space in the English medieval parish church' *Economy and Society* 18:3, 297–322.

Hanson, Julienne and Bill Hillier 1979. 'Tradition and change in the English house: a comparative approach to the analysis of small house plans' mimeo, Unit for Architectural Studies, Bartlett School of Architecture and Planning, University College London (London).

March, L. J. and J. P. Steadman 1971. *The Geometry of Environment*. R.I.B.A. Publications (London).

Moore, Henrietta L. 1986. *Space, Text and Gender: an anthropological study of the Marakwet of Kenya*. Cambridge University Press (Cambridge).

Muthesius, S. 1982. *The English Terraced House*. Yale University Press (New Haven and London).

Saalman, H. 1968. *Medieval Cities*, Series 'Planning and Cities' (Collins, G.R. gen. ed.). Studio Vista (London).

Steadman, J. P. 1973. 'Graph-theoretic representation of architectural arrangement' *Architectural Research and Teaching* 2, 161–72; repr. in L. J. March 1976. *The Architecture of Form*. Cambridge University Press (Cambridge).

Unit for Architectural Studies 1986. 'Spatial configuration and use density at the urban level: towards a predictive model', *Research Report*, Bartlett School of Architecture and Planning, University College London (London).

Five

The Late Neolithic House in Orkney

COLIN RICHARDS

Although Orkney provides the best known and best preserved remains of Neolithic houses and settlements in western Europe, this evidence is virtually ignored in previous social analyses. Instead it is the chambered tombs and henge monuments that tend to provide the foundation for competing schemes of social evolution. This paper examines the architecture and spatial structure of the house in relation to other forms of late Neolithic constructions. The idea of cosmology is examined as an overall principle of classification and order, within which human relationships are continually negotiated. This involves both the spatial and temporal elements of daily routines. In this way all areas of human activity may be examined within a single framework, overcoming previous synthetic difficulties.

Within the Orkney Islands a combination of factors present the archaeologist with an exceptionally complete structural and material record of the late Neolithic period. A lack of timber together with a geology of easily laminated sandstone apparently led to the practice of building houses, chambered tombs, and internal features of henge monuments in stone. The utilisation of sandstone as a building material was not restricted to the shell of the construction but also proved suitable for the internal furniture and fittings of the structures. Due to the lack of intensive methods of cultivation in modern times and the extraordinary weather conditions in the north of Scotland a number of complete late Neolithic 'villages' have been discovered in varying conditions of preservation.

The most famous and best preserved of these settlements is Skara Brae, which was revealed from beneath the sand dunes of western Mainland by a terrible storm in 1850. The condition of this settlement provoked both

Plate 5.1 The internal layout of stone furniture within the late Neolithic house.

Piggott (1954, 324) and Childe (1946, 25) to speak of its unique and miraculous preservation and, indeed, these are not overstatements since the majority of the houses at Skara Brae are standing to roof level and have intact internal stone furniture (Plate 1). This state of preservation is frequently commented on in the archaeological literature but never actually drawn on for analytical purposes. Moreover, in the majority of social analyses of the Neolithic period undertaken over the past few years, the architecture and organisation of the Orcadian settlements is completely ignored (e.g. RENFREW 1979; FRASER 1983; SHARPLES 1985; RICHARDS 1988). Instead, the chambered tombs and henge monuments tend to form the basis of interpretations (see, however, HODDER 1982).

Where the settlements are discussed (e.g. MACKIE 1977; HEDGES 1984; CLARKE AND SHARPLES 1985) the full potential of standing buildings, surviving almost intact, is never realised except in a purely descriptive or typological manner. Ironically, apart from descriptive praise, Skara Brae is treated in exactly the same way as if it were a ploughed out and eroded site remaining only as a two-dimensional plan. The presence of standing houses not only provides a further spatial dimension but should also promote a similar response in archaeological analysis.

Perhaps one of the main factors lying behind the reluctance to enter this area of study is the nature of architectural analysis, which necessarily focuses attention on the social arena. No longer should architectural variation be seen merely as the subject of typological classification, nor solely as a practical response to the physical environment. Instead, for any meaningful discussion of architectural form, social practices must occupy a central position (GUIDINO 1975, 7–11).

The actual process of building a house and delineating space effectively draws on social and cosmological ideas of order; architecture does not suddenly come into existence but is constructed by people and is therefore defined by their interpretations and intentions. As space has no intrinsic qualities any interpretation of spatial symbolism is dependent on the invocation of meaning through the presence of people. Understanding comes in terms of the social experiences of those who lived within the houses, moved around the settlements, and understood the organisation and classification of the world. Since the routines of life incorporate and recreate meaning, a recursive relationship exists in which spatial order may be frequently redefined without any alteration to the physical configuration of the spatial context (BLIER 1987). This contingency on social practices is, of course, not restricted to houses alone but occurs in all forms of constructed space, even in the most formal buildings such as a chambered tomb. If spatial meaning is derived from a conjunction of cosmology and everyday situations, then importantly it must also involve the co-ordination of space and time.

As 'time and the way it is handled has a lot to do with structuring space' (HALL 1966, 163), it is important to recognise in architecture an ability to situate the subject in space and time. For it is the presence of people at specific and appropriate places throughout the day, week, month, and year which constitutes and reproduces the routines and cycles of everyday life. As Bourdieu (1977, 162) recognises, 'it is simply a question of being in the right place at the right time.' In this way it is possible to understand why in preliterate societies time is often conceived in the form of events and the places at which they occur (GIDDENS 1981, 36).

Place and architecture, therefore, combine to structure and reproduce the essential routines of life by representing fixed points in the endless cycles of life and the cosmos. However, where people may or may not go, and what may or may not be witnessed at a particular place and time, is crucial in emphasising differences between people and thus structures of authority. In this aspect, architecture constitutes a powerful social instrument of restriction and manipulation (see GOFFMAN 1968).

Within the architecture of the Orcadian Neolithic house there exists a spatial medium in which systems of classification, and their cosmological basis, are continually realised in the various tasks and activities of everyday life. Here too lie the social divisions of inequality. The symbolism of the house, in all its ambiguity, remains an architectural expression embodying both ontological and metaphorical knowledge of the world (BLIER 1987).

In their method of construction, the late Neolithic houses of Orkney display a remarkable similarity (Figure 5.1). Grouped together in villages, the

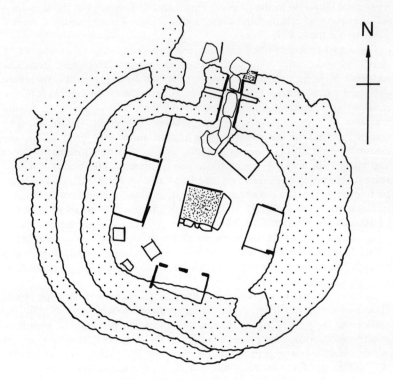

Figure 5.1 The Neolithic house.

regularity in the internal organisation of space is a consistent feature of design. Whether such homogeneity represents a high degree of cultural integration and 'harmony regarding the goals, norms, and values of life' (STOKLUND 1980, 122) is open to question. However, it clearly shows the importance attached to spatial interpretation in establishing order 'at the level of architecture as inserted into the social environment and at the level of cosmological referent' (GUIDINO 1975, 9).

The interior structure of the house is formed by the cruciform positioning of the stone furniture and entrance around a central hearth. Stone box beds are situated on either side of the hearth and at the rear of the house; opposite the entrance is the stone dresser. As others have recognised (CHILDE 1946, 28; HODDER 1982, 222; CLARKE AND SHARPLES 1985, 70), this apparently symmetrical organisation belies subtle differences in size and position. For instance, the right-hand bed is always larger than the left; frequently the ambry or keeping-place set in the wall above the bed maintains

Plate 2. View of the interior presented to a person entering the house.

the same difference in size, and the entrance is often situated slightly right of centre.

The hearth constitutes a central point of the house and the lives of its inhabitants. Indeed, it is the centre of the world, the *axis mundi*, providing an eternal reference point from which all things and people take their position and orientation. The fire it contains provides light and heat which, in the extreme climatic conditions of Orkney, are vital to the maintenance of life. Traditionally the fireplace symbolises the unity and well being of the whole family; the most serious offence to be committed within the house was to allow the fire to go out. The keeping in of the fire for over forty years was a common occurrence in the Northern Isles.

As Leach (1977) stresses, the cultural, transformational qualities of fire transcend the physical changes occurring in cooking and ceramic production, and fire assumes a supernatural and mythological significance (LÉVI-STRAUSS 1986). Consequently, elaborate sanctions surround fire and its use; this extends to ignition (INGOLD 1986, 268–71), and its residue, ash (MOORE 1986, 102–6). The construction of the square hearth, composed of four upright stone slabs set into the ground, certainly constituted a primary element in the building of the Neolithic house, and when the house was altered, rebuilt, or demolished, the original hearth tended to be left in position (RICHARDS in prep.). Thus, the hearth would seem to have been an extremely potent symbol embodying many disparate meanings.

When approaching a house, the subject had an initial view, through the entrance, of the central hearth and adjacent area to the right and the rear shelving with its contents (Plate 5.2). At Skara Brae the principal use of decoration was to mark paths of movement, either to emphasise and draw attention towards different areas of the house or in conjunction with threshold slabs to delineate space within the long entrance passages running through the settlement (RICHARDS forth.).

On crossing the threshold of the house, the internal organisation of space would have become visible, especially the right-hand side of the habitation, which would tend to receive more light coming through the entrance. In contrast, the left side would frequently appear in semi-darkness and the whole interior would probably be further obscured by smoke rising from the central fire. These differences, which can be distinguished in the varying quality of light available to the interior, are reiterated in the greater ease of access that a person is given to the right-hand side of the house.

The appropriate path of movement within the house is difficult to discern and would almost certainly have been dependent on an individual's social position and the activities being undertaken. However, in some houses the direction of entry is clearly defined. At Skara Brae the paving slabs leading into the interior of House 7 form a path into the right-hand area (Figure 5.2). Indeed, the position of stone furniture to the left of the

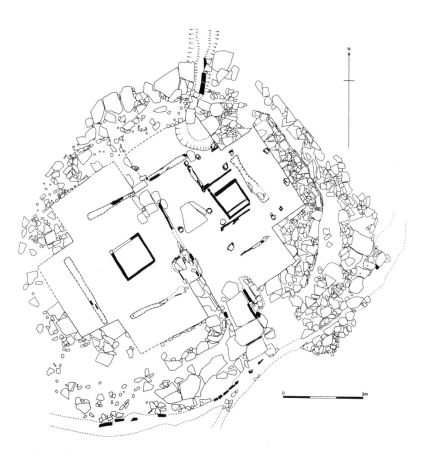

Figure 5.2. House 7 at Skara Brae with paved path leading into the right-hand area.

doorway effectively prohibit dignified entry. This rule of passage is clearly stated within the architecture of the large central House 2 at Barnhouse, where the position of the doorway ensures that visual access into the left 'inner' area is only possible after the subject is completely inside the building (Figure 5.3). In fact, the architecture of this house draws on and emphasises restriction to the degree of exclusion.

Whether movement into and within the house was restricted by a concern over the area illuminated by natural light (see RAPOPORT 1969, 75), which for houses situated in the open would vary throughout the day according to the position of the sun, is difficult to determine. Of greater

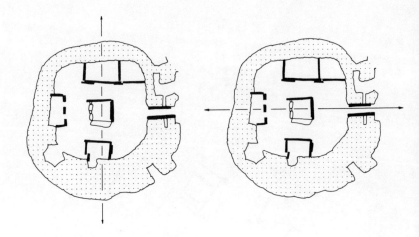

Figure 3. Plan of House 2 at Barnhouse.

clarity is the effect on the internal organisation of space which is redefined
by virtue of entry into the right-hand area. Although in many social circumstances the rear dresser will have represented the innermost area within
the house, perhaps with the 'dresser' assuming sacred qualities (COLLETT
1987, 109), when people enter the house into the right-hand side the
darker left-hand area becomes the deepest spatial unit.

With symbolic meaning contingent on particular activities within architectural form, spatial redefinition would have been a constant occurrence
within the house. In discussing spatial representation, Childe (1946, 32)
noted the similarities between the architecture of the Skara Brae houses
and the blackhouses of the Western Isles, where 'the right-hand side of the
single room was the men's side and the left reserved for women.' Within
the blackhouse, gender distinctions, particularly the women's role in food
preparation and cooking, assume spatial significance. This same space,
however, was redefined when guests entered the house. Seating was
arranged around the central fireplace; the status of the visitor was represented by the position offered relative to the rear of the hearth (CLARKE
AND SHARPLES 1985, 70). In this situation a front/back distinction comes
into play with the most important or prestigious position being directly
behind the hearth facing the entrance. Although a direct analogy is not
suggested, these examples do serve to demonstrate how the symbolic
meaning of a given spatial structure can be completely altered through different social practices.

Having stressed the importance of the internal organisation of the house

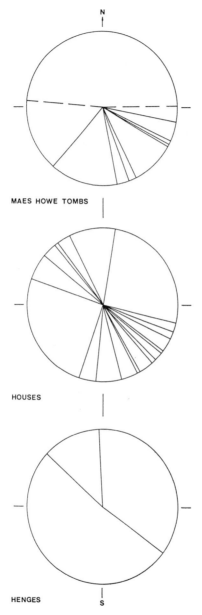

Figure 5.4. The orientation of late Neolithic houses and 'Maes Howe' type passage graves in Orkney.

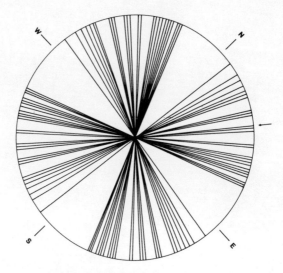

Figure 5.5 The orientation of hearths.

as a microcosm of the socially constructed world and the necessary links
with wider spatial and temporal principles and cycles, a broader understanding must be sought in terms of symbolic classifications. It is here that
the question of orientation may be introduced. Since the four main
features of the house interior are set in a cruciform arrangement around
the central hearth they have the bearings of four Neolithic cardinal points.
The entrance orientation of excavated houses at Barnhouse, Rinyo, and
Skara Brae shows that 80 per cent lie on a south-east/north-west axis,
which is also characteristic of the Orcadian passage graves (Figure 5.4).
However, a greater sample number is achieved by examining the alignment
of hearths (Figure 5.5), which always correspond to the cruciform spatial
arrangement within the houses, even when it is impossible to establish the
entrance orientation.

It is clear that this alignment is a consistent feature of house architecture.
Its significance, however, lies in the fusion of space and time. Each of the
four components which delineate space within the house, the entrance,
rear dresser, right and left beds, correspond to the key temporal points of
the annual cycle; midsummer sunrise and sunset, and the winter sunrise
and sunset.

A conscious concern with these annual events is displayed within the impressive architecture of Maes Howe, a house of the dead (Figure 5.6). This
notable deviant from the other Orcadian passage graves is orientated

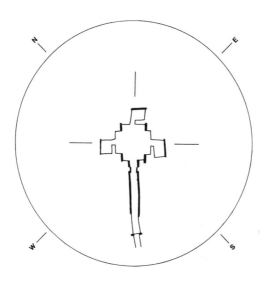

Figure 5.6. The alignment of Maes Howe on the winter solstice sunset.

towards midwinter sunset, marking the end of the day, having the longest period of darkness in the year. In Orkney the contrast between light and darkness, heat and cold is a major component of the annual cycle (Figure 5.7). Midwinter sees over eighteen hours of darkness as opposed to eighteen hours of sunshine at midsummer, when the night-time is merely a twilight zone and it never really becomes dark. In this context the marking of the darkest day by a symbol of the dead introduces a further element into an already elaborate classification scheme.

Just like human action, classifications are not static but only take on concrete expression in certain places at appropriate times. In linking the expression of ideas of left, inside, darkness, and death with midwinter, and right, outside, light, and life with midsummer within the architecture of the house, it is important to consider what occurs when the subject steps out of the house into the outside world. Then the house itself has to be categorised (BOURDIEU 1977).

In this rather brief canvas the architecture of the Neolithic house has been examined as an expression of social classification and cosmological themes. The ideas of order and correctness employed within the architecture of the house are suggested to be homologous to wider spheres of experience. These categories are drawn on in different social situations and in turn influence the course of events. The significance of such spatial representation is that by invoking wider themes of meaning and drawing

Figure 7. The hours of sunshine at midsummer and midwinter in Orkney (drawing Paul Carrington).

on such symbolism, everyday activities and routines assume ontological status. In this conjunction is visible the naturalisation of authority and domination and significantly the power of architecture.

Acknowledgements

I would particularly like to thank Patrick Ashmore, John Barrett, Pam Graves, Jane Downes, and all my colleagues at Glasgow for discussion and help in making these ideas coherent.

Bibliography

Blier, Suzanne P. 1987. *The Anatomy of Architecture: Ontology and Metaphor in Batammaliba Architectural Expression.* Cambridge University Press (Cambridge).

Bourdieu, Pierre 1977. *Outline of a Theory of Practice.* Cambridge University Press (Cambridge).

Childe, V. Gordon 1946. *Scotland Before the Scots.* Methuen (London).

Clarke, David V. and Niall Sharples 1985. 'Settlements and subsistence in the third millennium BC' in C. Renfrew (ed.) *The Prehistory of Orkney,* 54–82. EUP (Edinburgh).

Collett, David 1987. 'A contribution to the study of migrations in the archaeological record: the Ngoni and Kololo migrations as a case study' in I. Hodder (ed.) *Archaeology as Long Term History,* 105–16. Cambridge University Press (Cambridge).

Fraser, David 1983. *Land and Society in Neolithic Orkney.* B.A.R. BS117 (Oxford).

Giddens, Anthony 1981. *A Contemporary Critique of Historical Materialism.* MacMillan (London).

Goffman, Erving 1978. *Asylums.* Pelican (Harmondsworth).

Guidino, Enrico 1975. *Primitive Architecture.* Electa (Milan).

Hall, E. T. 1966. *The Hidden Dimension.* Doubleday (New York).

Hedges, John 1985. *Tomb of the Eagles.* (London).

Hodder, Ian R. 1982. *Symbols in Action.* Cambridge University Press (Cambridge).

Ingold, Tim 1986. *The Appropriation of Nature.* Manchester University Press (Manchester).

Leach, Edmund 1977. 'A view from the bridge' in M. Spriggs (ed.) *Archaeology and Anthropology,* 161–76. B.A.R. SS19 (Oxford).

Lévi-Strauss, Claude 1986. *The Raw and the Cooked.* Penguin (Harmondsworth).

Mackie, E. W. 1977. *Science and Society in Prehistoric Britain.* Paul Elek (London).

Moore, Henrietta L. 1986. *Space, Text and Gender.* Cambridge University Press (Cambridge).

Piggott, Stuart 1954. *Neolithic Cultures of the British Isles.* Cambridge University Press (Cambridge).

Rapoport, A. 1969. 'The Pueblo and the hogan' in P. Oliver (ed.) *Shelter and Society.* Praeger (New York).

Renfrew, Colin 1979. *Investigations in Orkney.* Thames and Hudson (London).

Richards, Colin 1988. 'Altered images: a re-examination of Neolithic mortuary practices in Orkney' in J. Barrett and I. Kinnes (eds.) *The*

Archaeology of Context in the Neolithic and Bronze Age: Recent Trends, 42–56. Collis (Sheffield).

Richards, Colin forth. 'Skara Brae: revisiting a Neolithic village in Orkney' in W. S. Hanson and E. A. Slater (eds.) *Remaking Scottish Archaeology*. Aberdeen Univeristy Press (Aberdeen).

Richards, Colin in prep. *The Neolithic Settlement Complex at Barnhouse Farm*.

Sharples, Niall 1985. 'Individual and community: the changing role of megaliths in the Orcadian Neolithic' *Proceedings of the Prehistoric Society*, 59–74.

Shee Twohig, Elizabeth 1981. *The Megalithic Art of Western Europe*. Oxford University Press (Oxford).

Stoklund, Bjarne 1980. 'Houses and culture in the North Atlantic Isles: three models of interpretation' *Ethnologie Scandinavice*, 113–32.

Six

Domestic Organisation and Gender Relations in Iron Age and Romano-British Households

RICHARD HINGLEY

In this paper a tentative model for the organisation of the Iron Age and Romano-British household is explored. It will be proposed that all Iron Age and many Romano-British houses were created according to the same conceptual model and that this model is expressed in spatial terms by the division of the house into 'public' and 'private' areas. The same conceptual model can be identified within some Iron Age and Romano-British settlements and patterns of settlement. Finally, some potential methods for exploring gender relations are examined.

Introduction

Symbolic space and the settlement

In many pre-modern/pre-industrial societies the house was (or is) of great symbolic significance to those who lived (or live) within it. In some societies the house serves as a microcosm for the social universe of its inhabitants – in other words the house expresses the people's perception of the organisation of their society and world. Social factors are therefore responsible for the form of the house – its shape, the number and distribution of rooms and also the distribution of activities within those rooms. The important principle is that among many communities:

> The Cosmic may be reflected in a microcosm at a whole range of scales, from an entire land through a city, a village, a house as a whole, the space within a house, and the furniture within it. Each,

or all, may reflect the shape in which the world is visualised
(RAPOPORT 1969, 50).[1]

Societies that exhibit this type of organisation include European examples
(RAPOPORT 1969, 51, 54).

A direction of interest for social anthropologists and some social historians and architects is an understanding of how the house was viewed by
those who built it and lived within it. It is evident that social concepts are
rarely directly reflected in the spatial structure of the house or settlement.
A structure of differentiation, or 'topology', is imposed on space by all individuals within society, and this topology enables other relationships to be
expressed in its terms (THORNTON 1980, 14). The extent to which archaeologists can determine this particular 'subjectivity' from the evidence which
is available in the archaeological record is debatable (e.g. DOUGLAS 1972;
BARRETT 1989a, 305; KENT 1990, 7).

The tools that are available to archaeologists who wish to develop this
type of model are those of spatial archaeology (CLARKE 1972; 1977). The
methods of spatial archaeology include the analysis of the number and the
distribution of rooms and patterns of access between rooms/resource
spaces within and between buildings. Another method is the analysis of the
differing uses to which individual rooms or areas of rooms were put. The
evidence for this type of analysis includes major structures (hearths, ovens,
benches, loom settings, beds, etc.) and the artefactual signature of a room/
resource space (i.e. the range of artefacts lost or deposited within the room
and found during excavation).

Previous studies of Iron Age and Romano-British houses

Prehistorians have adopted these methods; the best known example is
Clarke's influential analysis of the Iron Age settlement at Glastonbury Lake
Village (CLARKE 1972). Clarke identified a standardised and repetitive
'modular unit' within the settlement. This consisted of two major houses
associated with a minor house, a granary, and other structures. This modular unit is repeated several times within the settlement and Clarke's analysis
enabled an understanding of the development of the individual modules

---

[1] Among the Dogon (Africa) the house is thought to reflect a man lying on his right side and
procreating. The same pattern repeats itself continually at an ever-expanding scale, leading
from man to the cosmos (GRIAULE AND DIETERLEN 1954). The Pawnee (North America) earth-
lodge reflects its occupant's concept of the cosmos: the floor is the plain, the walls the distant
horizon, the dome the arching sky and the central opening the zenith (RAPOPORT 1969, 52). In
Kabyle (Africa) the house is organised according to a set of oppositions – fire:water, cooked:
raw, high:low, light:shade, day:night, male:female, fertilising:able to be fertilised. The same
oppositions are established between the house as a whole and the rest of the universe
(BOURDIEU 1977, 90–1). Among the Iraqw (Africa) the relationship between the inside and outside of the house is the same as the relationship between the settled land and the wilderness
outside its borders (THORNTON 1980, 31; see RAPOPORT 1969, 50–5; CUNNINGHAM 1973 and
KUS AND RAHARIJAONA 1990 for other studies).

and the whole settlement through time.

The detailed analysis of the evidence from Glastonbury and the organisation of the individual modules has now been discredited. The model is invalidated both by increased knowledge of the British Iron Age (COLES AND COLES 1986, 169) and also by the demonstration that it does not relate directly to the published evidence (BARRETT 1987, 421). The general argument made by Clarke in the article remains valid, however, and forms a powerful statement of the potential of spatial archaeology. Indeed a number of other prehistorians have adopted Clarke's methods in an attempt to analyse Bronze Age and Iron Age household organisation (see ELLISON 1978; 1981; DREWETT 1982; PARKER PEARSON forth.).

There have been few attempts to analyse household organisation from the available evidence for Roman houses. This is a consequence of the nature of the philosophy behind past studies (HINGLEY forth.). Accounts of Roman houses have concentrated on morphology and typology (RICHMOND 1969; APPLEBAUM 1972; HINGLEY 1989a), although on occasions some attempts have been made to build social models for the evidence (STEVENS 1966; APPLEBAUM 1972; SMITH 1973; 1978a; 1982). New directions are required in Romano-British archaeology (HINGLEY forth.). The spatial analysis of Romano-British houses forms one important new direction of study. The same arguments are generally true for Iron Age houses (PARKER PEARSON forth.), although there has been a greater interest in spatial analysis among prehistoric archaeologists, such studies are still rare.

The particular need for a new approach to the study of Romano-British houses is a reflection of the potential of spatial archaeology to reanalyse the available subject matter. There is a wealth of artefactual and structural evidence for the houses of Roman Britain. A range of simple and complex house types developed in the first to fourth century AD along with, in the civilian area of the province, a 'consumer society' which produced vast quantities of rubbish. There is the potential within the Roman period of Britain for useful analysis of household orgnisation. Many houses appear to have been kept very clean, but for unknown reasons a limited number produce large quantities of occupation material which forms a potentially rich source for social analysis of house interiors (see below).

The approach in this chapter

In this chapter an attempt is made to use some of the available evidence to investigate the organisation of Iron Age and Romano-British households. 'Household' is defined as those who lived within a single dwelling. It is evident that in many societies the family and the household are not identical groups (e.g. BENDER 1967). The relationship between family and household within society requires detailed social and historical analysis, as does the internal structure of the household in terms of any gender- and age-related groups (MOORE 1988, 54). In archaeological study it is possible to examine household organisation through the methods of spatial analysis. For the purposes of this chapter the household constitutes the group who used or resided within a single house or group of closely related buildings (HINGLEY 1989a). The organisation of the household refers to the size of the resident group and the allocation of activities and responsibilities between gender divisions and generational groups.

Three points are discussed in this chapter. Firstly, the evidence for a division of many Iron Age houses into two broad conceptual zones – a 'public' and a 'private' area – is reviewed. It is tentatively proposed that this division of space reflects a contemporary concept of the organisation of territory. A brief review of some evidence suggests that this conceptual model may also be reflected in certain settlement forms and landscape patterns of the British Iron Age. Secondly, it is argued that the majority of Romano-British houses can be reduced to the same simple spatial model that is reflected in the Iron Age round-house. It can therefore be argued that there is a broad trend of continuity from Iron Age to Romano-British house forms, or – to put the same argument another way – that Roman houses were derived from a strong indigenous tradition of architecture which was based on a particular concept of the world.

Thirdly, there is a brief discussion of the evidence for spatial organisation of the interior of Romano-British houses. The evidence that is presently available is very scarce but enables a possible connection to be made between the organisational model at the centre of Iron Age and Romano-British houses and a model for gender relations. The conclusion to this final section of the chapter is that while this approach has much potential, further work will be required if a detailed understanding of the Iron Age and Romano-British household is to be gained.

A conceptual model for Iron Age houses

The round-house typifies the Bronze Age and Iron Age settlement record in Britain (Figure 6.1, a-d). On rare occasions rectangular houses occur (e.g. HARDING 1973) and it has been argued that rectangular houses become the typical form over parts of eastern England during the latest part of the Iron Age (RODWELL 1978); round-houses, however, predominate throughout the whole of later prehistory and are common throughout Britain.

A tentative model for the organisation of late Bronze Age settlement places individual houses within compounds (ELLISON 1981; DREWETT 1982). The argument is that groups of related houses that are found belong to single family groups. Often two houses are found – a 'major' and a 'minor' house; the latter appears from its artefact signature to represent a food preparation hut and the former a food consumption hut. It has been suggested that women probably prepared the food and took it to the men for consumption – in other words there is a division of space within the

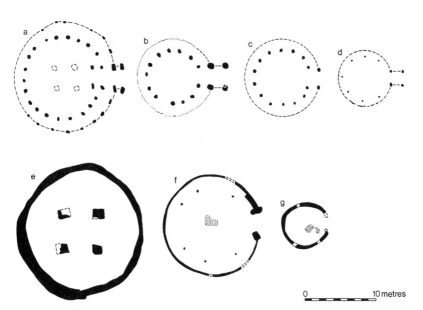

Figure 6.1 Round-houses of the Iron Age and Roman period: a. Little Woodbury (Hampshire), b. Moel y Gaer (Clwyd), c. Standlake Down (Oxfordshire), d. Moel y Gaer (Clwyd), e. Winterton (Humberside), f. Whitton (South Glamorgan), g. Thorplands (Northamptonshire). After Guilbert 1981, figures 7 and 8 and Hingley 1989a, figure 12.

compound according to gender. This general model appears to be applicable on a number of southern British late Bronze Age sites, e.g. Rams Hill (Oxfordshire), Weston Wood (Surrey), Chalton (Hampshire), Shearplace Hill (Dorset), Blackpatch (Sussex), Itford Hill (Sussex), and Thorny Down (Wiltshire).

Parker Pearson (forth.) has recently argued that a similar organisation may be visible on a number of excavated early Iron Age settlement sites, with a single major house for food consumption and a minor house for food preparation and craft activities.

Such compounds are difficult to identify in the archaeological record for the middle and later Iron Age. Parker Pearson (forth.) has argued that, in Wessex, middle Iron Age settlements appear to develop a linear form and this would also appear to be the case elsewhere, e.g. Ashville (Oxfordshire), PARRINGTON 1978, 39; and Claydon Pike (Gloucestershire) (HINGLEY AND MILES 1984, figure 4.4). How were family groups defined at this time?

Barrett (1989a, 312) has argued that during the late Bronze Age/early Iron Age 'activities previously divided between enclosures may now be found within large enclosures or buildings.' In other words, Barrett suggests that the compound of major and minor house disappears and is replaced by the single large round-house. The individual middle/late Bronze Age household may have resided within a single compound of major and minor hut. By the early/middle Iron Age each household may have occupied a single major round-house.[2] Barrett also suggests that this process is a general trend that occurs over a period of time, rather than a sudden and dramatic occurrence. This is supported by the evidence quoted by Parker Pearson, which indicates that the process took some time to occur. A gradual transformation in the organisation of the household is evident.

The cause of a general trend, from households defined by compounds with two buildings to households resident within a single round-house, is probably related to kinship and the broader structure of society (BARRETT 1989a) and is discussed further below.

In southern Britain Iron Age houses have usually been severely damaged by later occupation or subsequent cultivation. Two types can, however, be defined: simple single-ring round-houses and aisled double-ring round-houses. Well preserved round-houses often appear to have an inner ring of post-holes, forming a double-ring round-house, with an inner ring of posts and a solid outer wall (AVERY AND CLOSE-BROOKS 1969; MUSSON 1970; GUILBERT 1981; HILL 1982). Iron Age round-houses in northern Britain are often stone-built and better preserved and retain evidence for central hearths and sometimes radial stone-built partitions (REID 1989). In these cases the round-house has, in effect, an interior which is partitioned into central and peripheral areas, through the construction of an inner ring of posts or the building of stone radial partitions. It appears likely that, in Cunliffe's (1978, 175) words, 'two areas were created: a central area with a high roof-line where the principle activities of the house were carried out, and a surrounding area between the posts and the wall of the hut which would have served as storage or sleeping space.'

Some other simple houses without an internal ring of post-holes are also known (GUILBERT 1981, 311–2) and these possibly formed the majority on Iron Age settlements (ALLEN, MILES, AND PALMER 1984, 91).

Many southern British Iron Age round-houses also have a central, or roughly central, hearth. It is clear from published examples that not all hearths are exactly central (N. SHARPLES, pers. comm.) and also that the variable position of the hearth within the hut circle requires further investigation. In the great majority of excavated examples, however, the hearth occurs within the central area of the house. Central hearths occur in buildings that appear to have been of double-ring form and also in simple

---

[2] Certainly in the Upper Thames Valley throughout the Iron Age the single round-house appears to act as the basic unit (HINGLEY AND MILES 1984, 63). The same situation is apparent in the Avon Valley and in the Nene and Ouse Valleys, where the majority of enclosed Iron Age settlements appear to contain one house (KNIGHT 1984, 236; HINGLEY 1989b, 146).

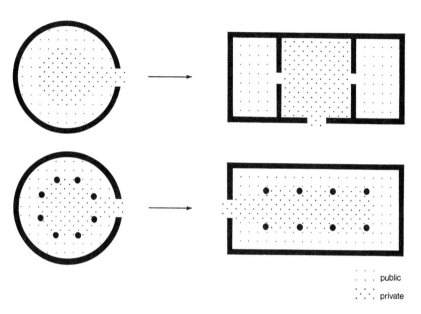

public

private

Figure 6.2 A general model for the transformation of Iron Age household space into Romano-British household space.

ring-post houses. In all of these cases it is likely that the central area was used for cooking and the peripheral areas for sleeping and storage (see Ross 1972, 115–6 for a discussion of literary sources which also suggest this two-part division).

Owing to their structure, both single-ring and double-ring round-houses embody a physical division between a central and a peripheral area. It will be argued here that this physical division is also a conceptual one, as the central and peripheral areas were not divided by barriers. The division between a central and a peripheral zone marks a division of the interior of the round-house into two areas: a 'public' central zone and a 'private' peripheral zone (Figure 6.2). The term 'public' is in some ways a misnomer as access to the house was controlled by its occupants. Presumably friends and kin were allowed access to the public area as guests, but would be excluded from the 'private' area. The public area would also be visible from outside the house when the door was open, while the private area was dark and would provide a greater degree of privacy from observation.

The central 'public' area is the location of the hearth and is also the area of the house which would receive most of the light let in by the doorway. It has already been argued that the location of the hearth in this area suggests that cooking occurred here. In addition it is likely that other communal activities such as eating, drinking, socialising, and entertaining went on in the centre of the house around the hearth.

In contrast, the private area of the house would always have been very dark and constricted because of the limited space available below the roof. In this area belongings would be stored and the individual members of the household would sleep. In addition cattle and other livestock could have been stalled in this outer area. In three well-preserved Iron Age houses in Wales (Moel y Gerddi, Erw-Wen, and Cefn Graeanog) phosphate analysis of the interior revealed high levels in the peripheral areas of the floor and low levels for the centre of the house (KELLY 1988). This indicates that the central area of the house was kept clean and may suggest the accumulation of organic material against the walls of these round-houses (this in turn probably represents the build-up of general organic waste or the storage of organic material in the periphery of the house KELLY 1988) or possibly the stalling of livestock in this area.

It can be suggested that this conceptual division of household space into public and private areas reflects a range of binary oppositions within the household. This is a structuralist model which defines the identification of binary oppositions within all human societies. By perceiving oppositions the mind builds up a picture of the world. Light and darkness are observed, as are contrasts such as winter:summer, culture:nature, cooked: raw, day:night and male:female. In many societies there appears to be some form of conceptual link between oppositions (for further discussion see LÉVI-STRAUSS 1978, 22–3; BOURDIEU 1973, 89–91; GARDENER 1976; MACCORMACK 1982a).

Evidently these oppositions are not culturally determined in all societies. It would appear, for instance, that the basic role of women in production within at least some small-scale agrarian societies results in a conceptual union between female and male rather than the identification of the two gender groups as in opposition to each other (MACCORMACK 1982b; HARRIS 1982; MOORE 1988, 13–24). Nevertheless the concept of the existence of binary oppositions as a basic structuring principle within human society has received widespread support from many social anthropologists. The task of the individual who studies a society is to examine the way in which binary oppositions were perceived within that particular society.

The binary opposition of central and peripheral areas within the Iron Age round-house reflects a range of additional oppositions within the community. It has already been shown that there is a division of peripheral dirt from central cleanliness in at least some Iron Age houses; in addition the division of the light communal area from the dark peripheral area has been identified. The division of raw from cooked is also relevant – with food perhaps stored in the periphery of the hut and cooked and consumed on the central hearth. The following range of oppositions can be identified:

'Public'	'Private'
Open access	Constrained access
Central space	Peripheral space
Light	Darkness
Cooked	Raw
Clean	Dirty

It may be possible to argue for a range of additional oppositions:

Day	Night
Summer	Winter
Culture	Nature
Fertility	Infertility
Life	Death

Another possible association is:

Male	Female

although this final opposition is debatable and requires further discussion (see below).

The round-house and the symbolic universe of Iron Age people

The stability of later prehistoric architecture, with the failure of rectangular houses to replace round-houses (e.g. PARKER PEARSON forth.) may be a result of the symbolic importance of the spatial organisation of the round-house. This may be taken further to suggest that, as in many other societies, the Iron Age round-house reflected the symbolic universe of society – in other words that it contained a conceptualisation of space that matched a view of the world that existed within the minds of the occupants of these houses.

As we have seen, it is possible that the centre of the round-house was identified with concepts such as summer, day, culture, and fertility, while the periphery was identified with winter, night, nature, and possibly infertility. This may form a microcosm for the organisation of the landscape – with a central area within which the settlement, the arable land, and pasture was situated, and a peripheral area forming waste land and the territory of other communities. This would appear to fit the suggestion made by Barrett that society in the Iron Age had begun to draw on the metaphor of agricultural production in order to structure material reality (BARRETT 1989b, 3). The round-house may have acted as a metaphor for the spatial organisation of the territory of a single community.

This conceptual model for the organisation of the land of the community may be a basic structuring principle within society and may identify a further relevant opposition between 'us' and 'them' in Iron Age society. I am not attempting to suggest that all single round-houses in the Iron Age

had a distinct area of land which was divided from other individual communities. Many houses appear to have been grouped into settlements
forming a community which can be identified as 'us'.

Elsewhere I have argued that groups of settlements can be identified on
the gravel soils of the Upper Thames Valley in the early/middle Iron Age
and I have termed these 'multiple settlements' (HINGLEY 1988, 75–81).
These multiple settlements are identified by a ring of settlement that
defines an area of fertile gravel terrace, ideal arable land, from lower
terrace and flood plain, which probably provided rough pasture (HINGLEY
1988, figure 7.5). This would appear to identify a homologous structure of
organisation to that of the round-house, with the settlements lying on the
dividing line between centre and periphery. Once again central communal,
or 'public', land is surrounded by 'private' space – land to which access was
constrained, the territory of other communities.

This multiple settlement could indicate that the model for communal
and private areas within the round-house is reflected by a similar division
of the landscape within at least some Iron Age communities. If this is the
case a number of binary oppositions are shared within both the house and
the landscape – these are as follows:

Centre	Periphery
Open access	Constrained access
Culture	Nature
Fertility	Infertility
Life	Death

I would also suggest that the same concept may exist within the spatial
organisation of some settlements, although this will not be discussed in
detail in this chapter. One example is Danebury hillfort (Hampshire) where
there is a transformation in the settlement pattern between an 'early' and a
'late' period (e.g. CUNLIFFE 1983, figures 30–1). In the early period the hillfort has two entrances and the interior appears to be divided into a peripheral and a central area. Huts occur in the periphery, while storage pits
occur in the interior; there are also possible 'shrines' near the centre. In
the later period one of the entrances is blocked, huts become more peripheral, and the centre is occupied by four-post granaries and small central
shrines. Both phases at Danebury reflect the same central/peripheral
dichotomy evident in the organisation of the round-house and in the
model for the Iron Age multiple settlement.

The later phase at Danebury, with its single entrance and more marked
centre/periphery division, is a clearer parallel to the organisation of the
round-house. The same conceptual model is probably in use and many of
the binary oppositions that are evident in the round-house and multiple
settlement find a parallel here. Once again the centre is associated with
fertility as large numbers of granary buildings occur in this area. It is of in-

terest that the supposed shrines are in a central position analogous to that of the hearth, and that this area was apparently cleaned and levelled before the construction of the shrines (CUNLIFFE 1983, 71). The houses are in the periphery and therefore should be associated with the ideas of darkness and dirt. A thick occupation deposit built up within the quarry hollows in the lee of the rampart. Once again a contrast occurs between central public space and peripheral private space.

I do not wish to explore this model for the organisation of Iron Age settlements and landscapes in any greater detail, as the purpose of this chapter is to consider the structure of houses. Iron Age architecture and settlement layout formed a strong tradition, however, and space was organised in a symbolic manner which reflected the beliefs and ideas of individuals.

As mentioned above, rectangular houses occur within the southern British Iron Age record. Many of these are not particularly well preserved. The majority, however, would appear from the limited evidence to represent one-roomed houses and may have contained the division into two conceptual areas represented in the Iron Age settlement record.

A model for Romano-British houses as a direct transformation of the Iron Age round-house

The majority of Romano-British houses reflect a parallel organisation of space to that identified in the Iron Age round-house; in other words, 'public' and 'private' space can be defined. This continuity in the basic conceptual structure of the house under new conditions is in keeping with a number of anthropological studies, which show that a change in the shape of houses from circular to rectangular masks continuity in the basic spatial organisation of the house.

A model for the transformation of round-houses into rectangular houses

It is appropriate at this stage to utilise a model derived from the ethnographic study of the influence of western societies on African communities. The process of the incorporation of Britain into the Roman Empire was very different from the incorporation of indigenous African societies into the various empires of western powers; however, many of the processes of change evident in the transformation of indigenous house forms were probably similar.

Among many African societies the introduction of new building materials and ideas has resulted in the transformation of building types from the traditional round form to a rectangular shape. The rectangular houses, however, commonly reflect the same spatial concepts – or the same social model – which is evident in the traditional round dwelling. The form of modern housing represents a minor adjustment to the conventional form and the effect on the organisation of family life is minimal. [3]

A range of Romano-British house types can be defined and these are discussed in detail in *Rural Settlement in Roman Britain* (HINGLEY 1989a). These house types can be arranged according to a sequence of complexity: round-houses, one-roomed rectangular houses, two- to three-roomed rectangular houses, aisled houses, 'cottage' houses, corridor houses, winged corridor houses, and courtyard houses (Figure 6.3 illustrates the main house types with the exception of courtyard houses).

The round-house typifies the Iron Age settlement record and continues as a common Romano-British building type (Figure 6.1, e, f, and g are Roman period houses). Houses of this type are particularly common in the West and North, but continued to be built even in some areas of southern Britain into the fourth century AD. These houses often have central hearths and presumably incorporate the same division into 'public' and 'private' space that is expressed in the Iron Age round-house. One-roomed rectangular houses (Figure 6.3 a) occur on some sites and it can be argued that these represent the same conceptual model.

Two- to three-roomed rectangular houses (Figure 6.3, b and c) occur on a wide variety of sites in southern Britain (LEECH 1982, 31; HINGLEY 1989a, 35–7). In these houses one room is always larger than the others and this large room often contains a hearth (LEECH 1982). In three-roomed houses the largest room is often in the centre and is flanked by smaller rooms. Leech has argued that the annexe rooms were used as private rooms for sleeping, while the large room was used for living and eating (LEECH 1982, 31). These houses also represent the conceptual model expressed above, again with the private one peripheral to the public zone.

Aisled houses (Figure 6.3, d), in their simple form, have a central room which runs the length of the building with aisles defined by posts or columns to either side. These buildings usually appear to have one entrance in one of the short ends and the hearth is often in the central

---

[3] In Bakosi (Africa) the introduction of new building materials and ideas has resulted in the architectural transformation of the basic house type from round to rectangular (LEVIN 1971). The house types that have developed, however, reflect the basic spatial concepts evident in traditional housing. The round-house comprises a central area which is a working/sitting area and spaces to either side which form storage and sleeping areas. All the main forms of rectangular house incorporate the same basic structure and give expression to it in differing forms. The modern house expresses the conventional form and has little effect on family life.

Among the Bemba (Africa) circular huts are traditional, while rectangular houses were probably introduced by the Europeans (RICHARDS 1950). The rectangular hut is a modification of the methods of building used for the round-house, but is in no way a new design. The internal organisation of the round-house and rectangular house are identical. The Iraqw (Africa) have been encouraged by the government to build rectangular houses to replace their traditional round-houses (THORNTON 1980, 31–2). In spite of superficial differences between round and circular houses, the Iraqw now living in rectangular houses have attempted to maintain the interior details and construction of the older round-houses (see also RAPOPORT 1969, 52 and note 19 for this point in a different form).

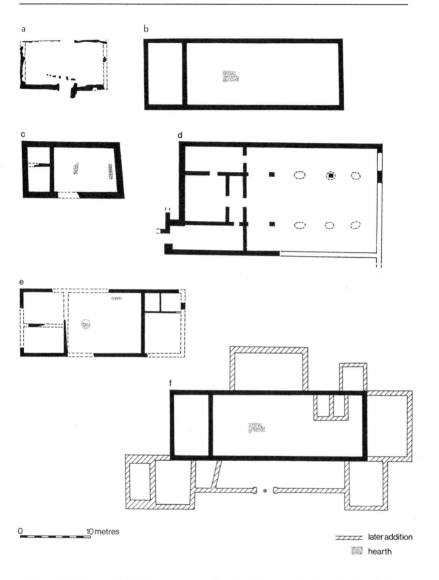

0 ⸻ 10 metres

⚡⚡⚡ later addition
░░ hearth

Figure 6.3 Romano-British house types: a. Studland (Dorset), b. Clear Cupboard phase 1 (Gloucestershire), c. Catsgore (Somerset), d. Combley (Isle of Wight), e. Carsington (Derbyshire), f. Clear Cupboard all phases (Gloucestershire). After Hingley 1989a, figures 15, 16, 17 and 21.

passageway. These aisled houses are common in Roman Britain from the first to the fourth century AD.

This basic undivided aisled hall is very little different from the double-ring round-house – the aisle posts in both house types divide a central public zone from a peripheral private zone. The aisled house relates directly to the double-ring round-house in the same way that the one-roomed house relates to the one-ring round-house (Figure 6.2).

In secondary phases the aisles and far end of aisled houses are often subdivided into a number of separate rooms. This represents the sub-division of the private zone of the house and indicates a trend towards greater privacy within the house – the same trend which is evident in the development of the two- to three-roomed house.

'Cottage houses' (Figure 6.3, e) are buildings with more than three rooms in a row (RICHMOND 1969; HINGLEY 1989a, 37–9). In most cottage houses one large room with a hearth can be identified and the peripheral rooms are, in effect, multiplied. This can be envisaged as a further trend in the process of development of the public/private model, except in these cases the development of private zones takes on a linear rather than a con-centric form.

Corridor and winged-corridor façades are added to all the above rect-angular building types (e.g. Figure 6.3, f, which represents the conversion of a two-roomed building into a winged corridor villa). The winged corridor façade represents a standardised pattern across the north-west of the Empire, related to the status of a particular household group (SMITH 1978b, 358). In these more complex building forms it is often possible to recognise the basic two- to three-roomed house at the core of the building (HINGLEY 1989a, 45, 47). This is also the case with some courtyard villas (e.g. Spoonley Wood in Gloucestershire). Even in these complex and ex-tensive Romano-British buildings the same basic conceptual model of public and private areas is evident.

The model and the settlement

At the level of the settlement, Richmond (1969, 64) has made the point that the Romano-British courtyard villa differs from courtyard houses on the continent: 'The difference lies in the fact that in Britain the courtyard is a thoroughfare leading to the main house, whereas the Classical court-yard is a garden-court within or behind the house and away from the main entrance.' This may indicate the existence of the same model for private and public space at the scale of the Romano-British settlement. The court-yard is entered from the outside and is the equivalent of the open public area within the round-house, while the courtyard building represents the peripheral distribution of private areas distributed around the central public zone (see further HINGLEY 1989a, 59–71).

It is not surprising that the basic public-private concept forms the model for many Romano-British houses. The house in many societies acts as a microcosm for the social universe of its inhabitants. Change due to contact with Rome occurs in the ephemeral aspects of architecture (the shape of the building, the trend from timber-built to stone-built structures and the addition of ornate façades), while the basic spatial concept remains the same. This merely indicates that villas and other Romano-British house types develop from a strong tradition of architecture and that Roman contact transformed indigenous social structure rather than replacing it (HINGLEY forth.).

Spatial distribution of activities and gender relations within the house

The position of women in the household – a specific example

As mentioned in the introduction to this chapter, evidence for the spatial distribution of activities within Iron Age and Roman houses is very scarce. Most attempts at spatial analysis have examined the division of activities between buildings within a single compound. It has been suggested that spatial analysis of Romano-British house interiors may be useful in the study of household organisation; this is a consequence of the complexity of many houses and the large quantities of occupation debris present in some cases.

Only one Romano-British house has been studied in this manner, enabling examination of the spatial distribution of activities; this is the aisled house at North Warnborough (Hampshire) illustrated in Figure 6.4. The excavator of this site argued that particular activities occurred within certain rooms in the house and that distinct areas occupied by males and females could be identified (LIDDELL 1931). Some of the categories of artefacts on which Liddell's distinction of male from female areas are based are open to discussion (e.g. EHRENBERG 1989, 144–5) and the site requires critical re-analysis. For present purposes, however, Liddell's arguments will be used in order to study a specific model of gender relations within this particular house.

The living areas of the house appear to have been situated in the hall and aisles of the house, and these can be divided approximately into two. The south-western rooms include a room with a hypocaust and a kitchen area indicated by a hearth and midden and these appear to have housed the women of the community. In contrast the men occupied the hall of the house (LIDDELL 1931). I have argued that the house may have been the home of a large extended family, probably of several generations and perhaps including as many as thirty to sixty individuals (HINGLEY 1989a, 43–5).

For the purpose of this chapter, however, the most relevant point is that it would appear that the women were living in the aisles and far end of the aisled house, while the men appear to have occupied the hall of the building. In terms of the model outlined above, it would appear that the women

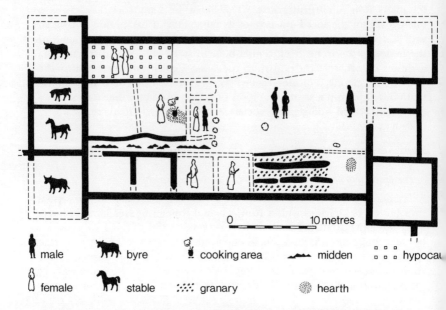

Figure 6.4 Social reconstruction of the aisled house at North Warnborough (Hampshire). After Liddell 1931.

are occupying the private zone of the house, while the men occupied the public area. It should be noted, however, that the hearth has become isolated to a peripheral area within the house.

A number of possible binary oppositions for the public and private areas of the house were examined above. It was tentatively suggested that there could be an association of women with the private area and men with the public area within the round-house, although the association of women with nature and of men with culture is not fully supported by anthropological studies of societies. The North Warnborough building, however, may support this association.

The association of women with the periphery of the house may indicate an association of the peripheral aisles of the North Warnborough house with the territory of others. If the community at North Warnborough had patrilocal kinship organisation, the women of this household would have been brought in from outside the territory of the community and would be, in effect, the daughters of 'outsiders' (see LÉVI-STRAUSS 1969, 136).

The general position of women in Iron Age and Roman Britain

It is clearly far too early to build a model for the organisation of gender relations within the Iron Age/Romano-British household on the basis of one case study. In fact recent studies of women in Iron Age and Roman Britain give attention to the relative power of women within both the domestic and the political domain. Ehrenberg (1989, 142–71) has argued that women in Iron Age Britain had power based on their position in the process of economic production and has discussed the military and political careers of some Iron Age women. Allason-Jones (1990, 190) has argued that women in Roman Britain had a stronger position in law than their contemporaries in Rome and elsewhere in the Roman Empire, possibly as a result of their involvement in the production and supply of food. Presumably Romano-British women derived their status from gender relations within Iron Age communities.

Even if the particular argument for the household at North Warnborough is correct, it is clear that the position of women and the organisation of gender relations within the household will have varied through time and also across space. Could the isolation of the hearth to the periphery of the house at North Warnborough actually indicate that no such distinction was made by gender in the majority of Iron Age and Romano-British houses? It is possible that in the majority of these houses men and women shared private and peripheral space.

Does the trend from the compounds of the middle/late Bronze Age record to the single round-house of the Iron Age indicate an increase in the status of women? Willis (1989) has discussed the position of women in society as reflected by their functions in the process of cooking and eating.[4] In Ufipa, Africa there is a strict and complementary division of labour between men and women in economic production, and the emphasis in the cooking and eating of food is on integration rather than on opposition and separation. This is in contrast to societies across much of the rest of Africa, where eating occurs in sexually segregated groups and strong gender-related divisions of labour occur (WILLIS 1989). The trend from compound to single round-house in British prehistory may indicate a transition from a social situation in the Bronze Age when women and men were strictly segregated and women subjected to men, to an Iron Age scenario in which the two sexes lived together and worked as a group, and in which there was a relatively greater degree of equality between the two gender groups. The continuity of the Iron Age scenario in the Roman province and any evidence for the down-grading of female status under Roman influence requires further study.

The house at North Warnborough is an aisled house and houses of this

---

[4] Willis has discussed the importance of eating and drinking as a reflection of the status and function of gender and age groups in African society and has also drawn attention to Elias's study of the civilising process in European society, as reflected in eating and drinking (WILLIS 1989; ELIAS 1978). The group composition and spatial organisation of eating and drinking are topics of importance in the study of Iron Age and Romano-British household organisation and require further detailed investigation.

type occur in large numbers in certain areas of Britain, particularly in Hampshire and in the Nene Valley. It is possible that aisled houses reflect a particular type of household group in which a marked division occurred between gender groups and in which women were subjugated to men. In the other types of round and rectangular houses that occur on Iron Age and Roman sites a marked division of areas by gender has not been found, although it has also not really been looked for.

Further assessment of houses is required in order to build alternative models of household organisation. In addition contradictions between age groups within households may also have been significant within Iron Age and Romano-British communities.[5] The North Warnborough model merely indicates the potential value of spatial archaeology to the study of family organisation and gender relations.

Conclusion

It has been argued that in the late Bronze Age an opposition may have occurred between major (male) houses and minor (female) houses (ELLISON 1978; 1981; PARKER PEARSON forth.). In the Iron Age this opposition is transformed into a division of space within the single large round-house. In the Iron Age it appears probable that this division of space is conceptualised according to a particular model of territorial organisation among communities with an intensive mixed economy.

As noted in the introduction, the model explored in this article is only tentative. It describes a general structuring principle which is evident in Iron Age and, to a lesser degree, Romano-British household space and settlement organisation. Lévi-Strauss's (1968, 132-41) discussion of the organisation of Winnebago settlement is of particular relevance to this point. The Winnebago are divided into two moieties (descent groups) called, respectively, 'those who are above' and 'those who are on earth'. Conceptions of the spatial organisation of one particular village varied between two extremes, the upper moiety describing the village as divided in two with the two moieties divided into separate areas, the lower moiety viewing the village as a single entity with both moieties living together and surrounded by cleared ground.

Lévi-Strauss has argued that these two conceptions do not relate to differing organisations, but to two differing ways of describing one organisation which is too complex to be formalised by means of a single model. Members of each moiety envisage the village in one way rather than the other depending on their position in the social order (LÉVI-STRAUSS 1968, 134-5). The same author makes the interesting point that both forms of

---

[5] Wilk has discussed a model for investigating conflict between age groups and the resolution of conflict within the Kekchi Maya household (South America) (WILK 1990). This model may be of use in considering the nature of wealth investment in the villas and other elaborate rural buildings of Roman Britain.

organisation described correspond to real examples which have been observed during fieldwork. These two models are described by Lévi-Strauss (1968, 135) as 'diametric structure' and 'concentric structure'.

My conception of Iron Age/Romano-British spatial organisation is a version of the concentric model outlined by Lévi-Strauss. The point which the Winnebago case study makes is that there may have been alternative structuring principles within a single society. Parker Pearson (forth.) has discussed the division of late Bronze Age and early Iron Age round-houses and enclosures into two halves and the differential distribution of activities and gender groups between them. This diametric structure may also be relevant within particular Iron Age and Romano-British communities. For instance, many Romano-British compounds appear to have two houses (HINGLEY 1989a, 59–71) and within some settlements a division occurs between a high status and a lower status compound (ibid., 80–6). The late Bronze Age to Iron Age may be characterised by a general trend from diametric to concentric organisation, but the former concept could still represent a concept that existed within the minds of many (? male) occupants of Iron Age houses.

Future studies of spatial organisation should acknowledge these possibilities, but must not attempt to reduce the settlement record to a single oversimplistic model or set of models (CHAMPION 1987, 106). Greater complexity and more imagination are required in the study of the social organisation of prehistoric and Romano-British households and communities (BRADLEY 1984, 2–4).

Acknowledgements

My thanks to Dr Mike Parker Pearson for permission to use a number of arguments from his forthcoming paper on Iron Age houses. I am also grateful to Niall Sharples, Dr Lesley Macinnes, Dr David Breeze and Christina Unwin for advice and information. My thanks also to Christina Unwin for drawing the illustrations for this paper.

Bibliography

Allason-Jones, Lindsay 1990. *Women in Roman Britain*. Batsford (London).

Allen, Tim, Miles, David and Palmer, Simon 1984. 'Iron Age buildings in the Upper Thames region' in B. Cunliffe and David Miles (eds.), *Aspects of the Iron Age in Central Southern Britain*, 89–101. University Committee for Archaeology (Oxford).

Applebaum, Shimon 1972. 'Roman Britain' in H. Finberg (ed.), *The*

Agrarian History of England and Wales I:II (AD 43–1042), 3–270. Cambridge University Press (Cambridge).

Avery, Michael and Close-Brooks, Joanna 1969. 'Shearplace Hill, Sydling St. Nicholas, Dorset, house A: suggested reinterpretation' *Proceedings of the Prehistoric Society* 35, 345–51.

Barrett, John 1987. 'The Glastonbury lake village: models and source criticism' *Archaeological Journal* 144, 409–23.

Barrett, John 1989a. 'Food, gender and metal: questions of social reproduction' in Marie Louise Stig Sorensen and Richard Thomas (eds.), *The Bronze Age-Iron Age Transition in Europe*, 304–20. BAR (Oxford).

Barrett, John 1989b. 'Further problems in the Iron Age of southern Britain' *Scottish Archaeological Review* 6, 1–3.

Bender, D. R. 1967. 'A refinement of the concept of household: families, co-residence and domestic functions' *American Anthropologist* 69, 493–504.

Bradley, Richard 1984. *The Social Foundations of Prehistoric Britain*. Longman (London).

Bourdieu, Pierre 1977. *Outline of a Theory of Practice*. Cambridge University Press (Cambridge).

Champion, Timothy 1987. 'The European Iron Age: assessing the state of the art' *Scottish Archaeological Review* 4, 98–107.

Clarke, David L. 1972. 'A Provisional Model of an Iron Age Society and its Settlement System' in D. L. Clarke (ed.), Models in Archaeology, 801–69, London, Methuen.

Clarke, David L. 1977. 'Spatial information in archaeology' in D. L. Clarke (ed.) *Spatial Archaeology*, 1–32. Academic Press (London).

Coles, John M. and Coles, B. 1986. *Sweet Track to Glastonbury*. Thames and Hudson (London).

Cunliffe, Barry W. 1978. *Iron Age Communities in Britain*. Routledge and Kegan Paul (London).

Cunliffe, Barry W. 1983. *Danebury: Anatomy of an Iron Age Hillfort*. Batsford (London).

Cunningham, C. E. 1973. 'Order in the Atoni house' in R. Needham (ed.), *Right and Left: essays on dual symbolic classification*, 204–38. University of Chicago Press (London).

Douglas, Mary 1972. 'Symbolic orders in the use of domestic space' in Peter J. Ucko, Ruth Tringham and G. W. Dimbleby (eds.), *Man, Settlement and Urbanism*, 513–21. Duckworth (London).

Drewett, P. 1982. 'Late Bronze Age downland economy and excavations at Black Patch, East Sussex' *Proceedings of the Prehistoric Society* 48, 321–400.

Ehrenberg, Margaret 1989. *Women in Prehistory*. British Museum (London).

Elias, N. 1978. *The Civilizing Process: the history of manners*. Blackwell (Oxford).

Ellison, Ann 1978. 'The Bronze Age of Sussex' in P. L. Drewett (ed.), *Archaeology in Sussex to AD 1500*. CBA (London).

Ellison, Ann 1981. 'Towards a socioeconomic model for the middle Bronze Age in southern England' in I. Hodder, G. Isaac and N. Hammond (eds.), *Patterns of the Past: studies in honour of David Clarke*. Cambridge University Press (Cambridge).

Griaule, M. and Dieterlen, G. 1954. 'The Dogon' in D. Forde (ed.), *African Worlds*, 96–7. (London).

Gardener, H. 1976. *The Quest for Mind: Piaget, Lévi-Strauss and the Structuralist Movement*. Quartet Books (London).

Guilbert, Graeme 1981. 'Double-ring roundhouses, probable and possible, in prehistoric Britain' *Proceedings of the Prehistoric Society* 47, 299–317.

Harding, Dennis W. 1973. 'Round and rectangular: Iron Age houses, British and foreign' in C. F. C. Hawkes and S. C. Hawkes (eds.), *Greeks, Celts and Romans: studies in venture and resistance*, 43–62. Dent (London).

Harris, O. 1982. 'The power of signs: gender, culture and the wild in the Bolivian Andes' in C. MacCormack and M. Strathern (eds.), *Nature, Culture and Gender*, 70–94. Cambridge University Press (Cambridge).

Hill, Peter 1982. 'Towards a new classification of prehistoric houses' *Scottish Archaeological Review* 1, 24–31.

Hingley, Richard 1988. 'The influence of Rome on indigenous social groups in the Upper Thames Valley' in Rick F. J. Jones, J. H. F. Bloemers, S. L. Dyson and Martin Biddle (eds.), *First Millennium Papers*, 73–98. BAR (Oxford).

Hingley, R. 1989a. *Rural Settlement in Roman Britain*. Seaby (London).

Hingley, Richard 1989b. 'Iron Age settlement and society in central and southern Warwickshire' in A. Gibson (ed.), *Midlands Prehistory* 122–57. BAR (Oxford).

Hingley, Richard forth. 'Past, present and future – the study of the Roman period in Britain' *Scottish Archaeological Review* 8.

Hingley, Richard and Miles, David 1984. 'Aspects of Iron Age settlement in the Upper Thames Valley' in B. Cunliffe and D. Miles (eds.), *Aspects of the Iron Age in Central Southern Britain*, 52–71. University Committee for Archaeology (Oxford).

Kelly, R. S. 1988. 'Two late prehistoric circular enclosures near Harlech, Gwynedd,' *Proceedings of the Prehistoric Society* 54, 101–51.

Kent, Susan 1990. 'Activity areas and architecture: an interdisciplinary view of the relationship between use of space and domestic built environments' in S. Kent (ed.), *Domestic architecture and the use of space: an interdisciplinary cross-cultural study*, 1–8, Cambridge, Cambridge University Press (Cambridge).

Knight, David 1984. *Late Bronze Age and Iron Age Settlement in the Nene and Great Ouse Basin*. BAR (Oxford).

Kus, Susan and Raharijaona, V. 1990. 'Domestic space and the tenacity of tradition among some Batsileo of Madagascar' in S. Kent (ed.), *Domestic Architecture and the Use of Space: an interdisciplinary cross-cultural study*, 21–33, Cambridge, Cambridge, University Press.

Leech, Roger 1982. *Excavations at Catsgore, 1970–3*. CRAAGS (Bristol).

Levin, M. D. 1971. 'House form and social structure in Bakosi' in Paul Oliver (ed.), *Shelter in Africa*. Barrie and Jenkins (London).

Lévi-Strauss, Claude 1968. *Structural Anthropology*. Penguin (London).

Lévi-Strauss, Claude 1969. *The Elementary Structure of Kinship*. Beacon Press (Boston).

Lévi-Strauss, Claude 1978. *Myth and Meaning*. Routledge and Kegan Paul (London).

Liddell, D. M. 1931. 'Notes on two excavations in Hampshire' *Proceedings of the Hampshire Field Club* 10, 224–36.

MacCormack, C. 1982a. 'Nature, culture and gender: a critique' in C. MacCormack and M. Strathern (eds.), *Nature, Culture and Gender*, 1–24. Cambridge University Press (Cambridge).

MacCormack, C. 1982b. 'Proto-social to adult: a Sherbro transformation' in C. MacCormack and M. Strathern (eds.), *Nature, Culture and Gender*, 95–118. Cambridge University Press (Cambridge).

Moore, Henrietta L. 1988. *Feminism and Anthropology*. Polity Press (Cambridge).

Musson, Chris 1970. 'House-plans and prehistory' *Current Archaeology* 2, 267– 75.

Parker Pearson, Michael forth. 'Food, fertility and front doors in the first millennium BC' in Timothy Champion and John Collis (eds.) *Recent Trends in Iron Age Archaeology in Britain*. (Sheffield).

Parrington, Michael 1978. *The Excavation of an Iron Age Settlement, Bronze Age Ring-Ditches and Roman Features at Ashville Trading Estate, Abingdon (Oxfordshire) 1974–76*. CBA (London).

Rapoport, Amos 1969. *House Form and Culture*. Prentice-Hall (London).

Reid, Malcolm 1989. 'A room with a view: an examination of round-houses with particular reference to northern Britain' *Oxford Journal of Archaeology* 8, 1–39.

Richards, A. I. 1950. 'Huts and hut-building among the Bemba: part 1' *Man*, 87–90.

Richmond, Ian R. 1969. 'The plans of Roman villas in Britain' in A. L. F. Rivet (ed.), *The Roman Villa in Britain*, 49–70. Batsford (London).

Rodwell, Warwick 1978. 'Buildings and settlements in south-east Britain in the late Iron Age' in Barry Cunliffe and Trevor Rowley (eds.), *Lowland Iron Age Communities in Europe*, 25–41. BAR (Oxford).

Ross, Ann 1970. *Everyday Life of the Pagan Celts*. Batsford (London).

Smith, J. T. 1963. 'Romano-British aisled houses' *Archaeological Journal* 120, 1–30.

Smith, J. T. 1978a. 'Villas as a key to social structure' in Malcolm Todd (ed.), *Studies in the Romano-British Villa*, 149–56. Leicester University Press (Leicester).

Smith, J. T. 1978b. 'Halls or yards? a problem of villa interpretation' *Britannia* 9, 349–56.

Smith, J. T. 1982. 'Villa plan and social structure in Britain and Gaul' *Caesarodunum* 17, 321–51.

Stevens, C. E. 1966. 'The social and economic aspects of rural settlement' in C. Thomas (ed.), *Rural Settlement in Roman Britain*, 108–28. CBA (London).

Thornton, R. J. 1980. *Space, Time and Culture among the Iraqw of Tanzania.* Academic Press (London).

Wilk, R. 1990. 'The built environment and consumer decision' in S. Kent (ed.), *Domestic Architecture and the Use of Space: an interdisciplinary cross-cultural study*, 34–42. Cambridge University Press (Cambridge).

Willis, R. 1989. 'Power begins at home: the symbolism of male-female commensality in Ufipa' in W. Arens and I. Karp (eds.), *Creativity of Power*, 113–28. Smithsonian (London).

Seven

Romano-British Villas and the Social Construction of Space

ELEANOR SCOTT

The appearance of winged-corridor façades and visually impressive gateways in Romano-British villas is linked to fundamental economic and social changes. Changes in an economy are linked to changing social relations and ways of perceiving the world. The environment of the new market world was seen as hostile. This perceived hostility was more than the physical threat of raiders: it was the less tangible yet relentless threat of vulnerability to market forces, inflation, and taxation, and the need to accept strangers over the threshold. The new architecture both reached out to embrace the Roman world by embodying 'Romanised' material culture, and at the same time drew its occupants back and protected them from it. This effect was heightened by the use of enclosures and monumental gateways which culminated in the large courtyard villas of the fourth century. These houses were more than fashionable retreats. Villas are a class of material culture which, like all others, reinforce and actively affect world views. Sometimes these world views rest uncomfortably upon society and contain contradictions which 'speak' through the manipulation of the configurations of social space.

The social logic of space

Hillier and Hanson conceived the idea of 'space syntax' in the mid-1970s (HILLIER AND HANSON 1984, xiii); Henry Glassie published his thesis on 'transformational grammar' in 1975. That archaeologists continue to apply these techniques successfully within specific historical contexts fifteen years later is a testament to their lasting importance.

A passage in Hillier and Hanson's *Social Logic of Space* (p. ix) is particularly pertinent for students of Roman villas:

> However much we may prefer to discuss architecture in terms of
> visual styles, its most far-reaching practical effects are not at the level
> of appearances at all, but at the level of *space*. By giving shape and
> form to our material world, architecture structures the system of
> space in which we live and move. In that it does so, it has a direct
> relation – rather than a merely symbolic one – to social life, since it
> provides the material preconditions for the patterns of movement,
> encounter and avoidance which are the material realisation – as well
> as sometimes the generator – of social relations. In this sense, archi-
> tecture pervades our everyday experience far more than a pre-
> occupation with its visual properties would suggest.

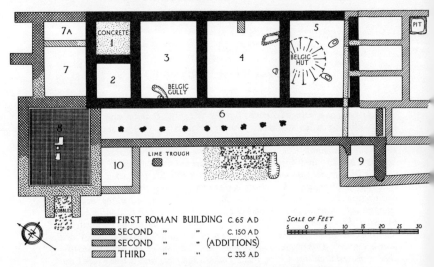

Figure 7.1 Lockleys Welwyn (from Ward Perkins 1938).

A meaningful application of 'space syntax' depends upon a thorough
knowledge of the position of a building's doorways. This enables levels of
accessibility and permeability to be measured. However, even a cursory
glance at Romano-British villa plans (e.g. Figures 7.1–7.3, 7.5–7.6, 7.8–7.15)
reveals that unfortunately the doorways have seldom been located with any
certainty. The published plan of Lockleys for example has no doorways indicated at all (Figure 7.1). The recently published plan of Piddington villa in
Britannia 1989 shows no doorways, yet some were in fact found.

There is, however, hope for the analytical study of Roman villas. Glassie
(1975; 1985) has used the idea of 'transformational grammar' to suggest that

general principles can be identified which have explanatory power and which can be useful for the meaningful interpretation of changes in house plans. Glassie analysed Middle Virginian folk housing and postulated that the causes of the changes in house form he observed were related to social and political change. He divided the 335 houses in his database into two groups.

In the first group, the most integrated room (the one with the most doorways leading in to/from it), or the 'integrative mechanism', was the living room, or 'functioning room'. In this old-style house, if you took one step in from the outside you would be in the house, because the front door opened directly into the living room. The front door of such a house would be visible to an observer standing on the outside, and consequently the observer would know automatically the whereabouts of the living room in relation to the rest of the house. It was clear where the occupants of the house would be sitting, and any guest brought in to the house would necessarily step straight into this living space. The front door was not centrally placed, but was slightly off-set, giving the house an asymmetrical frontage.

The second group of houses contained a vestibule, and this vestibule was the 'integrative mechanism'; it was the room with the most doorways leading into/from it. This change in house planning meant that after one step in from the outside, one would be not in the living room but in a corridor-like vestibule. The front door was symmetrically placed, disguising the exact position of the living room.

This change from 'open' to 'closed' architecture represents a change in a way of perceiving the world and organising world views. It is interesting that it occurred c. 1760, for Glassie's explanation is that these fundamental changes came about as a response to a period of increasing social tension in the years leading up to the war of 1776.

Glassie pursued this idea at the Glasgow TAG conference of 1985, where he discussed the Virginian data and enhanced his hypothesis by reference to other field studies in Ireland and Turkey. One critisism of Glassie's work is that he offers an uncomfortably simple cause-and-effect explanation of architectural change. He should perhaps have been at more pains to observe that both the known conflicts in the USA and Ireland and the changes in house plans there were symptoms of underlying social and economic change and tension in a wide arena, and that the impending existence of physical conflict did not *directly* cause architectural change. Note that 'new orders' of 'closed' symmetrical domestic architecture have developed in many contexts, and for a variety of economic and social reasons.

The introduction of closed, uninformative façades with doorways leading into vestibules or corridors can be shown to have occurred in a number of temporal and geographical locations at times of underlying tension. That social, economic, and political tensions can manifest themselves in house planning should be a concept of great interest and significance to archaeologists working with Romano-British data, for we now have a number of excellent studies of the contemporary economy and social relations, and a great number of excavated house plans. Houses are the living space of people, and how that space is constructed tells us much about how these people live and perceive the world. This is as true of Roman Britain as it is of eighteenth-century Virginia. Although 'the social construction of space' is a crucial concept in the study of buildings and settlements, studies of both Iron Age and Roman sites tend to consist solely of broad descriptive statements. Many villa reports in this country are still little more than an account of where the walls were. Many descriptions of villas – 'well-appointed house with mosaics, wall paintings, and detached bath house' – could have been produced by an estate agent.

It is possible to do more than merely describe morphological changes in house plans. We can consider the configurations of space involved and, by concomitantly examining the historically specific context of the houses, assess how the space is used as a means of expressing social relations. Spatial patterns not only represent but also constitute aspects of culture and social organisation (GLASSIE 1985, 28–9; HILLIER 1985, 28). When we erect the walls of a building, we do more than create walls; we also construct the space between, and immediately without, these walls and we create façades which present symmetrical or asymmetrical aspects to the world. Some house plans require only one 'step' in from the outside world to the living space, while others will require a number of steps. Space is not an accidental by-product of architecture, it is the intention. Space is used and manipulated in such a way that it reveals much about and helps form the structures of society.

Winged-corridor villas

In his study of winged-corridor villas in Britain, D. J. Smith (1978, 120) notes briefly that the winged-corridor frontage was 'regarded as a requirement' even of simple farmhouses of the German provinces, and that 'Romano-British farmers appear to have been slow to adopt this feature in its entirety.' He does not consider this statement any further. But it is important that we understand why the architectural change occurs in the form it does and when it does. What underlying factors governed the change from the simple oblong block of rooms to the winged-corridor house, a process seen so often in Britain? The insistence that this architectural development directly reflects social ambitions, 'fashion', migrations, or even population increase, is strong in the literature (e.g. FRERE 1982, 139; BRANIGAN 1976, 51; O'NEIL 1971, 26). The use of the term 'Romanisation' is not explanation, for it omits any real analysis of social and economic change, and is not an adequate discussion of the manipulation of Roman material culture in Britain.

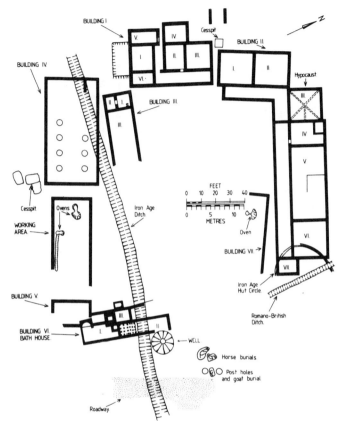

Figure 7.2 Tarrant Hinton (source: Giles 1982, Britannia 13, 386–7, fig. 23).

Early villa houses

It is no surprise that many villas are known to have occupied the sites of Iron Age settlements. Some, such as Tarrant Hinton (Figure 7.2) and Brixworth actually lie over round-houses (BRANIGAN 1982, 88), while others such as Faversham (Figure 7.3) were built on or near Iron Age ditches or have produced Iron Age artefacts or features.

The indigenous timber building tradition remained in use for some considerable time at many villa sites. A large number of villas are known to have been built initially completely in timber and wattle, and some, like Alrewas, appear to have remained in timber into the second and perhaps third centuries. Wherwell is a corridor villa, with mosaics, built entirely of timber,

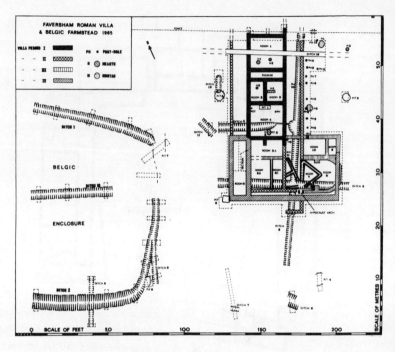

Figure 7.3 Faversham (source: Philip 1968, Excavations at Faversham, Kent).

dating to the late third to fourth century.

Because I aim to highlight a general trend among British villas – the development from simple rectangular to winged-corridor plans – little attention will be paid to the very early, large, and luxurious establishments of Fishbourne and Eccles, for it is possible that they were official residences, and subject to different social constraints.

The sites around Verulamium (St. Albans), which have featured prominently in British villa studies, are some of the earliest native villas to appear in the British landscape. The first stone-footed oblong blocks of rooms appear *c.* AD 75, though that at Lockleys may have appeared as early as AD 60 (WARD-PERKINS 1938, 339–76; WALTHEW 1975, 197, n. 73). Later at Lockleys a simple lean-to porch was added, and *c.* AD 150 a stone-footed corridor and additional rooms including wings were erected (Figure 7.1). Park Street developed much the same way as Lockleys (SMITH, D. J. 1978, 120). Other villas which are known to have begun as simple oblong blocks of rooms include Faversham (Figure 7.3), Frocester Court, Hambleden, Brixworth, Boxmoor, Cox Green, and Huntsham.

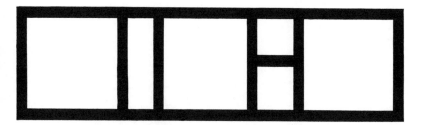

Figure 7.4 Recurring permutation of rooms found in Romano-British villas.

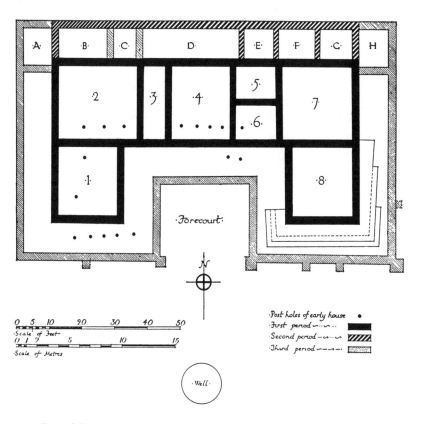

Figure 7.5 Ditchley (source: Ralegh Radford 1936, Oxonensia 1, 30, figure 9).

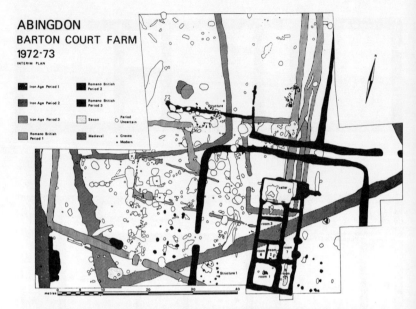

ABINGDON
BARTON COURT FARM
1972·73
INTERIM PLAN

Figure 7.6 Barton Court Farm (source: Miles 1974, Britannia 5, 456, figure 22).

Significant permutations of rooms

One simple rectangular plan in particular can be identified in many villas in
Britain, indicating that these were not random designs. Figure 7.4 is a
schematic representation of this recurring permutation of rooms (cf. DRURY
1982b; and see below). It is found to be the basic building block of many
British villas: Ditchley (Figure 7.5), Barton Court Farm (Figure 7.6), Maid-
stone, Frocester Court, Farningham, Little Milton, and it is found in the
north wing of Chignall St. James. Slight variations of this design are found at
Lockleys, Northchurch, Rockbourne, Llantwit Major, in the north and west
wings of Chedworth, and in the west wing of North Leigh.

The scale of dimensions and proportions of these blocks of rooms are
much the same: *c.* 20–30 m. long and *c.* 7–10 m. wide, giving proportions of
3:1–4:1. The area of floor space of these blocks is in the range 140–300
square metres. Comparisons with available floor space in the Iron Age are
notoriously difficult.

There have been suggestions that villas may have been two-storied, which
would of course add to the floor area of roofed space. The evidence was reviewed recently by Neal (1982, 153–70). He concluded that although some
parts of some buildings may have risen to a height above that of the adjacent
rooms (granary towers, for example), there is no evidence for more than a

single storey. Branigan (1982, 95) was on the right lines, describing villas as bungalows.

It is possible that the pairs and trios of round-houses which housed and comprised the late Iron Age extended family unit were transmogrified in the early villas into the three larger rooms which are often apparent. The smaller rooms (the 'H' and the 'I') probably represent the 'dividing space' that used to exist between the separate round-houses. An analysis of their space syntax, where doorway identification allows, shows that these smaller rooms and 'through-passages' served to control access to the large rooms. The 'passages' cannot actually be 'through-passages' at all, because in many other types of domestic buildings – especially *mansiones* (official inns) – it has been demonstrated that these thin rooms are flanked by porticos and other features which are *themselves* passages (DRURY 1982b, 295). These rooms acted as 'barriers' between larger pieces of social space.

It must be significant that the block plan which has been identified here is also found in British towns and *mansiones*, and as a central feature of 'estate villas' in northern Gallia Belgica, such as Anthée in Belgium. Variations on this theme appear as the central rectangular range of rooms at Odrang in Germany, at Guiry, Seine-et-Oise in France, and at a whole host of villas discovered by Roger Agache during relatively recent aerial surveys of northern France, including a large number of probable first-century enclosed villas like Anthée: Malpart, Grivesnes, and Warfusée Nord, for example (AGACHE 1975).

Romanisation and the 'ideology' of villa building

The fact that these standardised blocks are seen in northern Belgica, and at an early date, suggests that although these blocks replaced round-house architecture in Britain as early villas, they were not a uniquely indigenous British response to the introduction of masonry rectangular plans. Rather, we should consider that these simple plans were suggested to or imposed upon the 'upwardly mobile' British; that is, architectural ideas of assistance were provided by the new Roman provincial administration. The 'testimony' of Tacitus (*Agricola* c. 21) is thus:

> He encouraged individuals and assisted communities to build temples, fora, and private houses. He praised the energetic and scolded the slack. Competition for honour took the place of compulsion. And he had the sons of the leading men educated in the liberal arts. He expressed a preference for the natural talents of the British over the trained abilities of the Gauls, so that those who used to reject the Roman tongue now coveted its eloquence. Thence our manner of dress became fashionable and the toga was often to be seen.

Drury has isloated blocks of rooms (Figure 7.7) which are the heart of fig-

Figure 7.7 Drury's 'standard unit' of rooms.

ure 10 in a number of *mansiones* in towns such as Silchester. He (1982b, 295) observes that:

> The repetition of suites or rooms of similar plan, coupled with the generous provision of baths, suggests that their function was to accommodate separate groups of people.

The so-called *mansio* at Silchester in *insula* VIII was probably planned *c*. AD 90–120. There is no proof that this building was the *mansio* for users of the *cursus publicus*, although there are a number of features that suggest that this was no ordinary house. It was a large building, covering as much ground as the forum, and larger than any other house at Silchester. The bath house was of considerable size, and it adjoined an open courtyard running the whole length of the eastern side, which in turn was separated from the main building by a substantial wall. Although it is not impossible that this was the residence of a wealthy citizen, its size alone and early date indicate a public use and certainly official involvement in the planning (WACHER 1976, 262–4).

It may be that the earliest simple oblong villas were adapted copies of the 'apartments' seen in early towns in Britain, themselves transported from early 'Romanised' contexts in northern Gaul. Sets of rooms reminiscent of those which comprise the earliest simple villas such as Brixworth and Lockleys can be recognised at Verulamium as early as *c*. AD 49 in the timber 'Claudian shops' of *insula* XIV (*ibid*. 204, 213). It is possible that the construction of these 'shops' was overseen by military architects who had access to military supply bases for materials (FRERE 1971). These sets of rooms could well have provided a 'blueprint' for the first Britons who had these villas built or who had villas 'commissioned' for them.

In light of the British provincial origins of aisled farmhouses (SCOTT 1988, 102–6; in prep.), the possibility must be considered that, left to their own devices, the British would have more probably developed the aisled house as their response to the stimulus and imposition of new architectural forms and materials. The British had, indeed, already developed a simple form of aisled building by the late Iron Age (NEAL 1983, 115–21). It was the direct involvement of the Roman administration in the lives of the British which altered and speeded up the course of cultural change.

In the passage quoted above, Tacitus stressed and idealised the conscious involvement of Britons in Roman provincial life by Agricola. It is presented as a deliberate set of actions by the Roman governor. Hanson (1988, 58–9) observes that, as the passage pointedly states that compulsion became unnecessary, one might reasonably infer that compulsion was, nevertheless, a possibility. The indigenous people were possibly not enthralled by their new financial commitments. What real honour could there be for prominent Britons in spending money which was not really theirs on public buildings which they did not own, and all with the 'encouragement' of an occupying force? The actions of Agricola would have been a massive contribution to the erosion of traditional power bases, and former paramount lineages would not necessarily appreciate Agricola's efforts to civilise the province.

The addition of winged-corridor façades and its effects

By the early second century it was usual for villa houses to have a corridor façade, often with 'wing' rooms, and for new villas to be built complete with such a façade.

Building B at Shakenoak, constructed at the end of the first century, is at present the earliest instance known in Britain of a villa built complete with winged-corridor frontage (BRODRIBB et al. 1971, 14–28). Wings were adopted in the contemporary or slightly later house at nearby Ditchley; a surrounding corridor was added in a later phase (Figure 7.5). Also c. AD 100, wings were adopted at Boxmoor and corridors at Cobham. Corridors were adopted at Faversham c. 100–150; wings were added c. 150–200 (Figure 7.3). It was only in the mid-second century that a winged-corridor frontage was added to the house constructed as long before as c. 65 at Lockleys (Figure 7.1), and only then or later in the second century that houses were erected complete with winged-corridors at High Wycombe, Gadebridge and Gayton Thorpe. According to David Smith (1978, 120), Lockleys, High Wycombe, and Gadebridge 'seem to represent the typical sequences and chronology.'

The winged-corridor frontage influenced access to the living rooms. The entrance – wherever it had been before – was now placed centrally and conspicuously in the corridor. This process can be seen, for instance, in the west and east ranges of the inner courtyard at Woodchester (Figure 7.8), the west

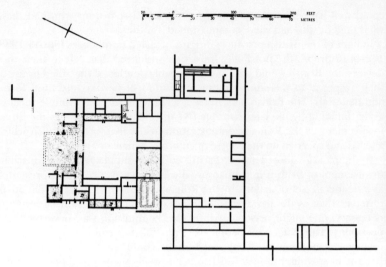

Figure 7.8 Woodchester (source: RCHM Glos. Cotswolds 1976, 133).

range of Chedworth (Figure 7.9), Great Staughton (Figure 7.10), the west building at Beadlam, Lockleys, Huntsham, Clear Cupboard, Brislington, Lullingstone, Ely, Witcombe, and Bancroft.

One of the rooms in the oblong block would previously have been the most integrated room, that is, the most accessible in terms of numbers of doorways. It is probable that the corridor now became the integrative mechanism. Doorways from the corridor lead both into the living rooms and into the wing rooms, as at Kingsweston (Figure 7.11). Certainly the adoption of a corridor resulted in an extra architectural step being needed to enter from the outside to even the most accessible of the original inside living rooms. This new feature, together with the axial entrances which produced symmetrical or near-symmetrical façades, became a convention in British villa architecture from the second century onwards. A tendency towards a more 'closed' architecture can be detected: the symmetrical façades acted as an architectural deception. The flanking wings act to guide the visitor unambiguously towards the central main entrance and the corridor, and the corridor itself maintains control over access to the living rooms behind it.

The corridor acts both as a spatial barrier between the outside world and the living rooms and as a reception area. These functions are most marked in the fourth century in villas such as Witcombe, where a portico entrance leads into a corridor, from where a right-angle turn and a twenty-metre walk was necessary to reach the ranges of living rooms. Keynsham took the trend to its limit; it was a courtyard villa built in the early fourth century with long

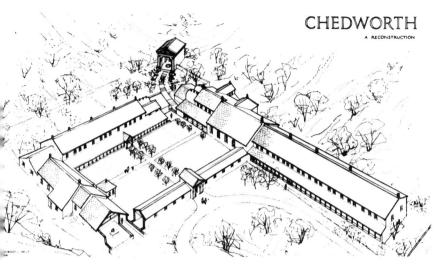

Figure 7.9 Chedworth (print in possession of D. J. Smith).

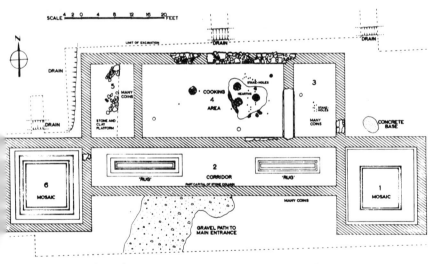

Figure 7.10 Great Staughton (source: Greenfield 1959).

corridors on each side. Long 'walkway' corridors are also evident at Bignor (Figure 7.12).

While the living rooms such as the kitchen may have had 'back doors' for informal family use, entry by visitors would have been more formal. Indeed,

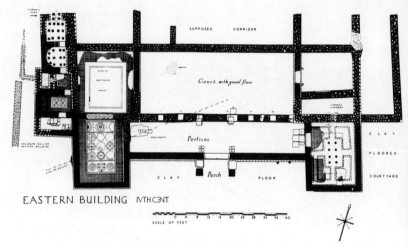

Figure 7.11 Kingsweston (source: Boon 1957, Guidebook).

the different path or mode of entry would make a social distinction between informal and formal visitors. The architecture exerted control over the movement of 'outsiders'. This phenomenon can of course be seen today: friends and family are permitted, even encouraged, to come through our back door and directly into our kitchens, but strangers and formal visitors are required to approach the front door and pass through the hallway. It is interesting too that different modes of request for entry exist in Britain today: a ring on the doorbell signals a formal, impersonal caller; a knock on the door is probably somebody known to the householder; a rapping of the letter box is usually a close friend, relative, or neighbour. Thus the formalisation of villa house plans from the second century onwards represents much more than just increasing social ambition, and the changes cannot properly be explained by invocation of the shibboleth 'Romanisation'.

A social and economic explanation for the architectural change

Why did the British wait generations to adopt these winged-corridor façades, this 'requirement' as Smith called it, and can we suggest what the adoption of these new configurations of space meant socially? It is an empirical fact that from the second century onward it became the norm for villas to have added to them, or for new villas to be built complete with, a winged-corridor frontage. There is no recognisable geographical 'trajectory' for this development. The earliest known winged-corridor façade is from Shakenoak in Oxfordshire, and the others mentioned above appeared soon after in Northamptonshire, then in Oxfordshire, Kent, Buckinghamshire, and Hert-

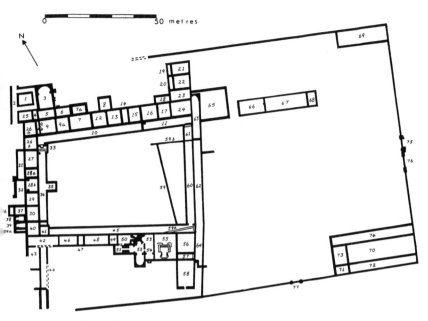

Figure 7.12 Bignor (Black 1983, Oxford J. of Arch. 2, 95).

fordshire. These known examples undoubtedly reflect the overall pattern of
villa exploration in the past rather than an historical reality.

The winged-corridor façade was often added at the same time as the villa
was given more rooms, sometimes including an elaborate reception room,
such as Room 1 at Woodchester (Figure 7.8) (CLARKE 1982, 218–9) which
contained the Great Pavement. Large axial rooms and the reception areas
comprising corridors and possibly wing rooms were frequently decorated
with mosaics in the early fourth century (and possibly from the late third).
The 'reception area' of Great Staughton (Figure 7.10) was very fancy relative
to the living area behind it: the only mosaics present in the house were
found in the corridor and wing rooms, and the axial entrance was graced
with stone columns (GREENFIELD 1959, 118). The corridors at Ely were tessellated. The large wing room, Room 8, at Lockleys was tessellated. The corridor between the wings at Frocester Court, and only the corridor, contained mosaics. The corridors at Bucknowle Farm were tessellated and one
part was furnished with a figured mosaic. The implication is that the owners
of the villas wished to keep their formal reception space visually impressive.
They did this in the early fourth century by inserting mosaics; prior to this
elaborate rugs may have been *de rigeur*. (The fact that mosaics 'fossilise'

symbolism of the early fourth century is too often neglected.)

Because social relations are inextricably bound up with economic transactions (MALINOWSKI 1922, 156–94; POLANYI 1944; 1959; HODDER 1979, 189–96; WELLS 1980, 7) – and no economy is ever fully disembedded – one should expect a changing economy to have an effect on social relations, and this in turn to affect the use of social space. The study of the ancient economy is a contentious area, but a number of general trends in the development of the Romano-British economy can be isolated. A coin-based market economy did not arrive in Britain with the Romans; it only gradually replaced the socially embedded economy which saw economic transactions taking place primarily within the sphere of social obligation. By the early second century, however, an economic system based upon money and market forces had begun operating in Britain. In a recent study of the evidence of pottery from Northamptonshire, Griffiths (1986, 5) demonstrated that samian wares were found in some quantity in even 'humble' rural roundhouse sites by this time, and that the the most likely mechanism to explain this is a market economy.

The social effects of the establishment of monetised interactions on a large scale and throughout the whole community were myriad. The money economy offered not just prospects of wealth, which had to be protected, but also prospects of inflation, taxation, and relative poverty, which were best kept at bay; there was now also the need to accept bureaucratic administration and strangers over the threshold. This major economic upheaval, and the resulting social tensions, are reflected in the changing architecture of the Romano-British villa.

The formal reception space was important to the functioning of society. As the intensification of the money economy eroded traditional social relations, so the British sought order through their use of social space. The new and closed use of social space reflects a profound change in the social and economic life of the inhabitants of the villas, and the fact that the winged-corridor frontage appears from the early second century onward indicates that its appearance was fundamentally linked with the emergence of a market economy. The number of known, suspected, and possible villa/rural Roman building sites in Britain – c. 2,250 – (SCOTT 1988, Appendix 1) demonstrates the vast scale of material wealth present in the countryside of the province in the fourth century, and this alone would argue against Finley's (1973) minimalist view of the Roman economy (cf. GREENE 1986, 170–1).

At a basic level it can be argued that the introduction of corridor façades and other reception areas is a reordering of space which is a response to the emergence of a reordered economy and reordered social relations. Visitors, often complete strangers, could be expected to arrive on business connected with commerce, taxation, administration and so forth. The new architecture guided them to the central doorway and into a formal and often highly decorated corridor. Access was subtly controlled. The configurations of space served not just to reflect social custom but reinforced the new social relations which arose out of the necessity for new types of economic transaction. The coin-based monetised economy of the Roman world, and the material culture of the Roman world in the form of closed villas, combined to constitute a new social order – and *this* was 'Romanisation'.

Villa enclosures and monumental gateways

Oswald (1937, 138) described the villas of Norton Disney, Ely, Langton, Castle Dykes, Cwmbrwyn, and Bartlow as 'fortified'. This raises two points. First, enclosures do not necessarily have to constitute fortifications; rather they can be used to control access, movement, and encounter. They define private property, and they also exist as social barriers. Enclosures embody the symbolism of possession, authority, and power, reinforcing the authority held by those who control or own the settlements. Second, it is not often appreciated that villas such as Norton Disney had such visually impressive enclosures because standard published plans frequently depict only the surviving masonry foundations.

Many of the enclosure ditches associated with villas clearly pre-date the masonry buildings. At Whitton a large ditch was found surrounding the villa buildings but the foundations were built over the tail of the internal upcast bank (JARRETT 1969, 200). Scott (1973, 189) believed that this villa had some bearing on the general question of the fortification of villas: because the enclosure pre-dates the villa it cannot have been fortified according to his argument. Elsewhere villa buildings are known to overlie what seem to have been Iron Age enclosure ditches, as at Ely, Tarrant Hinton and Gorhambury.

It might be suggested that these enclosures had become redundant, perhaps as a result of early official disapproval. The Roman administration may have viewed these enclosures as 'defensive' and unacceptable. They were certainly levelled before the villas were built. However, many late villa enclosure ditches and walls are known. From the third century onward villas tended to become enclosed, often by masonry walls, sometimes by earthworks. Single (e.g. Wellow (Figure 7.13) and Spoonley Wood), double (e.g. Chedworth, Bignor and North Wraxall (Figures 7.9, 7.12, 7.14)), and even triple (e.g. Woodchester (Figure 7.8)) courtyard villas became a feature of the British landscape. Entry into these courtyards was through monumental gateways. Often, as at Darenth (Figure 7.15), a water shrine or a well acted as a focus (cf. SMITH, J. T. 1978, 157).

The large ditches were constructed fairly late at Norton Disney. At Barton Court Farm the villa house was enclosed by a palisade and ditch, which cut through the 'corn drier' of the early fourth century. Elsewhere regular enclosures were associated with the villa buildings uninterruptedly throughout its history, as at Chilgrove 2.

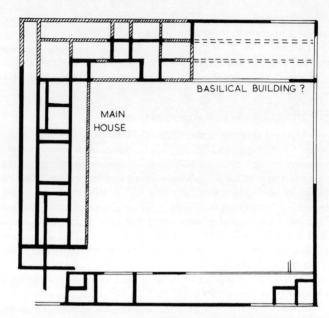

Figure 7.13 Wellow (source: Branigan 1976,
The Roman Villa in South-West England, figure 16B)

The classic 'courtyard villas' recognised by Richmond in his problematic typology of Romano-British villas (1969, 59–64) are Chedworth, Bignor, Chedworth, Keynsham, and Woodchester. They all appear to have reached their greatest extent in the early fourth century. The estate walls of these courtyard villas may have replaced enclosure ditches. Recent small-scale excavation at Woodchester, for example, detected a V-shaped ditch which seemed to run parallel to and about 5 metres from the eastern aisled farmhouse which formed one side of the centre courtyard. The ditch lay close to the enclosure wall, but unfortunately only a small part of the ditch was excavated and its relationship to the wall and the buildings could not be fully established (CLARKE 1982, 205). The appearance also of aisled farmhouses in the third and fourth centuries suggests that farming activities and people were being increasingly drawn into a centralised demarcated area. This may have less to do with defence than with reorganisation of the estate for economic reasons, for a number of villa buildings are attached to the *outside* of their enclosure walls, as at Clanville, Combley, Sparsholt, and Stroud. It is also possible that the aisled farmhouses were being run as 'home farms' by a younger branch of the family (SCOTT 1988, 146–9), and we may be seeing a desire for an increased control over inheritance.

It is extremely difficult to recognise general trends in the use of villa en-

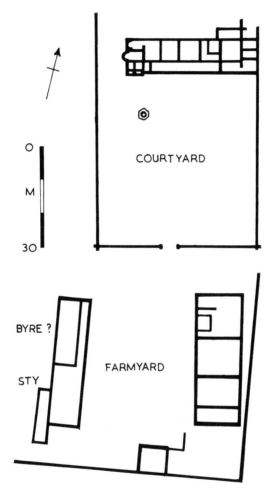

Figure 7.14 North Wraxall (source: Branigan 1976, The Roman Villa in South-West England, figure 31).

closures. However, what can be said is that these enclosures with their monumental entrances served as formal access routes. The routes through the courtyards of some villas would have been more like processional ways. Such architecture was the culmination of the process which began in the second century with the addition of winged-corridor façades.

Although the idea for the general form and style of enclosure walls may have spread from the Continent, from the estate villas of the Somme perhaps, it should be remembered that British farmers had a long tradition of

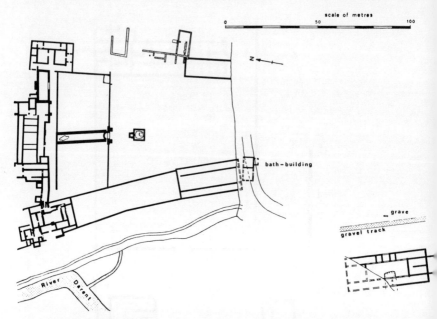

Figure 7.15 Darenth (source: Locke 1970, Current Archaeology 19, 221).

site enclosure and that such enclosures had social and psychological as well as functional meaning. Physical barriers set up and reinforce social barriers, and reveal much about how people perceive the world. In an established monetised market economy prosperity and poverty exist side by side, and in the Roman period this led to increasing social tension and increasing formalisation of villa plans.

It has been argued here that one of the roles of a settlement enclosure is to embody private property. It has also been shown that villas become more enclosed with time, and that this development reaches a peak in the fourth century.

This is not to deny, however, that there were no tangible physical dangers in the countryside to threaten the sense of the security of the villa occupants. There were a great number of bandits (*latrones*) in the Roman Empire (SHAW 1984). (Bandits may perhaps be regarded as another by-product of a money economy.) The tendency for villas to become more enclosed through time could indicate a desire for the villas to appear well-protected. Boundaries also impart knowledge. A visible boundary says 'this is where private property begins and there will be consequences for you if you cross this line.' In the fourth century, and probably before, the 'official' entrances and walkways into villas were highly visible and elaborate – typical would be a monumental gateway in an enclosure wall leading into a courtyard or courtyards, and thence to verandas and corridors.

In the Roman world, of course, the consequences of trespass were severe, and bandits were executed. The forbidding enclosures of villas would act to reinforce the knowledge that there were penalties for transgressing Roman law. To scale an enclosure wall, or to cross an earthwork, requires conscious and severe physical effort. It is a clear trespass.

The problem of roaming bands of reprobates in the countryside grew worse on the continent by the early fifth century. The *Bacaudae* movements and revolts are historically documented, and it has been suggested that they may have been a force in Britain (THOMPSON 1977, 303–18) in the years 409–10. However, the villas of Britain were enclosed long before this date, so the question of the presence of *Bacaudae* cannot be held to be the impetus for the building of Romano-British villa enclosures.

Conclusions

It has been demonstrated that even with relatively few villa plans a pattern of development can be seen to emerge. This, when analysed in terms of 'transformational grammar', allows us a powerful insight into changes in Romano-British social relations, economic structure, and perceptions of the outside world.

We must eschew the simplistic notion that villas were merely the homes of people somewhat Romanised in manners. They were the homes of Britons who were being increasingly drawn into an unprecedentedly complex world of market forces, political upheavals, new religions and a standing army; their universe was, to all intents and purposes, continually expanding.

An analysis of the changing configurations of space in Romano-British villas suggests that there were significant economic changes and social tensions from the second century onward. The establishment of a true money market economy led to a vast increase in the number of economic transactions which took place outside of the social sphere. In villas a distinction was made from the early second century onward between private living space and reception or guest space. No two villa plans are the same, but this apparent freedom of development occurred within a number of recognisable constraints. The general trend was for the erection of symmetrical façades that obscured the rooms and thresholds behind them. The winged corridor façades and later the courtyards acted as buffer zones between the private family rooms and the outside world. The new architecture was of course visually impressive, and was a conspicuous display of wealth, but it also had these 'deeper' effects. The formal façades and paths through courtyards controlled access to the house by unambiguously guiding the visitor toward the main central entrance. Any deviation from the 'official' route – permitted or not – would have social meaning. The private living apartment was now set back an extra step or steps from the outside.

This new architecture expresses a fascinating duality of purpose – on the one hand a sophisticated attempt at entry into the Romanised world of markets and civilisation ('Romanisation'), and on the other an attempt to distance the household from an environment thought to be potentially hostile. This recalls some basic Marxist ideology which asserts that man's social existence determines his consciousness, and that one can explain this consciousness by the contradictions in material life (MARX 1962, preface). That is, people may think they are saying and doing one thing when in fact they are doing another – 'civilisation', it has been said, is merely 'organised hypocrisy'.

In Roman Britain the hostility that was perceived – albeit subliminally – led to a change in the world view of the villa inhabitants. This hostile environment was not just the perceived physical theat of barbarians. A more insidious threat existed: vulnerability to market forces and therefore poverty, inflation, taxation, and the need to accept strangers over the threshold. These latter concepts were outside the villa owners' intimate social networks and were therefore not controlled by them. Through architecture they sought to re-establish some form of control over the world. The architecture both reached out to embrace the Roman world and at the same time drew its occupants back and protected them from it. Further, it controlled the movement of people; this effect was heightened by the use of enclosures, culminating in the large and impressive courtyard villas of the fourth century.

The new architecture would of course have exterted a controlling influence over the movements of the occupants of the villa estates, possibly particularly women. Further studies of changing gender and household relations in Roman Britain will be relevant here (see SCOTT 1991 forth.).

On this note, and finally, we must beware of the 'country house' analogy and the androcentrism to which it is prone. In traditional farming societies it is usual for women and children to perform arduous manual labour. Women do 90 per cent of the world's work, but own only 10 per cent of the world's wealth; they consequently have been given a low profile and their contribution to labour both now and in the past is underestimated. We do not yet understand the relationship of villas to towns, and must not assume the widespread existence of 'gentleman farmers' with servants, slaves, town houses and wives and daughters dedicated to the pursuit of leisure.

Bibliography

Agache, Roger 1975. *Atlas D'Archeologie Aerienne de Picardie*. (Amiens).

Branigan, Keith 1976. 'Villa settlement in the West Country' in K. Branigan and P. J. Fowler 1976, 120–41.

Branigan, Keith 1982. 'Celtic farm to Roman villa' in D. Miles 1982.

Branigan, Keith and Fowler, Peter J. (eds.) 1976. *The Roman West Country*. (London).

Braund, D. (ed.) 1988. *The Administration of the Roman Empire 241 BC to AD 193. Exeter Studies in History*, 18.

Brodribb, A. C. C., Hands, A. R. and Walker, D. R., 1971, *Excavations at Shakenoak II*.

Burnham, B. C. and Johnson, H. B. (eds.) 1979. *Invasion and Response: The Case of Roman Britain*. BAR 73, British Series (Oxford).

Clarke, G. 1982. 'The Roman villa at Woodchester', *Britannia* 13, 197–228.

Cook, O. 1982. *English Cottages and Houses*.

Drury, P. J. (ed.) 1982a, *Structural Reconstruction*. BAR 110, British Series (Oxford).

Drury, P. J. 1982b. 'Form, function and the interpretation of the excavated plans of some large secular Romano-British buildings' in P. J. Drury 1982.

Finley, Moses I. 1973. *The Ancient Economy*. University of California Press (Berkeley).

Frere, Shepard S. 1971. *Verulamium Excavations I*.

Frere, Shepard S. 1982. 'The Bignor villa', *Britannia* 13, 135–96.

Fried, Morton (ed.) 1959. *Readings in Cultural Anthropology*. Crowell (New York).

Glassie, Henry 1975. *Middle Virginian Folk Housing*. University of Tennessee (Knoxville).

Glassie, Henry 1985. 'Structural analysis of vernacular architecture: transatlantic comparison of results', *Abstracts*, Theoretical Archaeology Group Conference, Glasgow.

Greene, Kevin 1986. *The Archaeology of the Roman Economy*. Batsford (London).

Greenfield, E. 1959. 'Great Staughton', *Journal of Roman Studies* 49.

Griffiths, Karen E. 1986. *Market Exchange Systems Within the Roman Economy of the First and Second Centuries A.D.* Unpublished PhD Thesis, University of Newcastle upon Tyne.

Hanson, William S. 1988. 'Administration, urbanisation and acculturation' in D. Braund 1988.

Hillier, Bill and Hanson, Julien 1984. *The Social Logic of Space*. Cambridge University Press (Cambridge).

Hodder, Ian 1979. 'Pre-Roman and Romano-British tribal economies', in B. C. Burnham and H. B. Johnson 1979.

Malinowski, B. 1922. *Argonauts of the Western Pacific*. Routledge (London).

Marx, Karl 1962. *A Contribution to a Critique of Political Economy*, Marx/Engels, *Selected Works*, Moscow, 1962, Volume 1.

Miles, David (ed.) 1982. *The Romano-British Countryside*. BAR 103, British Series (Oxford).

Neal, D. S. 1982. 'Romano-British Villas: one or two storied?' in P. J. Drury 1982, 153–71.

Neal, D. S. 1983. 'Gorhambury', *Current Archaeology* 87.

O'Neil, H. E. 1945. 'The Roman villa at Park Street, near St. Albans, Hertfordshire: report on the excavations of 1943–45', *Archaeological Journal* 102, 21–110.

Oswald, A. and L. H. D. Buxton 1937. 'A fortified villa at Norton Disney, Lincs.', *Antiq. Journal* 17, 138–78.

Polanyi, Karl 1944. *The Great Transformation*.

Polanyi, Karl 1959, 'Anthropology and economic theory' in M. Fried 1959.

Richmond, Ian 1969. 'The plans of Roman villas in Britain', in A. L. F. Rivet 1969, 49–70.

Rivet, A. L. F. (ed.) 1969. *The Roman Villa in Britain*. Routledge (London).

Scott, Eleanor 1988. *Aspects of the Roman Villa as a Form of British Settlement*. Ph.D. Thesis, University of Newcastle upon Tyne.

Scott, Eleanor 1991 forth. 'Animal and infant burials in Romano-British villas: a revitalisation movement?' in P. Garwood *et al.* (eds.) *Sacred and Profane*. OUCA (Oxford).

Scott, Eleanor in prep., 'The function and status of aisled farmhouses on Romano-British villas'.

Scott, P. R. 1973. *Roman Villas in the North of England*. Unpublished M.A. Dissertation, University of Durham.

Shaw, B. D. 1984. 'Bandits in the Roman empire', *Past and Present* 105.

Smith, D. J. 1978. 'Regional aspects of the winged-corridor villa in Britain', in M. Todd 1978, 117–48.

Smith, J. T. 1978. 'Villas as a key to social structure', in M. Todd 1978, 149–56.

Thompson, A. E. 1977. 'Britain A.D. 406 – 410', *Britannia* 8.

Todd, M. (ed.) 1978. *Studies in the Romano-British Villa*. Leicester University Press (Leicester).

Wacher, J. 1976. *The Towns of Roman Britain*. 2nd Edition. Book Club Associates (London).

Walthew, C. V. 1975. 'The town house and villa house in Roman Britain', *Britannia* 6, 189–205.

Ward-Perkins, J. B. 1938. 'The Roman villa at Lockleys, Welwyn', *Antiq. Journal* 18, 339–76.

Wells, Peter S. 1980. *Culture Contact and Culture Change*.

Eight

Comment on Eleanor Scott's 'Romano-British Villas and the Social Construction of Space'

ROSS SAMSON

Eleanor Scott has convincingly shown that architectural changes (the addition of corridors to façades, wings, and enclosures) in Romano-British villas from the second to fourth century represent increasing formality in the organisation of space, and that the activities occurring in those spaces were less visibly evident from exterior façades. She suggests that the increasing formality was related to changes in society and economy, in particular the growth of a monetised economy. The changes, argues Scott, necessitated more strangers than ever before crossing the threshold, be they tax collectors, representatives of municipal or imperial administration, or merchants.

My first comment is a relatively minor objection. Not everyone is at home with Scott's contention that the economy had become monetised by the late Empire. I myself remain in the shrinking Finley camp, believing that most production, exchange, and consumption occurred in the form of rents, tribute, slave exploitation, taxation, plunder, and gifts. Sale and purchase by coin I doubt played a significant role. Her characterisation of early and late Empire as respectively societies with a socially embedded system of exchanges and a monetised economy is overstated. It produces the opposed images of socially-motivated exchange between kin, friends, and superiors and the asocial, self-seeking exchange between strangers. This opposition of exchange with those you know and with those you do not allows Scott to put 'strangers' firmly in the third- and fourth-century picture. It is these strangers, their formal entrance through courtyard gates,

their passage through faceless corridors, and their entertainment on tessellated or mosaic-inlaid floors, in short their controlled meeting with villa
dwellers, that Scott uses to explain the changes in Romano-British villa
architecture. But this increase in the amount of social intercourse with
strangers is quite in keeping with Finley's view of the ancient economy.
The supposed importance of coinage and prominence of neutral exchange,
to use Marshall Salins' term, opens the door to dissent (and my objection
here is proof) that is unnecessary, for Scott's interpretation does not necessarily hinge on it.

This difference of opinion is, as I have said, relatively minor. However, it
will later be clear that my different emphasis (on the importance of forms
of social dependency and that they were not the result of or mediated by
the exchange of coin) leads me to an entirely different explanation of the
architectural changes of Romano-British villas.

Scott's interpretation remains largely on the cosmological level. She
expressly relates the changes in architecture to changes in world views.
Such quasi-anthropological analyses of cosmological meanings in architecture are often very convincingly made by archaeologists, especially when
a whole range of symbolic meanings in society are studied, and the society
is treated statically (both papers by HINGLEY and RICHARDS in this volume
are good examples). Even at its best, however, cosmological interpretations
are weak when it comes to explaining relations of power or attempts at
subversion of those relations. The re-creation of belief systems by archaeologists or anthropologists usually has little place for the social action of
individuals. I probably can say it no better than Saunders (this volume):
social space is interpreted as if it were mental space. When society changes,
world views usually change with it. But the explanation of change in beliefs
on the cosmological or structuralist level usually stops with the recognition
of 'tension', be it related to war, the industrial revolution, collapse of
empires, or whatever. The new beliefs are meant somehow to ease or deny
that tension or the changes that were wrought in society's fabric, or perhaps simply come to terms with the new order. What I would like to see
(and would be the first to agree is extremely difficult) is the relationship of
ideologies to the re-creation of social structures through everyday actions,
to the employment of power, to the claims of authority and denial of
authority, to the struggle against structures of power, to a variety of social
discourses.

In the case of the western Roman Empire, society and the villas it produced changed between the first and fourth centuries AD. Changes surely
occurred in world views so that Gauls, Germans, and Britons came to see
themselves as 'Romans' and built homes that expressed it. But can the
architectural changes not be related more closely to some of the social
changes, and how people used those physical structures to increase their
own power or deny others' authority? Instead simply of fears of going to

the wall, of taxation, and of the general hostility of a free-for-all economic system, can the architectural changes not be related to real-life situations? For example, did new building styles hide their wealth from tax collectors or merchants who could not estimate how well-off the inhabitants were because so much of the villa was hidden from view and external judgement? Or did formal control of strangers aid villa-dwellers to hide their poverty from important guests who did not venture beyond the lavish reception areas?

One home truth about Hillier and Hanson's applications of their spatial analyses and the work of Glassie is that they concentrate on the confrontation of inhabitants and strangers. There may be degrees of formality distinguishing strangers, but always movement through space is seen in terms of how it affects the outsider. Chapman (this volume) says that 'Access within settlements and inside buildings for inhabitants, visitors, and strangers lies at the heart of their model.' Scott's chapter is primarily concerned with the mediation of dweller-stranger meetings, as are some other papers that acknowledge inspiration from Hillier or Glassie (e.g. FOSTER 1989). Perhaps because Hillier, Hanson, and Glassie deal with recent history and the ever-popular nuclear family, internal social relations and their spatial constraints are largely ignored. But this can only be done with peril in prehistoric contexts, and even more so with Romano-British ranches. To quote Scott, 'The appearance of aisled farmhouses in the third and fourth centuries suggests that farming activities and people were being increasingly drawn into a centralised demarcated area.' To this internal development of the villa *familia* I want to direct the remainder of my comments.

To any student of the early modern English house the corridor instantly calls to mind the increasing formality of the master-servant relationship. Corridors and back stairs were introduced to grant the heads of the household more privacy and to push servants out of view. The corridor in Roman villas cannot function in quite the same way as back stairs, for it must have made activities within the household in some ways more visible. This busy highway of a corridor was used by visitors and perhaps there was no 'service entrance' so that high and low, friend and foe mingled, and the corridor thronged with activity (Figure 8.1).

Perhaps rather than the sedate early modern English country house, where chamber pots seemed miraculously to empty themselves and rooms were neither noisome nor noisy, the Roman villas employed a corridor to increase contact between the inhabitants. Perhaps the intention was to display the number of servants to guests, just as the long approach through an outer courtyard exposed the serried ranks of agricultural buildings to view and the wings of the villa-dwelling themselves enveloped anyone approaching when they could easily have receded back from the *domus*, out of sight. Perhaps constant meetings gave welcome opportunities to the villa-masters to receive the subservient rituals of obeisance by their slaves. Seneca (*Epist.*

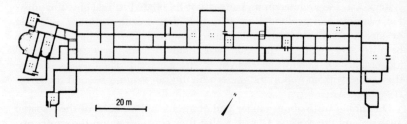

Figure 8.1 L'Hostée, Belgium, with an exceptionally long fronting corridor or portico.

47) wrote that 'proud Roman fashion decrees that a crowd of slaves shall stand around their master while he dines . . . the unfortunate slaves are not allowed to move their lips . . . and the slightest sound is checked with the rod.' Doubtless there was correct etiquette to be observed when the master passed in the corridor too. Sidonius Apollinaris (*Epist.* 2.2.10) tells us of the portico at his villa Avitacum, its pillars, its roof, its lack of a view, and that 'At the end of this passage, however, a part is stolen from it to form a very cool chamber, where a chattering crowd of female dependants and nurse-maids spread a feast for the gods, but sound the retreat when I and my family have set out for our bedrooms.'

Formality introduced by the corridor would have occurred most notice-ably within the *familia*, rather than between inhabitants and strangers. Out-siders were easily held at bay in certain reception areas, but movement within the house was uncontrollable if passage was gained only from one room to the next. Servants, carrying out chores, were not easily excluded from rooms if they had to pass between them to go about their business. If access to any room was possible by external passage there was no excuse for being in a room in which one had no call to be.

Formality in the spatial arrangement of villa inhabitants is clear in the case of double-courtyard villas such as Le Mesge (Figure 8.2), provided there were residents in the outer court, that is. While the dwellings of resident workers is seldom the object of archaeological concern, it is clear the much smaller, modest replicas of the great villa dwelling are sometimes found in the outer courtyard. These are usually interpreted as the resid-ences of the overseer, the *actor*. Presumably many of those who were supervised by the *actor* also lived in the courtyard. The separation of these lowly workers from the villa owners is quite marked. Perhaps we can assume that no one who was resident in the outer courtyard except the *actor* passed through the villa's second monumental gateway.

The enclosure around villas has traditionally interested no one (exceptionally, see ELEANOR SCOTT'S unpublished thesis and HINGLEY 1989),

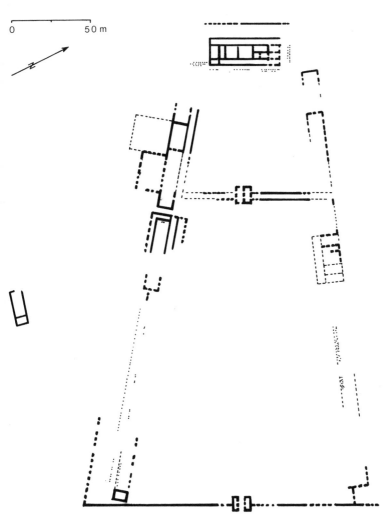

Figure 8.2 Le Mesge, Picardie, France (after Agache).

unless they are sufficiently large to be considered in some way defensive, and yet they still stand complete in part of their circuit at some Italian villas, such as Settefinestre and Villa della Colonne. Passing comments may touch on the ideological content of enclosure: the representation of power, authority, or possession. And thus it has been noted that the towerlets of the enclosure at Settefinestre, Villa della Colonne, and at least one other neighbouring villa seem to be imitations of town walls and towers in miniature. In my own work on early medieval Frankish villas, I (1985) noted that the barbarian law codes suggested a legal distinction between offences inside and outside the courtyard. One can just make out the idea of trespass. I further suggested that the enclosure marked a sphere of lordship and dominion greater in extent than outside the courtyard. It was difficult to pursue one's rights, such as the recovery of lost or stolen cattle, beyond the threshold of the villa enclosure gate. Rather than being physically protected by the massive ramparts at the Merovingian villa, the Camp de Larina, I thought the position of the peasants within the *curtis* was better defended by the lordly protection they clearly enjoyed. To harm them meant not just to harm the lord's dependants, but also to cross the enclosure barrier, to trespass, and to violate the sanctity of the lord's tiny private kingdom. At this point I had just gone beyond the ideological meanings and connotations inherent in the enclosure, but not by much. The question of times of crisis and social tension was raised by me in good Glassian tradition.

In Scott's paper a more immediate consequence of social importance is brought home concerning the physical barrier of villa enclosures: they ensured that the point of entrance and direction of approach were rigidly defined. The villa enclosure was absolutely essential if visitors were to be kept from approaching the villa from its sides or rear. But I cannot come down on Scott's side of the fence, for while I agree with her in part, there is more to the villa enclosure. I called attention to Scott's observation that farming activities and people were increasingly drawn into a centralised and demarcated area. Perhaps the demarcation line, the wall surrounding the villa, was related primarily to the peasants' relationship with the villa owners. Recently I (1989) argued that archaeologists have long ignored the labour force on villas and have markedly avoided discussion of their status, and that I believed rural slavery to be much more common than generally believed.[1] The position of these 'farm hands', as they are often called by archaeologists, within an enclosure under the eye and presumably supervision of the villa owner or *actor*, must have been fairly low. The legal status, *servus* or *colonus*, is probably less important than the implication of the spatial arrangement that these peasants did not control their own labour or enjoy its fruits. This is effectively slavery or severe serfdom unless it was wage labour, which I very much doubt.

The question of fleeing Roman slaves is the topic of whole books (e.g. BELLEN 1971) and was an obsession of the Visigothic law codes (KING

---

[1] Since then Hingley's *Rural Settlement in Roman Britain* has appeared, in which the traditional Romanists' 'farm-hands' (who always appear very close to being wage-labourers) are radically replaced by 'kin'. Slaves are boldly mentioned, but clearly their importance is considered minimal in comparison with family and distant kin.

1972). I (forth.) argue that the villa enclosure is a physical prerequisite for recognising slaves' intention to run away. Slaves found outside the enclosure at inappropriate times lost all ability to argue innocence; having had to climb the wall prevented any ambiguity about their actions. If gate-crashing is usually seen by archeologists as having only one direction (in), it is time now to add out.

My interpretation differs from Scott's. I suggest firstly that the changes in spatial organisation relate to changes in the social relations between the villa dwellers themselves, rather than between them and outsiders. Increasing formality was the product of greater social distance between the inhabitants. Rather than a fear of economic failure or external forces beyond their control, I believe villa owners, pillars of their society, expressed a self-assured, even arrogant, attitude to the world in their architecture, which controlled the movement of strangers, penned in their agricultural slaves, kept domestic servants at arm's length, and put all these inferiors on display to visitors. If the Romano-British villa was no setting for a Jane Austen novel, no Mansfield Park, it is because there was no genteel Georgian country folk, no Sir Thomas or Lady Bertram, resident. Eleanor Scott (1990) has shown elsewhere that the Romano-British were not 'just like us', were not 'modern-rational', but must have had quite different behaviour, morals, and perceptions of the world, given the way they disposed of dead babies on villas, who were almost certainly the victims of infanticide. Their attitude towards human life was not like our own; by our standards the Romans were frequently sadistic:

> Does Rutilus display a lenient temper and a sense of restraint when dealing with trivial faults? Does he hold that the bodies and souls of slaves are made of the same material and elements as our own? No, he does not! What he teaches is brutality: there is nothing he likes to hear more than the sound of a cruel flogging, no siren song (he thinks) is sweeter. To his trembling household he is a complete monster, never happy until he has called for a torturer and some poor wretch is being branded with a hot iron – and all because of two missing towels (Juvenal, *Satires* 14.15 ff.).

Perhaps the villa is better seen as a setting for a novel crossed between *Uncle Tom's Cabin* and *Gone with the Wind*. In it Lupus Tiberius, *vir illustris*,

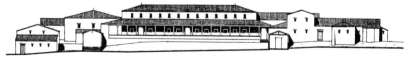

Figure 8.3 Seeb, Switzerland, possible model for Lupiacum, setting for a novel of the harsh but short life of Italia, the servant spinning maid.

and Septimia Flavinia make Lupiacum, their villa (Figure 8.3), a working farm by beating the *rustici*, while for the readers' titillation Gaius regularly ravishes the villa *ancillae*. Lupiacum is less Mansfield Park than it is Scarlet's Tara, but stripped of the romantic nonsense of happy, contented, singing negroes. It doubtless had something of both in terms of extremes in ostentatious, pretentious gentlemanly or ladylike behaviour, if not in form, then at least in arrogance.

Bibliography

Bellen, Heinz 1971. *Studien zur Sklavenflucht im römischen Kaiserreich.* Steiner (Wiesbaden).

Foster, Sally M. 1989. 'Analysis of spatial patterns in buildings (access analysis) as an insight into social structure: examples from the Scottish Atlantic Iron Age' *Antiquity 63*, 40–50.

Glassie, Henry 1975. *Folk Housing in Middle Virginia. A structural analysis of historic artifacts.* University of Tennesse Press (Knoxville).

Hillier, Bill and Hanson, Julienne 1984. *The Social Logic of Space.* Cambridge University Press (Cambridge).

Hingley, Richard 1989. *Rural Settlement in Roman Britain.* Seaby (London).

King, P. D. 1972. *Law and Society in the Visigothic Kingdom.* Cambridge University Press (Cambridge).

Samson, Ross 1987. 'The Merovingian nobleman's home: castle or villa?' *Journal of Medieval History 13*, 287–315.

Samson, Ross 1989. 'Rural slavery, inscriptions, archaeology and Marx: a response to Ramsay Macmullen's "Late Roman slavery"' *Historia 38*, 99–110.

Samson, Ross forth. 'Knowledge, constraint and power: the defenseless medieval wall' in Paul Shackel and Barbara Little (eds.) *Meanings and Uses of Material Culture: an archaeology of an Anglo-American tradition.* Special monograph of *Historical Archaeology.*

Scott, Eleanor 1988. *Aspects of the Roman Villa as a Form of British Settlement.* Ph.D. Thesis, University of Newcastle upon Tyne.

Scott, Eleanor 1990. 'A critical review of the interpretation of infant burials in Roman Britain, with particular reference to villas' *Journal of Theoretical Archaeology 1*, 30–46.

Nine

The Feudal Construction of Space: Power and Domination in the Nucleated Village

TOM SAUNDERS

Social space is both the medium and the outcome of human practice. Any research into social dynamics therefore requires a spatial as well as a temporal dimension. However, the role of social space in the production and reproduction of social relations can only be assessed through concrete research. It is here that the discipline of archaeology has most to offer.

The concrete context utilised below is that of medieval feudal society, a society based on rent extraction through the private control of landed estates. Its social structure was thus constituted within a hierarchy of land rights and through a hierarchy of space. Hence the development of politically regulated space was part of the very essence of feudalism. The reflexive relationship between social and spatial relations is examined through an analysis of the nucleated village. The rigorous definition of feudal space, restricting access and physical movement, is seen as being intrinsically linked to the economic power of feudal lords and their domination of the peasantry.

Introduction

Making sense of space is an issue at the heart of archaeological theory. Spatial patterns are a fundamental component of the discipline's data and therefore their analysis forms an essential element in archaeological explanations. The interpretation of social space has consequently always proved a highly controversial area of study. However, the increased openness of archaeology to social theory has greatly stimulated the debate. Critical philosophical and methodological arguments have recently been raised. One central theme running through these arguments is the relationship between social relations and spatial structures. Are the patterns observed passive reflections of human behaviour? Or does the social use of space actively contribute to social practice? This chapter attempts to understand this problem through an assessment of the role of space in early medieval society. Drawing on contemporary research within human geography, a materialist interpretation of space is used to explore class and power relations between lord and peasant within the English nucleated village. The argument is structured into three parts: first, there is a methodological discussion on the spatial construction of society; second, a definition of feudalism is offered, outlining the feudal construction of space in the abstract; and third, a concrete examination is made of the spatial data so far recovered from the Raunds area project in Northamptonshire.

The spatial construction of society

The terms of the debate on space within archaeology have been defined by the two dominant approaches: a positivist conception thrown up by the underlying philosophy of processualism, and a structuralist approach fashionable among post-processual archaeologists. In this chapter it is claimed that, despite the clear differences of methodology, both perspectives have failed to adequately make sense of space. The core of the problem is that both embody a disabling conceptual dualism that hinders concrete research.

The positivists, by focusing on the immediate surface appearances of spatial patterns, have given space an illusion of transparency. Space is analysed as a collection of things, a relationship simply between objects, and explicable primarily through those objects. Social space is thus reduced to physical description. This tradition has been prevalent for many years within archaeology, particularly among medievalists. Village forms are merely described, and space is represented as naturally relating the different components of the village and is explained in terms of the function of these components (for example see ROBERTS 1987). This approach has produced accurate information on the physical appearance of settlements. However, because content is abstracted from form, very little is said about the social production of space. The connection between social organisation and spatial organisation is portrayed in an extremely mechanical manner, with spatial patterns seen as a passive and incidental reflection of social practice.

Although the structuralists search beneath the surface appearance of physical patterns to discover an underlying order, they too have produced a reductionist perspective. Space is represented as a non-verbal language structured by an internal grammar (FLETCHER 1988). This leads to the analysis of patterning strictly in terms of ideology, with social space interpreted as a mental construct. Such a perspective has been taken up by the post-processualists to illustrate the all-encompassing symbolism of material culture (for example see HODDER 1982). Space is not portrayed as a passive reflection of society, but as an active representation of it on an ideological plane, part of the arena in which social relations are constituted. However, the problem here is that space becomes fetishised. The structuralists abstract the form space takes from its content. Consequently spatial structures are given powers that are rightly due to its constituents, as if space had intrinsic qualities in itself. The fault therefore is one of basic idealism. The reduction of space to ideology means that the material processes underlying the production, reproduction, and transformation of social space are obscured.

To overcome this false dualism between form and content, the active and the passive space, we must reassert the basic premise that spatial structures are simultaneously both the medium and the outcome of human action (SOJA 1989, 118–37). Social relations embody spatial structures which form a fundamental material dimension to society. Physical space is a social product, constituted by historically specific social practices that shape its character and form. However, as a material embodiment of recurrent social practices, space also plays an intrinsic role in the reproduction of these practices, in part actively shaping social action. There exists, therefore, a reflexive relationship between social and spatial structures, a link between the production of space and the reproduction of social relations (for example see articles in GREGORY AND URRY 1985). This materialist interpretation of space leads to two further propositions. First, as space is constantly being defined and redefined by day-to-day social activity, the process of its reproduction presents a continuing source of struggle and contradiction. Space is consequently political, being the domain of social conflict and antagonisms. Second, as spatial structures are intertwined with social relations, they cannot be appropriately understood when divorced from the society in which they are embedded. Hence there exists no independent, universal, or formal theory of physical space. The realisation that spatial patterns are historically specific is the key philosophical starting point for archaeologists.

These general statements might avoid the polarisation between passive and active theories of space. However there remains a critical problem to be solved. The reflexive notion of space as it stands is too vague. The simple proposition that space is both the medium and the outcome of social practice does not explain the extent to which specific spatial structures either constitute or reflect particular social relations. Further methodological procedures are required to clarify and examine the actual difference space makes in various historic contexts. An essential part of this methodological development centres on the distinction between abstract and concrete research which lies at the heart of all realist philosophy and has been applied to human geography by Sayer (1984, 128–35). To summarise the argument briefly, abstract research is concerned with locating the necessary objects, relationships, and causal powers of particular social structures. At this level very little can be said about actual spatial forms. Abstract social theory need only consider space insofar as spatial structures form a necessary component of social structures. On the other hand concrete research, by definition, focuses on the historic effects of social structure, its causal powers in particular situations. Research, then, at this level involves an empirical analysis of the specific events and contingent relationships involved in day-to-day social practice. It is here that the spatial dimension to social relations can play a critical role in the reproduction of social structure. Thus concrete research must necessarily take spatial structures into account. It is only through concrete research that the role of space in social practice can be assessed.

The feudal construction of space

To make sense of the social use of space within the early medieval nucleated village, it is important to define the necessary structural components of feudal society before exploring the actual production and reproduction of feudal social relations at a localised settlement level.

The term feudalism or feudal society, however, is problematic. Throughout medieval scholarship, definitions of feudalism have been hotly fought over and so the term has remained highly ambiguous. A discussion of the breadth and depth of the debate need not concern us, and the definition employed in this chapter is drawn explicitly from the Marxist concept of a mode of production, a specific combination of forces and relations of production (CALLINICOS 1987, 41–52). The feudal mode of production had its material basis in agrarian societies in which the overwhelming majority of the population was engaged in the cultivation of the land, primarily for subsistence. In the abstract there are three key necessary structural relationships which define it.

First there is the social form in which surplus value is extracted from the direct producers. Under feudalism this takes the form of rent, appropriated by landowning lords from the peasants living and working on their estates (HINDESS and HIRST 1975, 183–93). Critically, this mode of surplus extraction is direct and individual, distinguishing feudalism from other agrarian-based modes of production (DE STE CROIX 1984, 105–7).

Although the character of rent extraction takes a variety of historically contingent forms – labour services, renders in kind, cash rents – in each case it is realised through extra-economic forms of coercion, the second necessary structural relationship defining feudalism. As the peasants remain in partial control of the land, and consequently their means of subsistence, surplus value extraction must necessarily take place after this subsistence production has been completed. The feudal lords, therefore, must rely on judicial powers, political coercion, or physical force to appropriate the rent of individual peasant families (BRENNER 1986, 26–35). The particular form of this extra-economic force would obviously vary in time and space.

Finally, the third structural relationship defining the feudal mode is based on the private ownership of property, the alienation of land. In order for the lords to extract rents from the peasants, it is necessary for them to own the land, to hold judicial and fiscal rights over defined units, private estates. Hence the feudal ruling class is fragmented, individual lords being separated from each other by their private ownership of individual estates (ANDERSON 1974, 147–53). This fragmentation exerts a structural tendency for the integration of lordship at a political level to give the feudal ruling class a degree of social coherence. Thus, the relative strength and dominance of particular feudal societies would partially rest on the scale of political unity. This structural tendency expressed itself in a whole variety of historically specific forms, through the state, church, military obligations etc.

This abstract formulation of the feudal mode of production has been outlined in a non-spatial manner, but the three necessary structural relationships identified all point towards areas of concrete research in which a spatial analysis is fundamental. The importance of a spatial dimension to concrete research can be examined on a number of levels; on a macro-level, by exploring integration within the non-producing class, the feudal lords; and on a micro-level by assessing the mode of exploitation between peasant and lord.

As land was an integral element of the feudal means of production, notions of bounded or regulated space constituted the relationships between the feudal ruling class. Indeed, in England, the rise of feudalism in the ninth and tenth centuries was shaped by one form of control over land and the acquisition of estates: the grant of immunities from royal dues and tribute, and the grant of jurisdiction. The hierarchy of social order in medieval society existed through a hierarchy of land rights and consequently a hierarchy of space. The formation of bounded space, estates which were tightly regulated and controlled, was part of the means by which society was perpetuated. Feudal social relations were set within a particular spatial framework. As argued by the historical geographer Robert Dodgshon (1987, 186): 'Under feudalism, spatial order became socially regulated. Far from being an unintended side-effect, I would see this structuring of relations in space as part of the very essence of feudalism.' On a macro-level the fragmentation of land and the creation of regulated space was linked to the build-up of the state. Through the imposition of the concept of vassalage, in which individual jurisdiction was granted over a territory in return for fealty, homage, and military service, English feudalism allowed the integration of larger and more heterogeneous territories. It meant that the state's relationship with lords was mirrored in the lords' relationship with their underlings. Thus, feudal relationships of servitude were reinforced on all levels of society – the feudal lord was the king of his estate. This ordering of land into a hierarchy of regulated space was not simply a passive reflection of feudal social relations. It also played an active part in the reproduction of feudalism, the means by which the state's power was projected over the realm.

Research into the articulation of the feudal state through the integration of a hierarchy of rights connected to the ownership of land has been a suitable subject area for historical geography (DODGSHON 1987, 166–92). A more archaeologically orientated research topic, however, is the analysis of the feudal construction of space on a micro-level, exploring the class relationship between peasant and lord.

The development of English feudalism was tied up with the rising power of landlords within late Anglo-Saxon society. Essentially, the power of the lord was linked to the acquisition of 'book-land' and immunity from royal economic burdens on landed estates. Once the feudal lord obtained judicial rights to collect food-rents which were previously rendered to the king, his economic power over the peasants living and working on his estate could be fully realised. Freed from the payment of the king's 'feorm', the lord could invest the resulting increased resources into reorganising the relationship between himself and the peasantry in his favour (SAWYER 1979). Feudal relations thus penetrated and dominated the day-to-day lives of the peasants. It was through the exercise of the structural powers of lordship that the relationships between lord and serf became firmly anchored to, and structured by, specific territories and specific spaces. Rents were appropriated directly from individual peasant families and linked to the size of the tenement which they possessed and the strips of land which they farmed. Surplus extraction was therefore mediated through a rigorous definition and demarcation of space.

> For the peasantry, feudal space became bounded space. It was no longer a world of boundless or unlimited opportunities to be colonised when the need arose. For each and all, it was a world delimited by the land assessment imposed on the settlement. In effect, the landscape became divided into a chequerboard on which occupation was legitimised in some spaces but not others (DODGSHON 1987, 192).

The early medieval landscape was divided into units of land, defined by measures of rents, services, renders, and dues. This structuring of social space was a significant part of the means by which English society was constituted. As exploitation required extra-economic forms of coercion, politics and economics were fused at the level of lordship and this fusion became incorporated within the fabric of the manorial village. The imposition of bounded space effectively fragmented the peasantry as a class and meant their physical movement could be regulated by the local lord. This was of critical importance for the maintenance of the class position of the feudal lords *vis-à-vis* the peasants. Restricting peasant mobility curtailed the formation of a collective consciousness and the mobilisation of forces that could successfully resist feudal exploitation. As argued by Abercrombie, Hill, and Turner (1980, 72): 'Given the general problem of communication in a society based on isolated rural communes, there was no coherent peasant class consciousness which could have mobilised the peasantry against the landlords as a class of oppressors. Material conditions ruled out the development of anything but localised sense of identity and solidarity.'

The spatial morphology of the medieval nucleated village was therefore an essential element in the lords' extra-economic means of coercion. Feudal space was thus the arena of class struggle.

Power and domination in the nucleated village

To explore the feudal construction of space at the level of lord/peasant relations in early medieval society, we need to turn to a concrete case study. In the ninth and tenth centuries the archaeology of rural settlements indicates a qualitative and quantitative change in village morphology. On a general level there appears to be a movement from dispersed and fluid settlements, typified by settlements such as Catholme in Staffordshire (LOSCO-BRADLEY, 1984) and Maxey in Northamptonshire (ADDYMAN 1964), to more stable and nucleated villages associated with the planning of the landscape through the introduction of open-field farming (TAYLOR 1983, 107–24). Although there are many examples where this process of village nucleation is suggested, such as at Wharram Percy in North Yorkshire (HURST 1984) and Goltho in Lincolnshire (BERESFORD 1987), there have been few projects that attempt to examine in detail the evolution of the early medieval rural landscape. A notable exception, however, is the Raunds area project in Northamptonshire (FOARD AND PEARSON 1985). By combining large-scale rescue excavation with field survey (Figure 9.1), the project has yielded extremely important information on the origins and spatial development of the medieval village.

Although the project is far from complete and the data not fully assessed, it is clear that the late ninth and early tenth centuries represented a watershed in the evolution of Raunds village. The extensive settlement which emerged at the time was not only nucleated and planned, but in embryonic and immature form it took on the appearance of the village which survived throughout the medieval period (Figure 9.2). Three important structural and spatial components of this settlement can be identified. First is the appearance of manorial property at the Furnells site: a proprietary church and a manor house. These two buildings, comprising a timber aisled hall measuring 18 by 10 metres (CADMAN 1983, 118) and stone-built church of nave and chancel (BODDINGTON AND CADMAN 1981), were by far the most substantial buildings of the settlement. This architectural difference was also reinforced by their spatial arrangement within the village. The manor and church lay adjacent and perpendicular to each other and were set

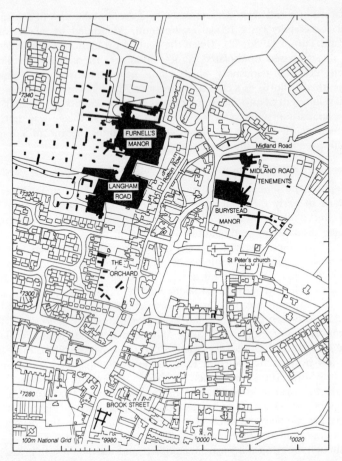

Figure 9.1 The extent of archaeological excavation at Raunds (after Dix 1987).

within ditched and banked rectilinear enclosures. These enclosures, which
were in fact linked, effectively separated the church and hall from the rest
of the settlement and formed a distinct manorial complex positioned at the
north end of the village on higher ground.

The second key component of the emerging Raunds village is the establishment of tenement rows. Immediately to the south of the manorial complex, at the Langham Road site, was an area divided up by a series of rectilinear ditched enclosures varying in width from 12 to 22 m. (AUDOUY AND
CADMAN 1987, 20). These tenements ran parallel to those of the manor,
fronting on to what later became known as Rotton Row to the east and

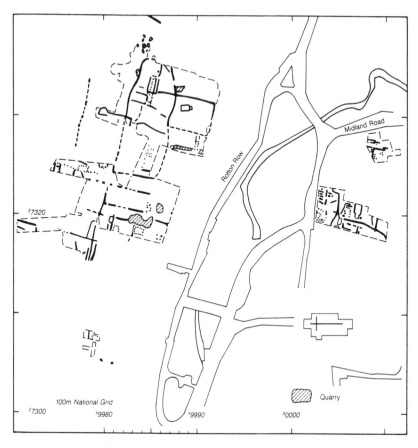

Figure 9.2 Late Saxon Raunds (after Dix 1987).

separated from the open-fields to the west by a headland, the southern continuation of the western manorial boundary. Set inside and outside these
enclosures was an area extensively covered by small timber buildings and
other features including stone quarries, clay extraction pits, and trackways.
Parts of a network of tenement ditches have also been identified at Midland Road and Burystead Manor, and on a small plot of land towards the
southernmost end of the village at Brook Street. Importantly, the establishment of tenement rows, which coincided with the construction of the
first church and manor, represents the creation of tofts, i.e. property
boundaries defining the homesteads of individual peasant families.

The third key element of the settlement is the imposition of roads or streets. The peasant tenements were all laid out at right-angles to clearly defined streets. At Langham Road the ditched enclosures ran parallel and perpendicular to Rotton Row, the main north/south village street. A similar tenement/street relationship was evident on the east side of the village at the Midland Road site and to the south at Brook Street. The imposition of streets, which strictly demarcated access routes, formed a critical structural and spatial component of the late Saxon Raunds village. For example Rotton Row, running perpendicular to the tenement plots and the manorial enclosures, framed and linked the two units together.

This particular morphological arrangement of Raunds village is not an isolated pattern within the immediate region. It is significant that the three components, manorial property, peasant tenements, and roads, perform a key role in the spatial structuring of the neighbouring hamlet of West Cotton, another site excavated as part of the Raunds area project (WINDELL 1987; 1988). In the late ninth and early tenth centuries the whole site was divided by a complex series of continuous timber-slots 0.8 m. wide and 0.6 m. deep (Figure 9.3). These gullies and ditches represent tenement rows aligned roughly east/west with a regular and consistent width of 19.5 m. Although the plots did not contain any major buildings, the substantial quantities of domestic refuse strongly suggest the proximity of buildings. These peasant tenement rows lay on either side of, and fronted on to, the main street of the settlement. At the north end of the hamlet, this street terminated at a gatehouse to a large enclosure which contained a substantial timber hall, possibly a manor house. Significantly, the manorial enclosure also contained a water mill lying beside the river Nene and fed by a leat which ran around the tenement plots (GAIMSTER, MARGESON, AND BARRY 1980, 204–6).

The rigorous organisation and definition of social space within these two settlements is an expression of the power and domination of the feudal lord over the peasantry. It not only reflects the changing nature of agricultural production, but also dictated the specific spatial structure of the settlements which aided the reproduction of these new productive relations on the land.

The nucleation of the villages in the Raunds area is associated with the introduction of the heavy plough and open-field farming (ROWLEY 1982). Fieldwork within the region clearly indicates that the organisation of the landscape into open-fields has its origins in the late Saxon period (HALL 1988). The move towards collective forms of farming, in which peasants, although owning individual strips, cultivated the land communally within a three-field system, was the stimulus behind this settlement change. The administration and implementation of this agricultural system was best organised through a village community. The heavy ploughs and oxen teams were often shared by a number of peasant families who farmed strips in a number of fields. The rotation of cultivation, pasturing, and laying fallow

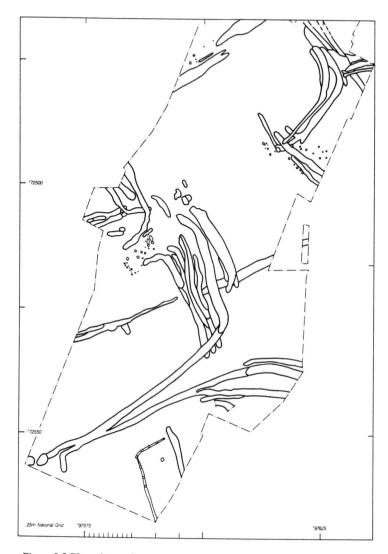

Figure 9.3 Plan of part of a tenement at late Saxon West Cotton (after Dix 1987).

required strict rules governing crop cultivation. Stock-raising on common land likewise required strict control of the number and types of animals involved. The nucleation of settlements into villages facilitated this new system of agriculture.

These changes in agricultural practices marked a period of intensive development of the forces of production. Collective forms of farming promoted a considerable increase in labour productivity, yielding far greater agricultural surpluses. The driving social force behind these developments, however, was always the material interests of the emerging feudal lords. As Sawyer (1979, 7–8) has argued:

> It was the labour and renders of their subordinate peasants that made it possible for lords to pay the food-rent owed to the king, or whoever else held the 'royal' estate. When these lords were freed from all, or part, of their obligation to pay this food-rent and to render other services, their resources were obviously increased, and it would not have been surprising if many of them attempted to re-organise their servile tenants to their own advantage.

Increased agricultural surpluses were therefore connected with the increased exploitation of the peasantry and the individual and direct extraction of rent by the local lord. This qualitative rise in the powers of lordship had dramatic consequences for the organisation of the rural landscape. Far from being a simple passive reflection of developments in agricultural production, settlement nucleation, as observed at Raunds and West Cotton, was also an active spatial embodiment of the growth of antagonistic class relations between lord and peasant, which characterised the imposition of feudal social relations of production in late Saxon England.

The creation of rows of tenement plots at Raunds and West Cotton was a result of establishing feudal relations of exploitation. Once the peasantry held land of a lord in return for feudal rent, then the need arose for the lord to fix that rent against the amount of land held. The feudal village then became divided into a fixed number of land measures, the size of the individual tenement being the basis of fiscal assessment. The regular tenement plots at West Cotton are a clear example of this. Thus, as the relationship between lord and peasant was constituted within bounded space, the organisation of the nucleated village was important: feudal space was part of the means by which the lords maintained their dominant class position.

Class struggle was rooted in the very structure of the feudal mode of production, forged by the character of surplus extraction. As argued above, as feudal rents were appropriated after the subsistence production had been completed, exploitation necessarily took the form of extra-economic forms of coercion. Thus the central problem facing the feudal lords was resistance from the peasant community. As outlined by Mann (1986, 394–7), there was no total monopoly of power within the rural landscape; it was divided between two institutions, the village and the manor. The class position of the lords *vis-à-vis* the peasantry, therefore, ultimately rested on physical force. It was because of this that politics and economics were intertwined within feudal society. For example, the political power of the feudal lord was fused with his economic position as landowner. The lord operated as king of his estate and thus social space became politicised.

This fusion of politics and economics at the level of lordship is expressed in the spatial layout of the nucleated village. The investment in manorial property, the construction of a large aisled timber hall and the building of a church, the only stone building at Raunds, were manifestations of the political dominance and power of the lord. This form of conspicuous consumption, the physical expression of lordship, gave the impression of permanence and stability within the village. The church and manor were clearly spatially related and represented and reinforced the integration of physical force and religious legitimation. Further, the social use of space facilitated the physical dominance of these two manorial units within the village. The church and manor at Raunds both lay at one end of the settlement on higher ground overlooking the rows of peasant tenements. As the political domination of the peasantry was a necessary component of economic exploitation, the positioning of these manorial property units provided a central focus for feudal surveillance, assisting the reproduction of class relations.

The importance of political power in the maintenance of feudal relations is also reflected in how property became rigorously defined through the establishment of tenement plots at Raunds and West Cotton. This rigid demarcation of space was not simply a reflection of the calculation of feudal rent, but also a means by which the peasantry could be controlled. The tenements were concentrated alongside streets, which enabled the lord to observe and restrict movement. The establishment of roads limited access in and out of the two settlements and so helped the lords' political supervision of the peasants' daily lives. The main street at Raunds and the single street at West Cotton linked the tenements to the manor so that traffic and the movement of people could be checked. Bounded space thus led to the creation of regulated space, the defining of legitimate and illegitimate places for peasant movement.

Finally, the creation of regulated space actively aided the feudal lords' control of critical resources and the monopoly of key elements of the means of production. The development of the forces of production with the establishment of feudal social relations not only saw the establishment of open-field farming, but also the introduction of new forms of technology such as the water mill. In the feudal village it was not unusual for the lord to have total control of the mill and to monopolise the milling process and so extract renders for its use from the peasants (HARFIELD 1988). The use of social space to aid this form of economic control is vividly illustrated at West Cotton. The hamlet's street terminates at a gatehouse which provided controlled and regulated access to a manorial enclosure which contained the manor house and water mill. This spatial relationship, therefore, reflected the lord's control of the milling process at West Cotton and re-inforced his economic and political dominance over the peasantry.

Conclusion

Although these comments on the relationship between the feudal mode of production and the archaeological information gained from the Raunds area project are very provisional, hopefully they illustrate the importance of integrating a spatial dimension into concrete research. In the articulation of the class relationship between lord and peasant at a local level, the social use of space was vitally important. The lord's reliance on extra-economic forms of coercion meant that feudal power and domination was critical for the extraction of surpluses. Its centrality was embodied in the spatial construction of the nucleated village.

To make sense of space, however, form and content cannot be separated. It is important not to reduce social space to the manor, church, peasant tenements, and roads – the components which define it – and thus to perceive space as a passive reflection of human behaviour. Neither should form be abstracted from content, with spatial patterns analysed simply in their own terms. There is no universal or independent theory of space. The relationship between social relations and spatial structures can only be understood through careful examination, involving both abstract propositions and concrete research of historically specific social structures.

Acknowledgements

I would like to thank Steve Roskams for all his advice, reassurance, and constructive criticism during the preparation of this chapter. Also, special thanks to Steve Parry and Dave Windell of Northamptonshire County Council Archaeological Unit for the information they gave me on the Raunds area project. Any errors are of course my responsibility.

Bibliography

Abercrombie, Nicholas, Stephen Hill, and Bryan Turner 1980. *The Dominant Ideology Thesis*. George Allen and Unwin (London).

Addyman, Peter 1964. 'A Dark-Age settlement at Maxey, Northants.' *Medieval Archaeology* 8, 20–73.

Anderson, Perry 1974. *Passages from Antiquity to Feudalism*. New Left Books (London).

Audouy, Michel and Graham Cadman 1987. 'North Raunds' in Brian Dix (ed.) 'The Raunds area project: second interim report' *Northamptonshire Archaeology* 21.

Beresford, Guy 1987. *Goltho: The Development of an Early Medieval Manor.* Historic Buildings and Monuments Commission (London).

Boddington, Andrew and Graham Cadman 1981. 'Raunds, an interim report 1977–80' in David Brown, James Campbell, and Sonia Chadwick-Hawkes (eds.) *Anglo-Saxon Studies in Archaeology and History*, 103–22. British Archaeological Reports, BS92 (Oxford).

Brenner, Robert 1986. 'The social basis of economic development' in John Roemer (ed.) *Analytical Marxism.* Cambridge University Press (Cambridge).

Cadman, Graham 1983. 'Raunds 1977–1983: an excavation summary' *Medieval Archaeology* 27.

Callinicos, Alex 1987. *Making History: Agency, Structure and Change in Social Theory.* Polity Press (Cambridge).

de Ste. Croix, Geoffrey 1984. 'Class in Marx's conception of history, ancient and modern' *New Left Review* 146.

Dix, Brian (ed.) 1987. 'The Raunds area project: second interim report'*Northamptonshire Archaeology* 21, 3–29.

Dodgshon, Robert 1987. *The European Past: Social Evolution and Spatial Order.* Macmillan (London).

Fletcher, Roland 1988. 'The messages of material culture: a preliminary discussion of non-verbal meaning' in Ian Hodder (ed.) *The Meaning of Things: Material Culture and Symbolic Expression*, 33–40. Unwin Hyman (London).

Foard, Glenn and Terry Pearson 1985. 'The Raunds area project: first interim report' *Northamptonshire Archaeology* 20, 3–21.

Gaimster, David, Sue Margeson, and Terry Barry 1989. 'Medieval Britain and Ireland in 1988' *Medieval Archaeology* 33.

Gregory, Derek and John Urry (eds.) 1985. *Social Relations and Spatial Structures.* Macmillan (London).

Hall, David 1988. 'The late Saxon countryside: villages and their fields' in Della Hooke (ed.) *Anglo-Saxon Settlements*, 99–122. Basil Blackwell (Oxford).

Harfield, Clive G. 1988. 'Control of resources in the medieval period' in John Gledhill, Barbara Bender, and J. Larsen (eds.) *State and Society: The Emergence and Development of Social Hierarchy and Political Centralisation*, 137–48. Unwin Hyman (London).

Hindess, Barry and Paul Hirst 1975. *Pre-Capitalist Modes of Production.* Routledge and Kegan Paul (London).

Hodder, Ian 1982. *Symbols in Action: Ethnoarchaeological Studies of Material Culture.* Cambridge University Press (Cambridge).

Hurst, John 1984. 'The Wharram research project' *Medieval Archaeology* 21, 77–111.

Losco-Bradley, Stuart 1984. 'Anglo-Saxon settlement in the Trent Valley' in Margaret Faull (ed.) *Studies in Late Saxon Settlement*, 101–4. Oxford University Committee for Archaeology (Oxford).

Mann, Michael 1986. *The Sources of Social Power: A History of Power from the Beginning to A.D. 1760*. Cambridge University Press (Cambridge).

Roberts, Brian 1987. *The Making of the English Village: A Study in Historical Geography*. Longman (Harlow).

Rowley, Trevor 1982. 'Medieval field systems' in L. Cantor (ed.) *The English Medieval Landscape*, 25–55. Croom Helm (London).

Sayer, Andrew 1984. *Method in Social Science: A Realist Approach*. Hutchinson (London).

Sawyer, Peter 1979. 'Medieval English settlement: new interpretations' in Peter Sawyer (ed.) *English Medieval Settlement*, 1–8. Edward Arnold (London).

Soja, Edward 1989. *Postmodern Geographies: The Reassertion of Space in Critical Social Theory*. Verso (London).

Taylor, Christopher 1983. *Village and Farmstead: A History of Rural Settlement*. George Philip (London).

Windell, David 1987. 'West Cotton' in Brian Dix (ed.) 'The Raunds area project: second interim report' *Northamptonshire Archaeology* 21, 25–9.

Windell, David 1988. 'West Cotton' *South Midlands Archaeology* 18, 51–60.

Ten

The Rise and Fall of Tower-Houses in Post-Reformation Scotland

ROSS SAMSON

*This chapter analyses post-Reformation Scottish tower-house architecture, reveal-
ing a coherence in its decoration, form, internal arrangements, and symbolic
meanings. It then discusses architectural forms in the early seventeenth century,
suggesting how the architectural system and internal spatial arrangements
changed.*

*The fall of tower-house architecture is traditionally ascribed to the growing
need for domestic comfort and an end to lawlessness. The chapter disputes this.
Most of the defensive elements were ineffective or essential to the whole architectural system of concentrated ornamentation on the skyline and strict division
between the ground and upper floors. Symmetry and changing function of the
ground floor in the early seventeenth century destroyed the martial appearance
of vernacular houses. Tower-houses are investigated within the context of
feuding in early modern Scotland, where killing was generally limited to specific
individuals. Wanton large-scale massacre was politically dangerous so assaults
on houses were rare. The end of tower-house architecture did coincide with the
end of feuding. Increased royal central authority demanded a monopoly on
violence, but violent death was no less common in the early seventeenth century;
it occurred within a new context of legal and illegal violence. Those closest to
central authority took royal office and with it some of the trappings of central
authority, including royal English Jacobean and neo-classical architecture.*

. . . and for anie displeasure, that they apprehend to be done unto
them by their neighbours, [they] take up a plaine feid against him,
and, without respect to God, king, or common-weale, bang it out
bravely, hee and all his kinne, against him and all his.

These were the words of King James VI in his book on kingship, *Basilikon
Doron*, about feuds (*feidis*) in Scotland. In comparison with England, feud-

ing survived late in Scotland and no discussion of the feud in early modern
Scotland is complete without a quotation revealing English confusion faced
with the concepts involved. Like the bewildered English ambassadors sent
to inform James of the execution of his mother, Mary, who could not comprehend the concept of assythment (compensation), modern historians
have, until recently, disparaged the feud as anarchic and lawless without
seeking to understand it.

The view of early modern Scotland as endemically violent supposedly
makes the peculiarity of Scottish tower-houses understandable (APTED
1980, 3): 'It is a significant indicator of the troubled state of Scotland that,
at a time when English landowners were raising houses which were out-
ward looking, and without obvious provision for defence, it should still be
necessary to make defensibility a major factor in the design of Claypotts'
(Figure 10.1). The same wording could be found in the introduction to
almost any guidebook to a Scottish tower-house. Nigel Tranter (1962–70 v.
1, 6) believes that Scottish tower-houses are unique in Europe because
elsewhere in the fifteenth to early seventeenth centuries 'the need for forti-
fying one's house was becoming progressively less urgent, when central
authority was growing and the rule of law being established.' Admittedly,
the defensive nature of these dwellings is generally played down by recent
writers, so that such a tower 'offered protection equally against hostile
human incursions, animal intruders and even, one might be tempted to
think, the climate' (STELL 1977, 159). The need for protection against rain
and bears, however, does little to explain tower-houses.

The equation of feuds and violence with Scottish tower-houses is so
strongly entrenched in historical writing that, apart from defence, few
other aspects of this architecture have been investigated, but I hope to
make clear that the architecture of Scottish tower-houses is much more
complex and, indeed, interesting.

The architecture of tower-houses

Scottish tower-houses were little more than rectangular stone towers, comprising three or more storeys. The ground floor was regularly vaulted in
stone while the upper floors were occasionally stone vaulted (usually taken
as evidence of greater antiquity) but more commonly of timber. The roof
was only occasionally stone vaulted, and generally likewise of timber. The
top of the tower walls might form a wall-walk with corner towers, and later
developments included the enclosure of the walk and ultimately its elim-
ination, with corner garrets or studies replacing former open towers.
Entrance to the tower-house was usually restricted to a single entrance
either at the ground or at the first floor (again a sign of greater antiquity).
Simple rectangular windows are found on the first floor and above, con-
sisting of fixed lead-framed glass, below which were small wooden shutters.
Often window seats were provided in the thickness of the wall. Externally,

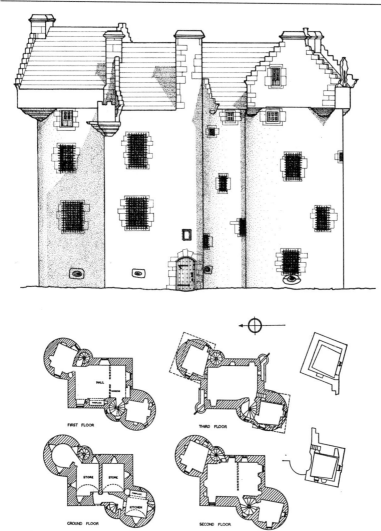

Figure 10.1 Claypotts (Angus) 1569–88. Measured drawing with hypothetical yetts. (Redrawn from Apted 1980 by permission HMSO).

windows were furnished with iron grilles or *yetts* and a similar iron gate was located behind the front door. The ground floor, by contrast, had no windows but arrow slits or, later, wide-mouthed gun ports. Arrow slits might be found in upper storeys in earlier towers, but gun ports are

Figure 10.2 Selection of post-Reformation tower-houses.
(Sketches from Tranter 1962–70).

relatively rare above the ground floor. Internal access was by turnpike
stairs. These might be built within the thickness of the walls or corbelled
out of re-entrant angles, often beginning above the ground floor. A more
spacious stair might lead from the entrance to the hall. Internal use of the
rooms followed a general pattern. The ground floor was used for cellars
and a kitchen, although the kitchen was also often located in an adjoining
building, again on the ground floor. Immediately above was the great hall.
This room was used to receive guests, acted as a living room for the family
and was where meals were taken. It acted as a 'court house or a meeting
place for the whole kin group' (SMITH 1970). It was the largest room,
although sometimes subdivided to allow one or two very small ante-
chambers which acted as serveries. Above the hall was the lord's room with
other family members' quarters either in upper storeys or in other wings.
The other wings were, in practice, adjoining towers. These were added, or

built in one piece to form L-, Z-, T-, or E-shapes in plan. This elaboration of tower-houses is very much a post-Reformation development.

Figure 10.2 shows a selection of post-Reformation tower-houses.[1] Kilravock (Nairnshire) is essentially composed of two building phases: the seventeenth-century five-storey range and the old fifteenth-century tower (c. 1460). This contrasts the pre- and post-Reformation styles nicely, although such a division cannot be maintained rigidly. Scotstarvit, generally believed to have been begun in 1627, although perhaps fifty years older, is frequently mentioned as appearing anachronistic, suited to the fifteenth century. It was also probably the product of Sir John Scott, director of the Chancery and keen antiquarian. It is not, however, alone. Castle Leod (Ross) (Figure 10.2) would appear to contain an older tower within the composite house, but the two dates of construction appear to be 1600 and 1616. Cakemuir (Midlothian) is effectively a fifteenth-century tower-house although built in 1565, while Strathendry (Fife) and Monimail tower (Fife), of late sixteenth century, are similar. Where fifteenth-century towers were

---

[1] The following list is by no means a complete record of post-Reformation tower-houses in Scotland. It includes only those houses, or major extensions which are very securely dated, primarily from inscription, to after 1560. At least the same number of houses again could be added on stylistic grounds or by probable documentary references to them. Descriptions and sketches of all are to be found in MacGibbon and Ross (1887–92) and Tranter (1962–70). The number of figures in this chapter have been kept to a minimum, but the reader is encouraged to refer to these works. References to Tranter in this chapter do not list volume or page, but this is easily calculated as his volumes are by shire and sites by alphabetical order, both given here throughout.

Aberdeenshire: Barra (1614–8), Corse (1581), Graigievar (1626), Craigston (1607), Fraser castle (1576–1617), Terpersie (1561), Tolquhon (1584–9). Angus: Braikie (1581), Colliston (1621), Gardyne (1568), Hatton (1575), Invergowrie (1568), Mains (1562), Pitkerro (1593). Argyll: Dundrave (1596), Carnasserie (1560s). Ayrshire: Auchans (1644), Greenan (1603), Kelburn (1581), Kirkhill (1589), Killochan (1586), Knock (1604), Penkill (1628). Banffshire: Blairfindy (1586), Fordyce (1592). Berwickshire: Greenknowe (1581), Thirlestane (1595), Nisbet (c. 1630). Caithness: Dunbeath (1624). Edinburgh: Bruntsfield (1605), East Coates (1615), the Inch (1617–34), Liberton House (1605), Stenhouse (1623). Dumfriesshire: Amisfield (1600), Fourmerkland (1590), Isle Tower (1587), Killywarren (1617), Spedlins (1605). Fife: Manse, Anstruther (1590), Airdrie (1588), Balcomie (1602), Earlshall (1547–1617), Fordell (1580), Wormistone (1612), Hillhouse, Dunfermline (1623), Kellie (1573–1606), Monimail (1578), Myres (1616), Pitfirrane (1583), Scotstarvit (1627). Inverness-shire: Dalcross (1620), Stewart Castle (1625). Kincardineshire: Balbegno (1569), Muchalls (1619–27), Tilquhillie (1576). Kinross-shire: Burleigh (1582), Cleish (1600), Tulliebole (1608). Lanarkshire: Barncluith (1583), Dalziel (1647), Gilbertfield (1607). East Lothian: Fenton (1577), Luffness (1584). Midlothian: Alderston (1626), Cakemuir (1565), Gogar (1625), Linhouse (1589), Roslin (1622). West Lothian: Carriden (1602), Midhope (1582), West Port House, Linlithgow (1600). Moray: Burgie (1602), Blervie (1598), Coxton (1644). Orkney: Birsay (c. 1574), Kirkwall (c. 1607), Noltland (1560–70). Peeblesshire: Drochil (c. 1578). Perthshire: Aberuchill (1607), Ashintully (1583), Cardross (1598), Claypotts (1569–88), Drummond (1630–6), Invermay (1633), Fingask (1594), Fowlis (1640), Grantully (1626), Innerpeffray (1610), Megginch (1575), Menzies (1577), Murthly (1617), Stobhall (1578). Renfrewshire: Dargavel (1584), Haggs (1585), Newark (1597–9). Ross: Leod Castle (1600–16). Roxburghshire: Branxholme (1570–6), Buckholm (1582), Corbet (1572), Commendator's House, Melrose (1590), Ferniehurst (c. 1598), Hillslap (1585). Shetland: Muness (1598), Scalloway (1600). Stirlingshire: Stenhouse (1622). Wigtonshire: Craigcaffie (157–), Kennedy Castle (1607), Park (1590).

incorporated into post-Reformation enlargements, they were regularly maintained in the original form. Thus at Blair Atholl the oldest tower stands out among the many which comprise this edifice of many dates. Fifteenth-century or early sixteenth-century battlements were maintained in post-Reformation extensions all over Scotland as at Brodie (Nairnshire), Skipness (Argyll), Brodick (Bute), and Castle Stewart (Inverness-shire), to name just a handful.

Sociological analyses of the architecture and spatial arrangement of tower-houses are seldom undertaken by architectural historians. When Dunbar (1978, 48) writes that the tower-house in Scotland was popular because 'it struck just the right balance between the claims of domestic comfort and those of defence', he echoes a long tradition which views architectural elements in terms only of physical comfort and defensibility (STELL 1981, 23). These two, it should be further added, are seen as conflicting, a position described by Coulson (1979, 77) as 'structural fundamentalism' and architectural changes are interpreted as a shift in the balance between them. Thus tiny arro- slit windows are seen as uncomfortable because they do not let in enough light, but they are defensive, for it is difficult for attackers to shoot arrows through and impossible to climb through. Simpson (1968, 216) suggested that arrow slits were really just a source of light, for it is difficult to shoot arrows (from the inside) through a slit in a wall eight feet thick. Perhaps a better functional explanation is that arrow slits appear most commonly on early towers when glass was uncommon and windows only became larger when people could see out of them! Turnpike stairways are seen as defensive for they are cramped and dangerous. Here we find the myth of the counter-clockwise turnpike designed to expose the attackers' undefended (right) side, with the delightful touch that one of the Douglas's castles contains a left- and right-handed spiral, one each for the left- and right-handed brother. But which military exponent notes that the stairway defendant, although able to protect his left side, is also unable to use his sword (right) hand? One important aspect of stairway arrangements is that they consumed little space, leaving as much as possible to the disposition of rooms. In the earliest towers they were built entirely within the width of the walls. As the walls became thinner, we find them corbelled outside of the tower-house walls into re-entrant angles, allowing rooms to enjoy a maximum of internal space. Later main stair towers were enlarged as at Glamis, or wider and grander stairs were inserted into an older tower as at Elcho (Figure 10.3) and Kellie. The importance of the grand stair leading to the main hall is seen in the use of scale-and-platt stairs (i.e. straight stairs), found very rarely, for example at Scalloway (Orkney), Sorbie (Wigtonshire), and Killochan (Ayrshire), and then restricted to this position within the house. Yet this is precisely where the danger would be greatest: the stair leading from the main entrance. Elsewhere the turnpike stairs continued in their functional

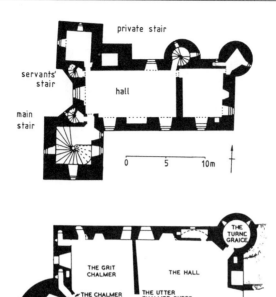

Figure 10.3 First-floor plans of Elcho and Huntly castles.
(From MacGibbon and Ross 1887–92 HMSO).

and unexceptional roles, linking rooms like a vertical corridor.

If turnpike stairs are grievously misprepresented by a fixation on explanations of security, other more overtly defensive measures also cause
problems. At Claypotts (Angus) (Figure 10.1), the walkway has all but disappeared, remaining only on two sides of the central square tower. The
'walkway' does not even extend over the main entrance and has become
nothing more than a balcony. A similar situation is found at Leod Castle
(Ross) (Figure 10.2) and at Strathendry (Fife) a wall-walk exists on only one
side, but it does not overlook the entrance and indeed overlooks a side of
the house that is all but windowless. This balcony effect is even more pronounced at Glamis and Craigievar. Pseudo-machicolations are some of the
most prominent features of fifteenth- and sixteenth-century Scottish tower-
houses. They are formed by pronounced corbelling, as at Leod Castle
(Figure 10.2) or Edzel but, strangely, no boiling oil could ever have been
poured through them, for they are not functional. By the time Craigievar
was built the machicolations had slipped down the side of the building to

form a rather tasteful string course (for a less obvious example see Fyvie, Figure 10.5). Crathes is not considered so 'tasteful', for its pseudo-machic-olation string course does not rise and fall with the skyline higher up. Very rarely does true machicolation occur, as at Killochan (Ayrshire). In such cases it is always over the door and, as a very small projection, looks for all the world like a garderobe, thus perhaps adding insult to threatened injury! The pseudo-machicolation almost invariably supports a wall-walk. It is often stated that the few feet by which such walks oversail the tower walls is a defensive feature, and Cruden stresses that it was from the wallhead that the 'real' defence of a tower-house was undertaken. But how? The inward cant of the tower walls was not so great that defenders would have had any difficulty getting their projectiles to clear the outside wall. On the other hand, such massive corbelling certainly draws attention to the wallhead.

The defensive gunloop features are also problematic. One peculiar feature at many towers is that they appear very low to the ground and in many cases this cannot be explained as a build-up of surrounding soil, such as at Spynie where they are placed on top of the ground level battered course. Were they designed to cut down the enemy at the knee? More significant still, at Claypotts one can read the guidebook to find that, in order to achieve raking fire along all sides of the house, gunports were in-serted into the back of the kitchen fireplace and behind a turnpike stair and that this reveals the lengths to which the Strachans went to ensure their safety. On the contrary, it might strike one that the arrangement shows how little their importance was, for it would have been difficult to have extinguished a large kitchen fire sufficiently quickly for the gunport to have been much use and the gunport behind the stair could only have been used with difficulty by a midget (admittedly a groove in the stair allows its use from the front rather than the back although this has the disadvantage of precluding the possibility of actually seeing the target). All-over fire might have been achieved more easily by situating the gunports higher up the walls, but this would have destroyed the consistent ground-floor height they now maintain. I return to this below.

Gunloops or shotholes not infrequently reveal artistic treatment. At Newark (Renfrewshire) the shotholes are heart-shaped. At Braikie (Angus) there is a small shothole in every window sill! At Fordyce (Banffshire) the shotholes are grouped in patterns which strike Tranter as interesting. When found other than on the ground floor, gunloops tend to occur in corner turrets or garrets. This nicely maintains the defensive link with castle towers, although by being placed awkwardly low in garderobes at Newark they appear functionally better suited to ventilation. The primary siting for shotholes, especially wide-mouthed gunports, on the ground floor raises one more problem. Were a tower-house to be attacked, these gunloops were quite useless until the enemy was inside the barmkin, the outer enclosure wall, by which time there was little hope for the house's

Figure 10.4 Kellie (Fife) 1573–1606. Yetts subjectively reconstructed.

defence. In other words, most sniping must have come, *not* from the especially fitted defensive features, but from the windows of the house.

It has been generally recognised that the introduction of elaborate plans
was not really to provide flanking fire across the faces of the main tower-
house, although this is sometimes claimed, but rather to provide additional
accommodation. The two round towers at Claypotts, for example, offer no
fewer than ten additional rooms. This becomes even more apparent when
we find additions to pre-existing tower-houses. Sir David Lindsay added
two ranges to his sturdy tower-house at Edzel and, like the addition at
Elcho or the joining range between two separate towers at Kellie (Figure
10.4), the new, longer, and lower additions were built to contain the new
great hall which could accommodate greater numbers of friends and
acquaintances for dinner. Post-Reformation towers and additions reveal a
growing and insatiable appetite for increased lodging space. Edzell Castle
and the earl's palace in Kirkwall reveal in their 'tusks' and the further
foundations at Edzell, that to the already spacious wings built by Sir
Lindsay and Earl Patrick even more building was planned.

Much of the tower-house architecture is, if not explained, at least appreciable when the structuring principles are made manifest. The principle

behind decoration is simply that it should be placed high or if possible on the skyline. Gables are crow-stepped and these are sometimes added as dummies such as at Kellie and Glamis to add to the 'busyness' of the skyline. Chimneys are coped or moulded and frequently unnecessarily tall. Dormer windows are ornamented while others within the body of the tower-house are unadorned, and they often interrupt the roof's edge in a pronounced manner (only one of Claypotts' four survive). Dummy dormer windows even exist in the corner garrets at Gardyne (Angus). Corbelling is often massive, in the shape of pseudo-machicolations, often to take walkways, corner turrets, or garrets. Claypotts is picturesque with its corbelled square rooms over round drums, an arrangement similarly found at Barra (Aberdeenshire), Burleigh (Kinross-shire), and Tilquhillie (Kincardineshire). This sophisticated architectural construction appears to be used for the sake of contrivance. Small attic rooms, caphouses, are often perched on the top of the square towers, thus recessed rather than corbelled out as at Claypotts. To some extent the English situation was similar. 'The most striking aspect of most sixteenth- and early seventeenth-century English houses is the remarkable richness of the rooftop' (HENDERSON 1985, 6). Where it differed in Scotland was that the roofscape contrasted sharply with the façade of the building. The walls of the tower-houses are quite plain, perhaps with the exception of string courses or pseudo-machicolations, although these too tend to be high up the walls. This arrangement can be seen as more striking if we remember that although internally the first-floor great hall is marked out as being the most noble, the windows of the great hall are quite plain on the exterior, unlike the dormer windows, yet these top rooms were of much lower social importance, sometimes lacking fireplaces altogether.

There were some exceptions to this decorative rule and these are almost invariably given the tag 'renaissance'. Most so-called renaissance decoration takes the form of small applied medallions or window pediments; both are found at Newark, medallions only at Glamis. Great oriel windows mark the hall at the earl's palace in Kirkwall, sometimes claimed to be the most 'mature and accomplished piece of renaissance architecture left in Scotland'. The earl's palace truly is exceptional and is the closest thing to Elizabethan manorial architecture in Scotland and Kirkwall palace makes Huntly Castle all the more remarkable. Returning from a year's exile in France the earl of Huntly added great ornamental oriel windows and a legend to his family house, the inspiration for which must have been the château of Blois. However, the windows do not ornament the first-floor hall and the earl's chambers, but rather the upper storey. Even at Newark, the window pediments are more restrained in the walls than over the dormer windows. Commonly medallions are restricted to a place above the door entrance commemorating the owner in the form of a heraldic device or motto. These panels, however, could be quite high up the wall, and initials and dates might be found on high, nowhere in greater profusion than Patrick Maxwell's numerous PMs at Newark. Although generally thought to represent Scottish incompetence, the restriction of renaissance decoration to such a limited range of isolated architectural features may have been a purposeful attempt to maintain general austerity.[2] There was, after all, no lack of profuse decoration *inside* the tower-house. As Malcolm Airs (1982, 41) says of the Tudor courtier's house, 'The somewhat forbidding exterior must have been deliberately contrived as a public demonstration of power and strength. Appreciation of the owner's taste was the preserve of the more exclusive audience.'

Unfortunately there is precious little information about the internal arrangements of tower-houses, although one suspects that this is in part the result of a lack of interest by historians.[3] There are no Scottish equivalents to the English household rules like those of Sir Francis Willoughby (*c.* 1572), Viscount Montagu (1595), Baron Berkeley (1601), Lord Ellesmere (*c.* 1603), the anonymous R. B. (*c.* 1605), the earl of Huntingdon (1609), and Lord Fairfax (*c.* 1620). However, such rules show a considerable similarity to later medieval rules and the broad similarity of house plans in Scottish post-Reformation houses encourages drawing on them for possible parallels.

The hall was the most important room and the most lavishly decorated. The grandest stair led to it, it was the largest room with the largest fire-place, and had the best ceiling decorations. It is also one of the few rooms about which we know anything (note the absence of other room labels in the Claypotts plan). The hall was sometimes referred to in England as the great dining chamber, revealing its primary function. Tabraham (1986) describes the importance of ceremony and ritual involved in seating arrangements, with the lord's table raised on a dais and the lord seated in a chair as opposed to benches for the less great. Such positioning was important and seating arrangements at Largo church were the occasion for a feud between two lairds. The earl of Angus was *forced* by his Douglas kinsmen to protest to the king and Huntly when in 1600 Huntly was pro-moted to the rank of marquis and demanded precedence over Angus in seating at Parliament. Otherwise the great hall was used for large functions, such as dancing, the performance of music or plays (particularly at Christmas), and the lying-in-state of the deceased lord or members of the family.

The first floor was the noble floor, the *piano nobile*, just as it was in medieval town houses. Each successive floor above was less noble. Originally the lord and lady had their chamber off the hall, and if the L- or Z-plan allowed it, this might also be on the first floor. Otherwise it would be

---

[2] A sad characteristic of the resurrected neo-baronial style of the last two centuries is the eclectic addition of ornamentation all over the walls in contrast to sixteenth-century bleakness.

[3] One exception is Warrack (1920), although he must be used with caution. Some of his statements, such as the move of the hall from the first to ground floor during the reign of James VI is wrong, although the move began during his reign.

immediately above the hall. The indeterminate term chamber reveals that the room was, in effect, a bedsitter. In England the term bedchamber only became common from the mid-sixteenth century. This was the result of the progressive development of an in-between room. It is argued that this developed from an ante-chamber to the private chamber and is perhaps reflected in the Scottish terminology of outer and inner chamber. The earl of Atholl's new building at Balvenie (c. 1550) had the chambers built as integral parts. At Huntly (Figure 10.3) the separation of the hall and 'grit chalmer' was achieved subsequently by the addition of a partition wall.

Whether or not it was hived off the bedroom, the outer chamber became, in England at any rate, the 'withdraughte', the (with)drawing room. Its name reflects its use as a room to which one might withdraw from the hall and the room usurped a number of the hall's functions, particularly of reception and dining. Reception of guests might then grade their social rank by how far they proceeded beyond the front door: to the hall, outer chamber, or even beyond to the private bedroom. This was so important in courtly politics that there was rivalry among James VI's nobles of the Privy Council and the Chamber. Access to the king was access to power and access was physically controlled. The public nature of the hall suggests that in earlier tower-houses the need to pass through the hall before being able to ascend to the upper storeys was not a defensive measure as is often claimed. Once inside the hall, the tower-house was as good as lost, for a fire kindled here would have killed everyone above. One of the few descriptions of the capture of a tower-house is that of Lochwood in 1547 which ends with the entry through the main door, 'so we entered and won Lochwood' (quoted in SIMPSON 1968, 223). Instead one could see this arrangement as purposefully controlling movement, for everyone must have passed under public scrutiny, and perhaps more importantly under the nose of the master or mistress. The lord of Elphinstone was presumably more secretive than most for he had not only an 'observation post' from the private stair leading to his apartment (which was a small unconcealed window), but also a spy-hole in the flue of the hall chimney. Elphinstone was pre-Reformation, but post-Reformation spy-holes are to be found as well at Maclellans (Kirkcudbrightshire) and there is a listening hole at Muchalls (Angus). The hall was thus central to lines of communication through the house and the lord's apartment lay off the hall, controlling it. Certainly his control of access is found in another important area, that of the wine cellar! This is the name given to the ground-floor storage room which is lockable from the inside with a communicating stair to the hall or lord's apartment. The arrangement is too common to need examples.

Elcho has sadly not been the subject of study in its own right, for its multiplicity of stair towers must surely hold the key to the social hierarchy of the building. The first floor plan (Figure 10.3) reveals the gracious main entrance stair, servants' stairs from the kitchen below, and a private stair presumably for the lord and lady which allows access to a storage chamber on the ground floor, the so-called wine cellar. The serving stair from the kitchen was the logical conclusion of ante-chamber serveries common at most halls; now not only were the servants not seen until needed, but they also did not have to use the main stair used by guests. At the earl of Huntly's castle a spy-hole is to be found in the servants' stair, apparently to allow the servants to remain out of sight until the lord and his guests were ready to be served.

One final spatial arrangement must be mentioned. Below the *piano nobile* existed an almost subterranean world. The ground floor with its great stone vault and tiny windows was unpleasantly dark, certainly damp, draughty, and cold. Such conditions were not necessarily unfavourable for the storage of wine or dairy products, although less so for grain storage, and the stone vault provided the tower with some protection from accidental fire in the kitchen. The ground floor thus was sharply opposed to the upper storeys in its use. Here there was no accommodation or living area. Such a division is immediately apparent from the outside, for the ground floor is marked off by its arrow-slit or gunport windows. Here the windows had no glass. At Noltland, the division is made more stiking by the fact that the ground floor is effectively very high, containing an entresol, and is marked by an amazing profusion of gunports and a string course which runs around the façade at mid-window height on the first floor. At Pitreavie (Fife), Ferniehurst (Roxburghshire), and Haggs (Renfrewshire) the string course more neatly separates the ground floor from upper storeys. The division is also marked by the frequent origin of stair towers corbelled out at the first floor level as at Kellie (Figure 10.4). In many instances, as at Kellie, the main stair at ground level is grand and entirely within the house, thus there is no 'need' for exterior stair space. But often a turnpike stair starts on the ground floor within the house or within the width of its walls before being corbelled out, although in building terms the stair tower would be strengthened and probably involve less labour were it to begin from the house foundations. In other instances, the external origin of the stair tower at the first floor also reflects a genuine internal absence of an internal stair between the ground and the first floor. This is most commonly found leading from the hall to the upper levels of accommodation, as at Newark. Such stair towers reflect their use by the well-bred by *not* communicating with the ground floor.

When tower-houses no longer had stone vaulted ground floors and adopted an English-style ground-floor hall, the whole ground floor could be rehabilitated. This process continued through the seventeenth century and the absence of gunloops at Pittencreiff House (1650) in Dunfermline has much less to do with safety than with the entirely new use to which the ground-floor rooms were put. Ironically, the division was to be revitalised by later fully classical houses as at Kinross House (Figure 10.6). Ground-floor windows, now glazed, were half sized (note this too at Kellie, Figure 10.4). The ground floor was also marked more effectively by rusticated ashlar, an arrangement which continued unbroken into this century.

It is tempting to associate this with the upstairs–downstairs complex, a development which dates in England to the seventeenth century, before which the ground floor often contained the hall, withdrawing room, and bedchamber(s). Certainly servants were associated with the kitchen and scullery on the ground floor of tower-houses. It is also regularly claimed that they might sleep there. While the kitchen might not be unbearable if a fire was maintained, other chambers would have provided inhumane accommodation in the winter. Not that the noble society which empowered lairds of southern Fife to force vagrants to work their coal mines would have baulked at such a prospect. However, the probability that most household servants slept in out-buildings must be accepted.

An attempt to understand architecture is necessarily difficult, a task not made easier by the purple prose of art historians – Jacobean architecture was not replaced by the classicism of Inigo Jones because 'it sank through its own weight' (GIROUARD 1983, 36)[4] – nor by such vacuous explanation of tower-house architecture as the 'innate conservatism' of the Scots or that it appealed to the 'frugality of the Scottish character' (SIMPSON 1961, 230). It also requires that we understand that the separation of the symbolic and the functional is a heuristic device that we use to facilitate our understanding of architecture, but that such a division is unreal and can even be unhelpful. We are accustomed to arguing the almost purely symbolic nature of ecclesiastical art and architecture, while stressing the functional defensive aspects of military architecture. This rigorous segregation is harmful for it precludes the recognition that symbolism has important social functions and that it may be expressed in functional forms. This sophistication is fortunately more necessary of thirteenth-century lordly architecture than of the sixteenth, when many defensive features are no longer functional.

To begin to understand tower-house architecture we must let contemporaries speak. Sir Richard Maitland described his Lethington home in poetry:

> Thy tour and fortres, lairge and lang,
> Thy neighbours does excell;
> And for thy wallis thick and strang,
> Thou graitly beirs the bell.
> Thy groundis deep and topis hie,
> Uprising in the air,
> Thy vaultis pleasing are to sie,
> They are so greit and fair.

---

4 It is not really fair to use Girouard as an example of an art historian trying to explain architectural change in aesthetic terms, for normally his architectural analyses and explanations are rooted in social history.

Maitland reveals two nearly universal characteristics of social behaviour among the elite: pride in their residences and competition with their neighbours. This is revealed more than once in the inscriptions occasionally found instead of heraldic devices or simple initials over the entrance to tower-houses, as at Muness Castle on Unst (Shetland):

> Listen you to know this building who began
> Laurence the Bruce he was that worthy man
> Who earnestly his heirs and offspring prays
> To help and not to hurt his work always
>
> The year of God 1598.

It is also interesting to note both that Maitland does not emphasise the protection Lethington affords him, and that the vaults might be described as great and fair. Fair is certainly not how most would see the ground-floor vaults of tower-houses today. Yet fair they might appear to Maitland because they were 'greit' or capacious, and voluminous cellars reflected an enormous stock-pile of provisions, of grain produced from his estates.

Lethington was also a 'fortres' to Maitland and although some hundred years old by then, the licence to crenellate issued in 1449 by James II to Lord Maxwell would have been readily accepted by Maitland as appropriate to his own home (quoted in TABRAHAM 1986, 45):

> . . . to build a castle or fortalice on the Barony of Mearns in Renfreshire, to surround and fortify it with walls and ditches, to strengthen by iron gates and to erect on top of it all warlike apparatus necessary for its defence.

Maitland did appreciate the thick and strong walls of Lethington, but they seem to function by carrying the lofty tower. Such a tone is continued by reference to deep 'groundis' or foundations and the height of the tower, 'uprising in the air'. Such licences have been studied by Charles Coulson (1979) who notes that unlike modern guidebooks and tourists, the medieval licence and mind was more impressed by crenellations than by the thickness of the walls. Things which are mentioned in such licences include ditches, barmkin, turrets, machicolation, corbelling, battlements, and iron *yetts*. Why the width of walls was not worthy of comment is easily explained: it could not be seen. Those elements most often mentioned were the most highly visible and the name of the licence to crenellate itself stresses the importance of this overtowering element of martial architecture. When Sir Robert Kerr wrote to Lord Lothian about proposed alterations to Ancrum House in 1636, his preoccupations were similarly fifty feet off the ground: 'By any meanes do not take away the battlement, as some gave me counsale to do . . . for that is the grace of the house, and makes it looke lyk a castle' (quoted in DUNBAR 1978, 55). The castle was

perceived as a symbol of rank and lordship. The common, massive but
functionless machicolations must be seen in the same light and indeed
were probably more common than crenellated battlements. It is interesting
that the 'warlike apparatus' should be erected on top of the tower, for
apart from the arrow-slits and gunloops, it is at the top of the tower-house
that the aggressive 'defensive' features gather, even if the cannon-shaped
water spouts, at Claypotts and Crathes for example, only ever threatened
people with a drenching. The bleak exterior of tower-houses becomes even
more explicable when one thinks of the austerity of fortified town walls or
the great fortresses of the realm. The gate tower of Edinburgh Castle
(1574) is effectively a great tower-house in its style. With façades as well
strewn with large windows as Claypotts, only the absence of decoration of
the window frames, pediments, and friezes maintains the martial aura. To
some extent the windows of lower floors are, 'cancelled' by their *yetts*. True,
iron grilles added to the defensibility of a tower-house, at least in as much
that it became more difficult to force an entry. Ferocious though they
looked, they scarcely hindered the firing of projectiles through the window.
The Privy Council decreed in 1606 that 'Irone Yettis in the bordouris
ordanit to be removit and turnit in plew Irnis.' The Biblical reference was
appropriate for it represented a symbolic act by James VI in his drive to
end feuding. The king, however, was also worried about waste. He had
even created a commission to investigate the state of the kingdom's coal
reserves. Conspicuous consumption and connotations of lordly intention
to defend one's rights meant that such *yetts* were common on the houses of
lairds and lords, nor were they 'removit' from James's palaces. Lord
Aboyne must have regretted such pretension in 1630 when he and many
other noble guests were burnt alive in Fredraught (Aberdeenshire)
following an accident when they were prevented from escaping out the
grilled windows.[5]

Coulson's work on English and French licences to crenellate reveals that
the crown showed little worry about granting such licences, that many of
the petitions came from lesser lords, and that it was perhaps only in the
cases of lesser nobles that the crown showed any reticence. In Scotland
kings showed themselves even less careful about making such grants. The
granting of such licences had little to do with the royal monopoly on fortifications but much more with the recognition of lordly status. Too often
the lesser castellated buildings are dismissed by historians as irrelevant,
'not true castles', or 'pathetic emulation', yet they are extremely important.
Coulson shows feudal interest in the size, elements, and quality of fortifications, *not* because of their military capabilities, but because of the social

[5]   This story is now regularly and wrongly attributed to Elcho (e.g. TABRAHAM 1986, 68),
seemingly because it is related by MacGibbon and Ross (1887 v.2, 101) under the entry for
Elcho.

implications of the nature of their relationship with dependent vassals. The castle was an active symbol of lordship and it is no accident that the 'tour', which continued to hold such connotations in sixteenth-century Scotland, should be the descendant of the donjon, for the name derived from *dominio*, the technical term of lordly dominion.

Any attempt to stress the aspects of lordship embodied by tower-houses is particularly frustrated by the loss of associated buildings. Generally enclosed within a barmkin, a barrier for kine (cattle), the tower-house was not hidden from view. The barmkin enclosure wall was relatively low and even the top of the sixteenth-century tower-house of the earl of Argyll can be seen peering over the top of the high thirteenth-century curtain wall of Dunstaffanage Castle. The visibility of the upper reaches of the tower-house was another good reason for the concentration of ornamentation there. The buildings within the barmkin were low, and often of timber, leaning against the enclosure wall. The tower-house thus rose above dependent buildings and at least the impression of such domination of the town's buildings can still be gained at Scalloway in Shetland. The tower-house also contrasted by being of stone, when many dependent buildings would have been of wood. Did it also contrast by being harled, by having slate roofs instead of thatch? We do not know.

One monument associated with tower-houses does survive and reveals how lordship might be expressed in mundane agricultural buildings. A saying, caricaturing the poverty of Scottish lairds, depicted their inheritance as 'a puckle land, a hantle o' pride, a doocot, and a law plea'. The proud, litigatious, and small landowing Scots laird stereotypically possessed a doocot, pigeonhouse. A source of fresh meat throughout the winter, it was also a lordly right. The resident rock pigeons could devour so much grain that legislation was introduced in 1617 limiting ownership to lairds who owned more than a 'puckle land', in fact, enough to produce 'ten chalders of victual', estimated to be about ten tons of grain. Lairds protected their rights against tenants angry at their loss of grain and against the starving who sought an unpaid meal. In 1567 shooting at a laird's pigeon was punishable by forty days in prison; a second offence could mean the loss of a hand; a third offence meant forty pounds Scots, and inability to pay could result in hanging. Probably nowhere is the doocot's position as an adjunct to seigneurial rights better displayed architecturally than at Newark (Renfrewshire) where it stands as a pseudo-tower at one corner of the barmkin, replete with its pseudo-machicolations.

That tower-house architecture was heavily imbued with connotations of power and authority can be seen from the various contexts in which it is found. There was no distinction between town and country. Maybole (Ayrshire) still contains a house of the earl of Cassilis, but it is said that there were once twenty-eight baronial dwellings within the burgh limits (TRANTER 1962–70). In the burgh of Irvine the so-called Seagate was a house belonging to the earl of Eglinton who is said to have entertained Queen Mary there. It is surely only urban growth that has made such tower-houses as Benholm's Lodging in Aberdeen a rare sight today.[6] In town, however, tower-houses were seldom enclosed and thus offered little more defensive strength than any tenement town house.

Tower-houses were residences of ecclesiastical as well as members of society. The archbishop of St Andrews had a tower-house at Monimail; Carsewell the bishop of the Isles built Carnasserie (Argyll); the archbishop of Glasgow had a tower-house opposite the cathedral. After the Reformation clergy seldom had the wherewithal to produce such houses, although Master James Melvill was an exception. Work began on his manse tower-house in Anstruther in 1590. Church authorities, quite remarkably, extended the architectural form even to their churches. The gatehouse of Crossraguel Abbey is effectively a massive square tower-house of fifteenth-century type, through which was a great entrance gateway into the monastery. Although Tranter (1962-70) believes it to belong to the post-Reformation period as the commendator's house, there is no reason to doubt that it was not earlier and belonged to the monastery. This is more acceptable when put into the context of Scotland's eccentric and insular ecclesiastical architecture of the sixteenth century. Although it maintained touch with other European late Gothic developments it readopted such Romanesque features as round-headed arches (especially in windows) and barrel vaulting, without making it baroque. Even more peculiarly, church towers commonly adopted a plainness which is the idiom of the tower-house. Not verbatim, however, for the walls are even more austere, broken only by small windows far up the tower and by heavily corbelled machicolations, as at Dunfermline Abbey, St Salvator's chapel in St Andrews, and most aggressively at St Machar's in Aberdeen. The tower-house idiom is even followed in the heraldic device of Archbishop Kennedy at St Salvator's, placed in a square panel over the gate entrance, analogous to that above the main door of a tower-house. Although the loss of church revenues meant that few immediately post-Reformation churches were built, the same tower-house style is found at Prestonpans church (1596). Even more bizarre, the tower-house is to be found at the student accommodation of King's College, Aberdeen (1658). This fascinating development raises little interest and even less enthusiasm among scholars. Cruden's (1986, 181-3) comments are that this reversion to tower-house tradition ignored the early renaissance developments (in secular architecture) and thus 'a great opportunity was lost', but the result was, even if 'backward-looking', 'totally Scottish'.

That such architecture was seen as appropriate to all forms of authority is almost inescapable when one considers its appearance on buildings ex

---

[6] Rare indeed, for Benholm's Lodging has recently been resited to an estate outside the town!

Figure 10.5 Fyvie. Upper parts were added c. 1599, producing a symmetrical façade. (From a measured drawing of MacGibbon and Ross 1887–92)

pressing municipal authority, such as tollbooths. The Musselburgh toll-booth (1590), for example, has a corbelled pseudo-machicolation above the first floor creating a partial wall-walk. It was presumably from this balcony that important declarations were made. The second floor thus rises like a caphouse on a fifteenth-century tower-house, but the internal arrangements reflect the administrative and jail functions of the tollbooth and could not be mistaken for a residence.

Seventeenth-century Scottish houses and Jacobean architecture

Discussing post-Reformation tower-houses, Tabraham (1986, 66) believes 'defensive considerations were noticeably exercising the minds of builders less and less as they contrived to improve on those aspects touching on comfort and domestic convenience.' Scholars tend to view the time follow-ing the wars of independence as progressively less violent, with concomit-ant growing emphasis on domestic comfort. The tenacity of the tower-house tradition is explained as 'old habits die hard.' One might expect therefore that the tower-houses would gradually disappear, but in fact the change was rapid.

Tower-houses continued to be built in quantity through the first two decades of the seventeenth century. They also continued to improve in quality, for the tower-houses put up in these early decades are among the most accomplished: Glamis, Castle Frazer, Fyvie (Figure 10.5), but above all others, Graigievar (1626). Yet with Craigievar the tower-houses had virtu-ally come to an end. Coxton (1644) and Leslie (1661) are two of only about

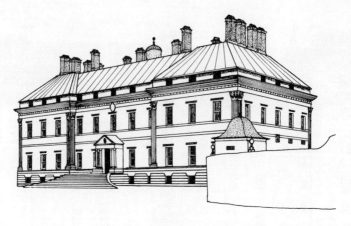

Figure 10.6 Kinross House (Fife) 1686–93, built by Sir William Bruce for himself.

a dozen that date later than this. The letter by Sir Robert Kerr quoted above reinforces the idea that Craigievar marks the end of tower-houses, for when he wrote in 1636 he was encouraging his kin not to *remove* battlements as friends had advised him to do. There was thus a move to remodel tower-houses which were becoming old-fashioned. By 1677 they were no longer built. In that year the earl of Strathmore wrote, 'such houses truly are worn quyt out of fashione, as feuds are, which is a great happiness' (quoted in DUNBAR 1978, 60) speaking of his own house at Glamis. The Englishman Thomas Morer recorded in 1689 the change which the early to mid seventeenth-century lairds and lords had initiated; 'the houses of their quality are high and strong, and appear more like castles than houses' but 'now they begin to have better buildings and to be very modish both in the fabric and furniture of their dwellings' (quoted in DUNBAR 1978, 55).

What architectural changes had occurred?[7] From 1660 onwards the change was radical. Following the restoration of Charles II Scotland witnessed its first fully classical country houses including Leslie House (Fife), Panmure House, Caroline Park (Midlothian), Yester House (East Lothian), and of course a whole series of houses associated with Sir William Bruce, including Hopetoun House, Thirlestane Castle, Holyrood Palace, and his own home at Kinross (Figure 10.6) (MACAULAY 1987). Before these 'foreign' homes were built seventeenth-century houses continued in much the same building tradition of the tower-houses but the few alterations that

---

[7] To my knowledge no one has ever studied the nature of early seventeenth-century Scottish architecture, except to say that it was a continuation of tower-house architecture without defensive elements. The following discussion may appear somewhat tedious, but it is my intention to show that a whole architectural system changed. The changes were interrelated and can not be singled out as the result of a growing search for comfort.

Figure 10.7 Early seventeenth-century houses. (Sketches from Tranter 1962–70).

Figure 10.8 Innes House. (From MacGibbon and Ross 1887–92).

did occur make them look more like 'ordinary' houses (Figure 10.7). Plewlands, Harlawhill (East Lothian) probably built in 1641, Sornhill (Ayrshire),
Pittencreiff House, Dunfermline (Fife), and the Mansionhouse, Rothesay
(Bute) are typical. None have corner garrets, corbelled stair towers, gunloops, or ground floor vaulting. Even dormer windows have all but disappeared. Pittencreiff House and the Mansionhouse, Rothesay are both T-
shaped in plan. Pilmuir House (East Lothian) is similar, dated 1624,
although it does and has a small round stair tower corbelled out of a re-
entrant angle, but it rises only two storeys with an attic. The lack of height
is also found at Monzie (Perthshire) dated 1634 and Monboddo House
(Kincardineshire) dated 1635. Both stand only two storeys high with an
attic, both lack ground floor vaulting, and both are furnished with large

ground-floor windows.

Sornhill is more typical in its L-shaped plan. In 1610 Innerpeffray (Perthshire) was built on identical lines without corner turrets or corbelling although it does have gunloops and a vaulted basement – we note again that the two tend to be inseparable. This seventeenth-century form must be said to culminate in the magnificent edifice of Innes House (Moray) (1640–53) (Figure 10.8). Here the renaissance style is elaborated with symmetrical window layout, string coursing which ties together each of the floors of the house, window pediments alternating triangular and arched, and finally the rustication of the ground-floor ashlar.

L-shaped tower-houses, by their nature, tended not to be symmetrical. Long before classicism was rediscovered by Inigo Jones, renaissance intellectualism demanded architectural symmetry in England. Fyvie (Figure 10.5) shows just how successfully symmetrical Scottish baronial style could be. Building on a large scale facilitated the production of symmetrical buildings. Methven (Perthshire) was remodelled for the duke of Lennox in the mid seventeenth century and achieved symmetry by extension to form a large four-storeyed square building (without a vaulted basement) with large round stair towers in each corner. Seventeenth-century alterations to Dunrobin (Sutherland) produced a similar façade although rather than square, two wings extended back from each end. This form is found again at Dudhope (Angus). The solution at Pinkie House (Midlothian) (1613) was to add in length, creating an impressive, if faceless, symmetrical façade of windows and chimneys to the exterior of the eastern wing.

T-shaped plans achieved symmetry on a more economical scale and might be said to be characteristic of the early seventeenth century, as the L-shape had been characteristic of the late sixteenth. But the best solution was found in the form of Gallery House (1680), where two jambs projected from the main range as pavilions. The window arrangement was impeccably symmetrical, although this made nonsense of some windows from an internal perspective. Because its internal arrangement is still that of the sixteenth-century tower-house, authors feel no qualms about putting it, with Innes House, beside them. Similarity of form, not fortification, unite them.

Pitreavie (Fife) (1644) was conceived along similar lines, although with a turnpike in each re-entrant angle corbelled out from the first floor and a vaulted basement it remained close to the tower-house tradition. L-shaped houses could easily be remodelled into such a symmetrical form as that represented by Gallery House, as happened at Careston (Angus) and Castle Stewart (Figure 10.9). William Bruce even tried to create something of a neo-classical house at Balcaskie (Fife) by adding corner pavilions to it and linking them with curved walls to two new neo-classical blocks. At Duntarvie (Linlithgowshire) the new tower addition created pavilions at the rear, rather than at the front of the house. More commonly extensions could produce a courtyard by the addition of wings, rather than pavilions

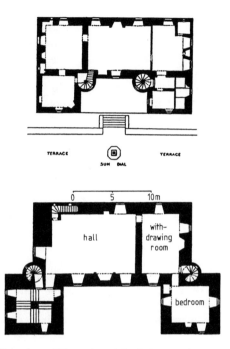

Figure 10.9 First-floor plans of Pitreavie and Castle Stewart. Compare with Figure 10.3.
(From MacGibbon and Ross 1887–92).

as at Wedderlie (Berwickshire). Maxwelton House (Dumfriesshire) (Figure 10.7) was built in 1641 to form three sides of a courtyard with symmetrical window arrangements all around and a central entrance. Maxwelton stands two storeys with an attic. Hamilton House (East Lothian) dated 1628 is similar but much smaller in all respects and rises only two storeys. Both have stair towers set in one re-entrant angle. Other early seventeenth-century alterations and constructions approximate to such a pavilioned or winged façade, without each pavilion or wing mirroring the other. This could be said to be true of Muchalls (Kincardineshire) (1620–30). Later alterations succeeded at Argyll's Lodging, Stirling (1632–74), but were only planned for Traquhair (Peeblesshire).

Most of these seventeenth-century changes can be seen as interrelated. The removal of ground-floor vaults meant that the ground floor could be used for more hospitable purposes, although the kitchen frequently remained here. Proper windows were necessary for proper rooms, hence the disappearance of little, open shotholes. The inclusion of proper windows was further necessitated by demands of symmetry. The three features are regularly found together. What amounted to an extension of habitable space on the ground floor reduced the need for upper-storey rooms. More importantly, perhaps, symmetry was served by adding pavilions or wings, creating a courtyard house. Where extensions were previously built up, they were now built out. The extensions and remodelling of Cawdor (Nairnshire) by Sir Hugh Campbell in 1660–70 consisted of two and a half storeyed wings built on either side of a very tall fifteenth-century tower. At the same time Glamis was remodelled, its low extended wings contrasting starkly with the older tower-house core which allowed access on to a balcony ninety-three feet above the ground!

A reduction in height decreased the emphasis on ornamentation along the skyline. Moreover, the symmetrical window arrangement courted attention. I argued above that the non-symmetrical windows of tower-houses were not only unembellished but were in some way further negated by iron *yetts*. The earl of Strathmore's remodelling of Glamis began with the removal of the *yetts*. The window pediments at Innes House and Winton House (East Lothian) draw the beholder's attention. The tower-house at Newark does something very similar, although elaboration increases with height. At Innes, Winton, Pinkie, and the new work at Linlithgow palace the attention is drawn further from height by the string courses dividing each floor.

Even the tall stair towers helped to reduce emphasis on verticality for the typical mid-seventeenth-century stair tower was built from the ground and very rarely corbelled out from a re-entrant angle at the first floor (Figures 10.7 and 10.8). This is partially explicable in terms of the new habitability of the ground floor: the external architecture no longer emphasised its distinction. MacGibbon and Ross (1887–92) noted that tower-house stairs gave the impression of descending from the roof. The mid-seventeenth-century stair towers, conversely, seem to rise from the ground. These later towers could rise higher than the remaining roof line because their greater width allowed the tower to house rooms, but despite their height they frequently emphasised house symmetry. They might do this by dividing the house into two parts, as in L- or T-shaped houses, or by flanking the façade as at Dudhope and Methven. The tall stair tower could, therefore, reflect lateral symmetry whereas turnpikes of tower-houses guided the observer's sight vertically to the roofline.

The changes in early seventeenth-century houses in Scotland appear to be related to English Elizabethan and Jacobean architecture (Figure 10.10) and more should be done to compare them, particularly the developments within the style Summerson has called 'artisan mannerism'. English external symmetry was essential, although internally it was certainly not. The symmetry was emphasised by numerous vertical and horizontal lines. The façade shimmered with light. So important was glazing that there even appeared in 1589 *A Booke of Sundry Draughtes, Principaly serving for Glasiers*.

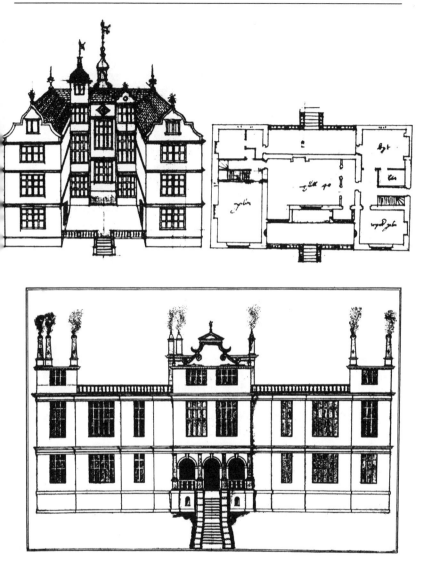

Figure 10.10 Two contemporary illustrations of Jacobean English houses.

The development of a similar interest in Scotland more or less demanded the removal of *yetts*. There was little attempt at producing great relief in projecting entrance bays, thus creating a somewhat two-dimensional aspect to façades, with the exception of great protruding wings, which were al-

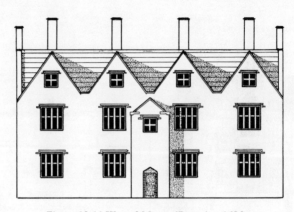

Figure 10.11 Wraxal Manor (Dorset) c. 1630.

most *de rigeur* in the great prodigy houses. The roof was often hidden, producing a façade with a flat roofline, which was often ornamented with a balustrade. In England, 'by the middle of the seventeenth century, interest in the roof was in decline' (HENDERSON 1985, 9). A central entrance to the house was occasionally gained by a grand stairway (NEWMAN 1985). Entrance led to the great hall, but the only internal compartment of particular relevance here is the gallery (COOPE 1986). The first is often said to have appeared at Hampton Court in 1530 but this only marks the beginning of its real popularity. It quickly became important so that they were inserted into older castles, such as at Haddon Hall or Penhurst in 1574. At Worksop the longest gallery in England, 212 feet long, was built in the new house in 1580. Although often said to have originated as a place to take exercise, from the beginning the gallery appears to have been used as a place to hang portraits of the family and for views of the gardens, but rarely as a connecting corridor.

Seventeenth-century architecture in Scotland can be seen to have developed or adopted several similar features. Gallery House (1680) is so named for its gallery, and galleries appeared in Scotland almost equally early as in England. Holyrood and Falkland palaces had each possessed galleries in the time of James V, and in the last quarter of the sixteenth century they appeared at Tolquhon, Newark, and Dunottar. A gallery was inserted into the tower-houses of Earlshall (1607) and Fordell, and built as part of new extensions at Pinkie House (1613) and at Aberdour (Fife) (1606–48).

Balustraded roof lines are not common in Scotland in the mid-seventeenth century, but they are found very often ornamenting the top of stair towers which have flat roofs as at Winton House (1620–30), Gogar (1625), Hill House, Dunfermline (1623), Castle Fraser, Innes House (1640–53), Cessnock (Ayrshire) (stair tower 1665), and Glamis (Angus). A glance at

Fyvie (Figure 10.5) shows how the former battlements might easily be adapted to follow an Elizabethan pattern. The very idea of hiding the roofline behind a horizontal balustrade partially conflicted with the tower-house tradition of concentrating ornamental detail there.

The corner pavilions of Gallery House and their planned completion at Traquhair House (Peeblesshire) as well as their extension into wings at various other houses reveals other connections. To some extent this has been overlooked by the tendency to create typological categories of castles which include the courtyard (MACGIBBON AND ROSS 1887–92, CRUDEN 1981). All tower-houses sat within their enclosing barmkin. The more important, usually royal (e.g. Linlithgow and Falkland) or nearly royal (e.g. Doune, Birsay) extended their ranges around the barmkin. At both Kirkwall and Edzell, already quoted above as revealing evidence in their building that more was planned, complete construction around the courtyard was intended. These differ from Dudhope, Maxwelton, Hamilton, and Argyll's Lodging where there was never an intention of enclosing the courtyard completely. Entrance to the main range was always intended to be along a central axis flanked by wings. Such an arrangement cannot be found in Scotland before the seventeenth century.

Finally, the removal of ground-floor vaulting reveals English influence. It was rare that the hall was then located on the ground floor as it was at Liberton House (1605), Hamilton House in Preston, and Argyll's Lodging, Stirling, but by the Jacobean period most formal entertainment in England had moved up to the first floor. As in England there was growing concern to create a grand staircase to the first floor. Scale-and-platt stairs were inserted and, again as in England, this remodelling was undertaken even if a new oak or pine stair replaced a former large stone newel stair.

Full-blown Jacobean-style houses were exceptionally rare in Scotland. Before James VI moved south the first Elizabethan-style house, Barnes House (East Lothian) was built for Sir John Seaton: a symmetrically-planned house with pavilioned forecourt with extruded staircase towers and central entrance leading to a scale-and-platt stair. Unfortunately nothing remains of the house today. Another precocious example was that of the house built for Lord Edward Bruce of Kinloss in the ground of Culross Abbey (1608). It was clearly a symmetrical Jacobean country house with a two-storeyed main range of plain façade and a string course dividing each floor. Four-storeyed pavilions advanced from each corner. It was replaced by a later house, but a small picture is preserved in Slezer's *Theatrum Scotiae*. The mansion built within Berwick Castle for Lord Dunbar (*c.* 1610) has elements reminiscent of Culross Abbey House and was the work of James Murray, master of the King's Works. The great construction of the pre-Restoration period is Heriot's Hospital in Edinburgh, begun in 1628. Drumlanrig (1679) was clearly modelled on Heriot's and the two are generally discussed together. They show little debt to the tower-house tradition, although they are frequently said to be in Scottish baronial style (e.g. SUMMERSON 1977, 535). Heriot's Hospital's great pavilions with turreted corners look much more like Robert Smythson's Wollaton Hall in Northamptonshire than any Scottish baronial house. Heriot's and Drumlanrig are both entered by a monumental stair approach, Drumlanrig's hall is on the first floor (by being perched on a ground-floor basement) and contains a gallery, both have roofs which have disappeared behind a flat façade top, with a decorative balustrade at Drumlanrig which is further decorated with classical pilaster columns. By English comparisons Heriot's Hospital and Drumlanrig seem unaccomplished and Drumlanrig seems particularly unfashionable in Campbell's *Vitruvius Britannicus* alongside the works of Jones and the young Palladians.

In a real sense the reason for this was that Scotland was indeed 'backward'. Elizabethan and Jacobean architecture was the product of a rapidly growing interest in architecture – during these two reigns the word architect appeared for the first time in the English language – which was reflected in the publication of John Shute's *The First and Chief Groundes of Architecture* (1563) and the translation of Serlio's *Architettura* in 1611. Serlio had been well known even before translation, as were other foreign books, such as J. Vredeman de Vries's *Variae Architecturae Formae* (1563) and Wendel Dieterlin's *Architectura* (1594–8). Bacon's essay *Elements of Architecture* appeared in 1624, and this rapidly growing interest in architecture led to the earliest examples of master masons and nobles purposefully noting architectural accomplishments abroad for future reference.

> The underlying assumption behind such expensive displays of ingenuity [in Elizabethan and Jacobean country houses] is that your peers would be as passionately interested in the novelty of your buildings as you yourself were, and it is abundantly clear that in the upper ranks of society, at least, architecture was a common subject for enthusiastic discussion. (AIRS 1982, 20–1.)

It was this burgeoning of interest and accumulation of knowledge that ultimately led Inigo Jones to 'discover' Palladio, Vitruvius, and Roman classical architecture.

The reason that Drumlanrig must have looked unfashionable in comparison with Clarendon House in London was that Scotland lacked the requisite knowledge to build otherwise, in the shape of formally trained architects. Despite the great modern reputation of the Italianate courtyard façade added to Crichton Castle by the fifth earl of Bothwell, the piece stands alone in post-Reformation Scottish architecture. Almost certainly it was not 'understood' by contemporaries. When Argyll's Lodging was originally built for Sir William of Menstrie in 1632, it was no tower-house with its ground floor hall and internal straight stair, but the masons could produce no classical house for Sir William. The place to have sought such pro-

fessional direction was the office of the King's Works. James Murray did
work at Berwick Castle and came into possession of Malleny (Midlothian)
in 1634. Although a previous house was here, the present building is a
typical mid-seventeenth-century T-shaped house. It lacks basement vaulting,
gunloops, corbelling, and turrets. The window arrangements, however, are
not symmetrical. It may be supposed that the work was that of Murray.
William Wallace built at Heriot's Hospital and Winton House. Mylne
carried out work at Heriot's, remodelled Methven, and may have been involved at the old college buildings in Glasgow. Aytoun was similarly involved at Heriot's and designed Innes House (Moray) (Figure 10.8). If
these masters of the King's Works produced nothing to rival that of Inigo
Jones, it was because the King's Works was a second rate business in Scotland. There was little time, money, peace, or direction for royal building
during the reign of Mary, and James VI gave little thought to building in
Scotland after his move to London. Wallace carried out work at Edinburgh
Castle and at Linlithgow palace, but even Linlithgow's New Work was only
undertaken after the wing had fallen down, although for some years James
VI had been warned of impending collapse if repairs were not effected.
The difference between the rather grandiose royal undertakings at the
palaces of Falkland, Holyrood, Linlithgow, and Stirling at the beginning of
the sixteenth century, and the general absence of building for the century
1550–1650, has frequently invited comment (DUNBAR 1984).

The king would not spend, and the Scottish nobles simply did not have
the cash to sustain the whole superstructure of architectural planning and
subsequent division of construction between perhaps as many as four
specialised building teams. Outside the prodigy houses, so-called artisan
mannerism flourished in England, a building style reflected more in the
method of construction than its physical form: one planned, organised,
and completed by masons. Construction in Scotland continued in the
hands of masons and artisans. For James VI's return to Scotland in 1617
London craftsmen had to refurbish Holyrood chapel, for as the Privy
Council recognised, 'this work could not be gottin so perfytlie and well
done within this cuntrey as is requisite.' The painted ceilings which are
closely associated with post-Reformation Scottish houses had a restricted
lifespan precisely because Jacobean plastered ceilings became fashionable
in the seventeenth century and it is from London and York that these
craftsmen are believed to have come. The infrastructure of the English
building profession was a prerequisite for the prodigy houses, as was the
architectural knowledge which made such 'tasteful' use of classical orders
appreciable. The union of the crowns helped to accelerate the process, but
it was not until the time of Sir William Bruce that they came together.
Bruce was the master of the King's Works and responsible for the completion of Holyrood Palace. He also had perhaps the first thing that could be
called an architect's practice in Scotland. Like previous masters of the

King's Works, Bruce designed houses for the nobility. Unlike those of previous masters, his designs were classical.

Feuding and the reasons for the demise of tower-house architecture

We turn now to the question of the tower-house's popularity and why its
architectural style changed. Can both questions really be answered by
reference to violence and security? The answer to be given here is no.

To explain tower-houses in terms of defensibility one must discount war
for several reasons. Tower-houses are not distributed primarily in the areas
affected by English invasions, the Borders. Instead they are very common
throughout Scotland, especially in the fertile areas with high population
density, and hence are scarce in the Highlands. When military engage-
ments and sieges do occur, we find them concentrated on the great
medieval royal castles of Stirling and Edinburgh or the towns of Roxburgh
and Berwick. If tower-houses are involved it is almost the result of accident.
Nothing reveals this clearer than the house built at Blairfindy (Banffshire)
in 1586 by the earl of Huntly. The earl's Catholicism led James VI to send
out more than one army against him. The only serious battle, that of Livet
in 1594, was fought between Huntly and the earl of Argyll's highlanders on
a hill by Blairfindy House. The house played no part in the battle, despite
Tranter's (1962–70) claim that it 'commands the pass of Livet'. Claims that
houses occupy commanding positions may easily be brushed aside in military terms. Blairfindy controlled movement along the Livet only in terms of
observation – cattle could not be driven through the pass unnoticed by
Huntly or his servants. Likewise Druminnor (Aberdeenshire) played no
part in the nearby battle of Tillyangus in 1571, although after being de-
feated the Forbes did flee to this, their tower-house. The functional milit-
arist would, in any case, note that tower-houses are quite inappropriate for
defence against even a small army. To Tabraham (1986, 61) Craignethan,
built in the 1530s, 'was the last private castle of high defensive capability
built in Scotland.' Later constructions are not seen as refuges or
strongholds, but rather as homes defensible against a surprise midnight
visit by angry and homicidal neighbours.

The connection between tower-houses and feuds may even be strengthened by the recognition of the number of post-Reformation tower-houses
built. This final efflorescence of Scottish tower-houses was once described
by Simpson as their Indian summer. But it is only with Keith Brown's
recent book, *Bloodfeud in Scotland*, that feuding has been examined sufficiently closely to reveal that the Indian summer coincided with a period in
which the bloodfeud had become endemic and particularly violent.
Brown's concluding chapter admits that 'fifteenth-century Scotland had
also been a feuding society, but it was not disturbed to this extent by
private violence, and the justice of the bloodfeud was able to maintain an
equilibrium of war and peace within communities.' The late sixteenth cen-

tury was different; between 1559 and 1594, Brown finds only twelve years not marred by civil war, rebellion, or coup. Feuding had not got out of hand, but was the result of general political instability as the Stewart monarchy and the Catholic Church both collapsed.

Brown's numerous citations of murders and attempted murders make it clear that the Scotsman's castle was not sufficiently secure that feuds did not come through the front door or window. Gordons seized Abercrumbie of Pitmedden from his house, killed him, and 'with their drawin sworids, cuttit him all in peeces; and as monsteris in nature; left nocht sax inche of his body, airmis, legis, and heid undevydit, and cut assunder' (BROWN 1986, 32). Campbell of Cawdor was shot dead through a window of his home, while the Ogilvies attempted to murder Lord Spynie by blowing in the gate and windows of his home with a petard (ibid., 22). Not even the Stewart kings were safe. The earl of Bothwell attacked Holyrood palace in 1591, Falkland palace the following year, and Holyrood again in 1593. The gunshot scars on the gate tower at Falkland are thought to date to this escapade. Admittedly Bothwell's activities were extraordinarily desperate. James VI, however, gave as good as he got, having the Ruthven brothers murdered in their Perth townhouse in 1600.

With the appearance of two recent publications (WORMALD 1980; BROWN 1986), anthropological work on feuding has made a long-overdue impact on Scottish history. The central name is that of Max Gluckman, but others include Evans-Pritchard and Leach and the ethnographically-studied feuding societies include Albanians, Corsicans, Sicilians, the Mafia, American 'hill-billies', Bedouins, and those fierce people, the Yanomamo, to name but the most common.

Anthropologists recognise that the bloodfeud is only the violent aspect of a system that regulates confrontations and disputes in societies where fission is impossible (practised among many hunting-gathering peoples) and no higher authority enforces its own version of justice on disputing parties. Bloodfeud is only part of a system which otherwise includes compensation and, most importantly, resolution. In the interests of peace, feuds must be ended in such a way that neither side is inclined to feel so dishonoured that it continues the feud. Thus compromise is the secret ingredient. It is made easier by the fact that in the complicated social relations of kin, neighbours, friends, and social superiors – all those whom an aggrieved party might seek for support in a feud – all may have conflicting loyalties and interests which would not be served by violence. They then form a pressure group for compromise, settlement, and peace. When, however, violence is in their interest, the bloodfeud may become very bloody.

Wormald, like Gluckman, chooses to emphasise the aspect of peace within feuding society, so that one reviewer feared that the feud had almost become a 'good thing'. Wormald, however, is generally recognised as having provided an invaluable service in making Scottish historians rethink the feud and it is only from her starting point that Brown is in a position to put the blood back into the bloodfeud. Brown even attempts to quantify the violence of post-Reformation Scotland, plotting relative increases and decreases in bloodshed. Whether or not early modern Scotland was a more dangerous and bloody place than other European nations is a difficult question, perhaps impossible to answer, but worth asking. It is possible that it was no more violent, but that European bloodshed was of an institutional nature; it was in the form of legitimate wars and of centralised violence – executions by the state. Bloodletting by central government was minimal in Jacobean Scotland, but state-sponsored death is more easily cloaked in the robes of justice. It was the private nature of violence that so shocked foreign visitors to Scotland, not the amount.

By tracing in great detail the participants, their political positions, their allies and their power, generally reckoned in numbers of followers, Brown can reveal post-Reformation feuds at almost all social levels from peers to lairds and even burgesses. He demolishes the myth that it was the exclusive reserve of robber barons. Quite the contrary, the supposedly unbridled anarchic lords of the realm appear much less frequently than the middling lairds in feuds. Feuding is primarily an aspect of political power and this is revealed by the fact that feuding 'partners' were of comparatively equal political strength; burgesses could not feud with lairds, nor lairds with lords. Neither did a lord's dependants feud among themselves, for the lord soon quashed any such violence. Feuds between lords and tenants were not common: quarrels might be, but the disparity of power meant that the tenant was generally incapable of pursuing a feud against his lord. Feuding was only feasible when greater political powers could be counted on to divide between the two parties, or remain aloof. The Scottish phenomenon of manrents, as Wormald (1985) has shown, were far from anti-royal treaties mutually assuring lordly autonomy, but were arrangements by which lords and lairds assured one another that feuding between their dependants would be resolved and that neither party would seek to support their men against those of the other party. It was here, precisely where political confrontation could occur because it was an area where political competition was possible, that special measures were needed. They were not needed where the political hierarchy was firmly established.

The close link between violence and superior power in general would greatly repay closer study. For early modern English society this has been done in the context of the family where power resided in the head of the household and those who were beaten included the wife, children, and servants (MACFARLANE 1978; STONE 1979; WRIGHTSON 1982; HOULBROOKE 1984). Discussions about castles and tower-houses tend to take no cognisance of this fact. Thus late fifteenth- and sixteenth-century castellated architecture in England such as Oxborough Hall elicits observations that bands of thieves still roamed the countryside. This ignores the fact that contemporaries were building great defenceless country houses and shows little understanding of the sociological context of violence in early modern society. The protection of property is apparently envisioned by scholars as aimed against gangs of burglars and yet Alan MacFarlane (1981, 198) argues that banditry probably never existed in England. The growing literature on crime and society (e.g. COCKBURN 1977; GATRELL *et al.* 1980; CAMERON 1983; SHARPE 1984) is seldom to be found in the bibliography of works on castles. Those brutalised by violence and most often the victims of theft were those in the lowest echelons of society and not because they could ill afford to decorate their homes with battlements.

When power was unequal there was little scope for protracted resistance, regardless of the defensive measures undertaken. The impotence of tower-house defences is seen most clearly in Orkney. There the Stewart earls reigned supreme. Their houses at Birsay, Kirkwall, and Scalloway (Shetland) all reveal defensive features. In James VI's Scotland there was probably no house less needful of a gunloop than the earl's Kirkwall palace, for it was precisely because there was no one to rival his power that Patrick Stewart became legendary for his tyranny. When, however, the king moved against him, the struggle was unequal and short, with Patrick ending his life on the chopping block in 1617.

Brown shows us that local issues such as land ownership, estate boundaries, control of moorland, fishing rights, local jurisdictions, burghal offices, and even royal offices, were most commonly the causes of feuds. What made post-Reformation Scotland even more violent than before, was that the monasteries had been dissolved and the collection of teinds became an additional and significant source of competition and conflict. This conflict was given more scope by the fact that dissolution occurred during the king's minority so that there was not always a legitimate moment of acquisition, and James VI took advantage of the many quarrels to appropriate the former Church resources for himself.

Because the feud was so closely bound to struggles for power and extension of lordship, the 'inemie' was always well known. Unlike our modern paranoia of the unknown murderous maniac, when Alexander Cunningham, earl of Glencairn complained in 1578 of an ambush outside his house, they were not unknown assailants. They were Robert Montgomery and accomplices who had a deadly feud with the Cunninghams because the earl of Glencain had murdered Montgomery's father and brother, the third and fourth earls of Eglinton, during the previous two years. He had begun the feud at the beginning of the 1570s by aggressively attacking Montgomery lordship in Ayrshire. Control of Kilwinning Abbey was at the centre of the feud. The fifth earl of Glencairn had good reason to fear for his life after the attempted ambush outside his tower-house in 1578, for the previous year he had complained that the Montgomeries were pursuing him for his life. In 1580, they got him. It took another twenty years before the Montgomeries finally shot Alexander Cunningham, laird of Aiket, out-side his house, and while John Cunningham, laird of Corsehill, survived, his son Patrick was murdered. So, because Alexander and John had murdered the earl of Eglinton with Glencairn's complicity, two paid with their lives, one with that of his son.

Scottish society came to terms with its violence, it could not do other-wise. It also condemned it. Brown's book covers the period during which the feud was to disappear from Scotland, but its eradication was not easy, despite the overt efforts of the king and church to end it and the general recognition of lords, lairds, burgesses, and peasants alike that peace was preferable. It also raises the philosophical question concerning the efficacy of the physical measures of safety employed, such as tower-houses. Despite the need, as modern writers often describe it, for such towers, post-Reformation Scotland suffered and survived extreme violence which tower-houses seem to have done nothing to curb. Indeed, Brown is right in show-ing that the prevalence of carrying pistols and rapiers led to more frequent bloodshed and an intensification of the feud. Only distance in time makes Brown's example of the death of John Graham comical (1986, 32). Walking with friends in Edinburgh he noticed his enemy Sir James Sandilands approaching with the duke of Lennox and a large company brandishing weapons. Graham's company attacked and Graham was killed, but the 'weapons' brandished by Sandilands' company were golf clubs for they were on their way to the links. The incident would surely not have occurred had the participants not been armed. Perhaps William Forbes would have agreed that pistols did not increase one's safety after he accidentally shot off one of his hands in his Lickleyhead tower-house (Aberdeenshire) in 1629. The 'necessity' of such self-defence measures sounds as hollow for early modern as it does for present-day Scotland.

Tranter (1962-70) writes of Pittheavlis (Perthshire), 'presumably nothing ever happened here of sufficient importance or excitement to chronicle, despite – or possibly even because of – the sturdy strength and amplitude of gunloops.' This defence by deterrent is unconvincing. No 'stirring deeds' (i.e. murder) may have been recorded at Pittheavlis because John Ross of Craigie, Robert Stewart, and Patrick Oliphant, the three known owners between 1586 and 1636, were men of lowly political status and are not recorded *themselves* to have been involved in political confrontations.

Admittedly there was transient safety offered by the tower-house walls and iron grilles. Fear of death and belief in the safety of his tower-house caused Thomas Jack 'to abyd continewallie in his hous for feir of his lyff' (BROWN 1986, 28). But it was not simply stout walls that offered safety, for violence was not without its restraints. Sadistic torture provoked outrage and a certain 'cruel man' was 'hangit for setting on ane woman's bare [arse] ane girdill quhen it was red hot' (*ibid.*, 23). The sanctity of the home was similarly protected. *Hamesucken*, the violation of another's home by, for example, breaking and entering was considered intolerable and is suggested by Brown as possibly contributing to the level of outrage engendered when Huntly murdered the earl of Moray at Donibristle.

Safety provided by the home is implicit in the number of attacks that took place out of doors. On the other hand, more often than not the site of the clash was the object of conflict. Lord Ruthven and Bruce of Clackmannan and their armed men clashed in the fields where teinds were to be gathered. A similar confrontation with large parties of armed men over teind gathering was resolved without bloodshed in a dispute between the earl of Cassillis and the lairds of Bargany and Girvanmains. Fighting broke out in the moors between the armed forces of Douglas of Cashogle and Douglas of Drumlanrig over the cutting of peat, as it did in the church of Largo over the right to seating arrangements between two lairds (BROWN 1986, 67–71). The object of conflict might even be a tower-house and in 1579 Alexander Porterfield had to complain to the Privy Council that the earl of Glencairn was preventing him from entering his father's castle at Duchal, although a decreet had found in his favour the previous year. The Kerrs and Scotts fired on one another in a dispute over Spielaw Castle and a feud between Bruce lairds of Clackmannan and Fingask led to the burning of a house by the rightful owner to spite his rival (*ibid.*, 71)! In 1624 the Chattans drove away the earl of Moray's servants and possessed themselves of the earl's 'handsome edifice', the Castle Stewart (Inverness-shire) (TRANTER 1962–70).

Two incidents which occurred during the most violent feud of James VI's reign, the Huntly-Moray feud, had tower-houses as the central scene of action. They are worth discussion at greater length to show how little tower-houses impinged on the nature or level of violence which formed part of the politics of lordship. In late November 1590 the earl of Huntly rode with a large force to the earl of Moray's house at Darnaway. Moray was reinforced there by the earl of Atholl and many other supporters. Huntly made a noisy show of surrounding the house, shots were exchanged, and only one Gordon was killed before Huntly withdrew. A little over a year later the earl of Moray was *en route* to Edinburgh in order to make his peace with Huntly. In February 1592 the earl of Moray was at his mother's house at Donibristle on the south coast of Fife. The earl of Huntly surrounded the house, shots were fired, again a Gordon was hit, but a fire forced the besieged out, and the earl of Moray was killed with the sheriff of Moray and five other men.

From a tactical perspective one might suggest that Donibristle reveals the tremendous vulnerability of tower-houses to fire but that Dornaway reveals that a tower-house could indeed hold out against attackers, given sufficient defenders and time for preparations. Such 'military' observations, however, would obscure the real importance of the two incidents. Huntly withdrew from Darnaway at a time when the earl of Moray was at the height of his success. Indeed, it was the first time he was politically able to challenge his enemy. Huntly also withdrew after receiving letters cancelling his commission to arrest John Grant, thus removing his legal right to storm Darnaway, and letters commanding him to ward at St Andrews. His fortunes were at a low ebb. At Donibristle, by contrast, the earl of Moray was on his way to Edinburgh to make peace with Huntly and the king. Now, a year later, the political situation was very different. As it was, Huntly only escaped the outrage over the murder by the king's extraordinary support, something which would not have been possible a year earlier.

The two incidents reveal another important point. A confrontation at Darnaway was avoided not because of tactical considerations, but by the simple fact that given the numbers of participants, it would have been a bloody affair, the political repercussions of which would have been terrific. At Donibristle, on the other hand, the earl of Moray was in effect murdered alone, for the others had no independent political connections. Most feuding seems to have turned on murders, counter-murders, or executions if pursued through the courts. Contemporaries rightly did not recognise a great difference between execution by a feuding enemy acting as a royal officer, and murder. The numbers actually killed during a feud might be kept down and, as the Montgomery-Cunningham feud shows, the targets for such killings were not random. At least such restraint seems to have been characteristic of feuding in the lowlands. Slaughter in the highlands seems to have been frequently on a greater scale. Doubtless Huntly would have preferred Donibristle to have gone more like the murder of the earl of Moray's ally, John Campbell of Cawdor, earl of Argyll. Huntly conspired to have him dispatched only eight days before Moray, but alone by an assassin's shot through the window of his house.

The political determination of other incidents rather than the defensibility of tower-houses is easily documented. In 1567 the earl of Caithness claimed wardship over the young earl of Sutherland. He was aided by the lord of Duffus, master of Caithness, and laird of Strathnaver against the bishop of Caithness. The town and cathedral of Dornoch were burnt, but the bishop's tower-house in Dornoch was manned by the bishop's dependants. A month passed, but with no change in the political situation – the king did not intervene – the bishop's men came to terms with the earl of Caithness and left the tower-house which the earl then burnt. Slaughter was unnecessary and defence pointless when the power struggle was uneven.

As the result of a feud, thirty men led by two Stewart lairds broke into Ashintully House (Perthshire) in 1587, only four years after it was built. They dragged off Andro Spalding and mistreated him. Tranter's (1962–70) description of the incident as a 'siege' is unhelpful. Spalding was not murdered and he later had them all 'put to the horn' and fined 100 merks. Spalding's survival was certainly due to his influence at court, for no less a person than the earl of Atholl had to become cautioner for the culprits. He had become too big to be murdered, but it was his political connections, not the strength of his house, that saved him.

Survival was literally a matter of politics. Danger did not lurk everywhere in a hostile environment, but only in areas where competing lordships might clash. These were areas frequently away from the home, and no ambitious lord or laird could remain neurotically locked away in their tower-house like Thomas Jack. It was precisely the most ambitious who were likely to be engaged in a feud and for them danger lay, as it did for the earl of Mar, not in the storming of his house, but from the assassin's bullet in a wynd in Stirling.

It becomes easy for historians to accept the equation of tower-houses with feuding, for the earl of Strathmore recognised in the later seventeenth century that both were a thing of the past. At least since MacGibbon and Ross, architectural changes in the seventeenth century have been associated with the growing peacefulness of society. What Tranter (1962–70) says of Plewland (West Lothian) built in 1641 is now traditional: 'There are no defensive features and this house represents . . . the end of the fortified period, with the need for defensive provisions no longer necessary, but the old habits of planning and architecture still remained.' The rule of law, it would appear, made tower-houses an unnecessary anachronism. True, the feud had disappeared. James VI began a campaign against feuding in 1595, legislated anent Feuding in 1598, and in 1649 Parliament abolished the principles of assythement – the essential compensation element of the feud. Settlement of disputes were now the sole preserve of lawyers and the end of the feud was bound to the sixteenth-century rise of the lay legal profession (WORMALD 1980). But neither the earl of Strathmore nor Scottish historians for generations could grasp that the feud was not simply anarchical slaughter for the sake of bloodlust. The rule of law did not necessarily reduce the amount of violence. While law courts could expect enforcement of its decisions by the crown, its justice, because more just, did not coincide with social realities, thus leaving many aggrieved parties with the power to seek their own justice. Compromise and reconciliation in the feud aimed at quashing just such resentment. As a mid-sixteenth century legal manual put it: 'Assythement . . . paid by the committers of slaughter to the kin, children, and friends of any person that is slain, is given to them to compensate for the hurt, damage, and loss sustained by them through the lack of the person slain . . . and for pacifying of their rancour. This was a more effective instrument for regulating violence than the authority of the courts (LENMAN AND PARKER 1980, 15).

The victory of the rule of law was also a triumph for the Reformed Church, which equated crime with sin and saw the merciless, God-fearing state as a tool for the punishment of sinners. From 1560, for at least two centuries, the zeal of kirk elders meant that Scots were more likely to end up in the parochial court, the kirk sessions, than in secular courts. While it was still the secular courts that tried the cases that feuding would bring, the Reformed Church's God could be counted on to encourage them to be merciless and indeed would claim His own victims. Only by being merciless could the courts eliminate murder as an acceptable political tool, and Scotland joined the European fraternity of state-monopolised violence. In 1603 James VI ordered that the MacGregors be 'extirpat and ruttit out' after they massacred the Colquhouons of Luss in battle (LENMAN AND PARKER 1980, 13).

The legislation of James VI and the end of the feud by the abolition of assythment did little to end violence. Brown's (1986, 276) graph of the incidence of feuding is a good general indicator of the level of violence in the years 1573 to 1625; it is striking how constant the number of feuds remained. There were not many fewer feuds in the two decades following 1600 than preceding it. Tabraham (1986, 71) ends the Scottish tower-houses on a note of peace and tranquility, in Edzell gardens. The guide-book to Edzell explains the 'artistic significance of the pleasance' (which ought to read 'historic') as the embodiment of 'stately equipoise and dignified calm' which had been achieved both between Church and state and between Scotland and England (SIMPSON AND FAWCETT 1980). Built in 1604, supposedly the wonderful pleasance 'could scarcely have been conceived' prior to the union of the crowns. Doubtless the gardens, summer house, and bath house were put to use by Lindsay as a place for deep contemplation and were a source of inspiration for the order of the universe (the eight 'planetary' spheres thought to encircle the earth are depicted along one wall of the enclosure) and for enjoyment of its tranquility (the wall contained nesting holes for song birds). Nevertheless, the union of the crowns was only a precondition to its conception inasmuch that before 1603 Lindsay would surely not have included the fleur de lys, with the rose, thistle, and shamrock ornamentation on the reverse side of the bust niches. A 'dignified calm' had existed between Scotland and England for two decades, but no such calm reigned within the Lindsay kin, for the laird of Edzell had a feud with the Lindsay earl of Crawford. One year after the pleasance was built, in 1605, Sir David's son was involved in street fighting in Edinburgh and the master of Crawford killed and hewed to pieces Sir David's brother. A few years later Sir David's son murdered the master of Crawford's uncle, Lord Spynie, and royal commissions had to be taken from the earl for fear that he would use them to destroy the whole Edzell branch of the family. The feud only ended in 1616 when the laird of Edzell swore that the killing of Lord Spynie had been an accident and that he had been trying to kill the earl of Crawford. Assythment was paid and land sold. Even in the very symbol for modern writers of the end of the feuding age and inauguration of a new law abiding epoch, we find murder and mayhem.

Brown's graph of feuding incidents extends to 1625 and in the final five years the numbers are certainly down on the previous four decades. Peace was not necessarily any nearer to hand, for James VI's son, Charles, brought unrest to Scotland unheard of even during the time of his grand-mother, Mary. The covenant was signed in 1639 and Scotland was drawn into the civil war a few years later. Scotland was occupied throughout the 1650s by Cromwell and his new model army and would see armies again following the 'glorious revolution' of 1689 and Jacobite uprising of 1715. Indeed, it was primarily in the civil war that any of these tower-houses were the sites of shots fired in anger. Cromwell besieged Dunbeath (Caithness) for all of a few days before it surrendered. But most houses only saw milit-ary action in the form of barracks for Cromwell's soldiers. Interestingly, the wings added to Kilchurn in 1693 by the first earl of Breadalbane are inter-preted as barracks for the men of the Campbell of Glenorchy. Fyvie was occupied by Montrose in 1644, but a ditched camp on a nearby hill was built in readiness for defence – there was no trusting the battlemented house. Any of these three civil wars or revolts saw more 'legitimate' destruction of homes of political enemies than all the feuding of King James VI's reign put together. Yet during and after, almost no tower-houses were built. Tranter's (1962–70) observation that Plewlands was built in a period when 'defensive provisions were no longer necessary' could not be further from the truth. The house was built in 1641 on the brink of civil war. A hypothetical but plausible explanation for similar houses built dur-ing the 1650s would stand Tranter's observation on its head. A good covenanter and republican might manifest his good faith in such trying times by building a house devoid of gunloops – such were for papists and royalists.

If it was not the dawning of a new peaceful era that sounded the death knell of the tower-house, what was? The answer lies in power. Tower-house or Jacobean country house, both were, in the terms of Girouard (1978, 2–3), power-houses, the houses of a ruling class:

> The size and pretensions of such houses were an accurate index of the ambitions – or lack of them – of their owners. When a new man bought an estate and built on it, the kind of house which he built showed exactly what level of power he was aiming at. If the head of an established family was ambitious to raise its status – or simply to keep up with new arrivals – one of the most obvious means towards doing so was to rebuild or improve his house.

The final efflorescence of Scottish tower-houses coincided partially with a period that Brown recognised as particularly violent. The cause of this flurry of building activity was not, however, due to an increase in violence or political instability. It has long been recognised that this immediately post-Reformation phenomenon is the direct result of the dissolution of the monasteries (MACGIBBON AND ROSS 1887–92). Cruden (1981, 150) recog-

nised that the resources previously dedicated 'to private and votive masses,
to the building and endowment of collegiate churches and to the founding
of chantry chapels in cathedral, parish, and monastic churches were now
available for castle and house building.' He recognised too that this was the
Scottish equivalent of the English phase of great Elizabethan constructions.

Unfortunately, although it is occasionally recognised that the relation of
incomes to building projects would form an interesting topic of research
(STELL 1981), the work has not been done.[8] A superficial glance recognises
that several houses can be related to secularised Church property.
Inglismaldie (Angus) was obtained by John Livingstone of Dunipace in
1588, recorded in a charter from James VI. The name is a corruption of
Ecclesmaldie, thus, ironically, the distortion of the name mirrors the
secularisation of the Church property. Names similarly reveal the ecclesiastical origin of Monkland, Monkcastle, and Kirkhill. Monkland
(Kirkcudbrightshire) was presumably built by Mark Ker who became commendator of Newbattle Abbey in 1587 and was created Lord Newbattle.
Monkcastle (Ayrshire) was built on land of Kilwinning Abbey which the
earl of Arran's son Claud, commendator of Paisley Abbey, received.
Kirkhill (Aryshire) was built in 1589 by the third son of Alexander Kennedy
of Bargany who had obtained Church land. Fourmerkland (Dumfriesshire)
was built in 1590 on former lands of Holywood Abbey. Maclellans
(Kirkcudbrightshire) was built in 1582 on former land of a Franciscan
monastery and Park (Wigtonshire) was built in 1590 by Thomas Hay of
Park, son of Thomas Hay, who became commendator of the abbey of Glen-
luce in 1560, to which Park formerly belonged. The equation of secularised
monastic revenues and new domestic building is inescapably obvious at the
commendator's houses at Melrose, Culross, and Dunfermline Abbeys.

The commemoration of ascent in rank is found everywhere among
tower-houses. James Drummond was made Lord Madderty in 1609 and
built Innerpeffray (Perthshire) the following year. John Carsewell's father
had been the earl of Argyll's constable. On his appointment as super-
intendent and bishop of the Isles, Carsewell built Carnasserie (Argyll). His
new position meant that he had outgrown Kilmartin. The earl of Morton
built Drochil (Peeblesshire) (c. 1578) with finances derived from his
guardianship of the earl of Angus (HEWITT 1982, 2). The tutor of Kintail
moved up in the world by marrying the heiress of Macleod of Coigeach
and built Leod Castle (Ross). Others might rise from even less noble
station. John Sinclair of Geanies built Dunbeath Castle (Caithness) in 1624.
His father had made his fortune as a merchant. John Halliday, son of an

8 Politics and architecture of Tudor England has been the recent topic of publication by
Howard (1987) and forms part of the present research of a contributor to this volume, Matthew
Johnson. This cursory sketch of a slightly later period in Scotland shows that something
comparable could be done and easily. Why it has remained of little interest to scholars is
something that Stell does not suggest.

advocate, built Tulliebole (Kinross-shire) in 1608, the year he was knighted. George Bruce earned his fortune and his knighthood from coal mining, something he celebrated by adding a wing to his house. As *parvenus* the new men might seek to endow themselves with a fictitious antiquity and hence respectability or they might seek to impress by adopting the most up-to-date fashions.

New men, unless they bought old houses, by definition had to build new houses. The earl of Morton began building Drochil as an expression of his position as regent to James VI, but established families with established homes tended to add rather than start anew. Thus the seat of the Mortons at Aberdour is composed of three or four separate extensions. Some of the most 'ancient' families still occupy their tower-houses today, as at Blair Atholl and Glamis, despite the earl of Strathmore's complaint three hundred years ago that it was out of date. When Campbell of Glenorchy added his north and west wings to Kilchurn (Argyll) in 1693 it was on the occasion of his promotion to the first earl of Breadalbane, he too must have recognised how old-fashioned the tower must have looked. But established families might not feel the need for new building to be pressing. The earl of Huntly's ornate windows announce his rise in status to Scotland's first marquis. New windows sufficed. At Elcho Lord John Wemyss added the initials EJW and the date 1633 to commemorate the creation of an earldom by Charles I at his coronation, apparently the earl's initials sufficed.

Building was a serious matter. A seventeenth-century writer thought that the earl of Morton had brought about his own downfall by 'making mansions with the subjects' coffers' (HEWITT 1982, 152). New construction not only commemorated changes which had taken place in the owner's status, but was part of the active politics of upward mobility. It is no accident that the new earl of Stirling died bankrupt, his heirs losing the Stirling residence to Argyll. Kellie was sold to Viscount Fentoun in 1613 immediately on the death of the fifth Lord Oliphant, a man of 'vast estates' but who spent to maintain his position. Some of that spending was lavished on Kellie. In the same year, the earl of Dunfermline commemorated construction at Pinkie House with the inscription, 'Dominus Alexander Setonius hanc aedificavit, non ad animi, sed fortunarum et agelli modum 1613.' He did not build according to his spirit, or wishes, but according to his fortune and means. He was apparently apologising for his modest improvements; the modesty was possibly false, but it was still only a pale reflection of the monumental scale and politics of expenditure by aspiring members of Elizabeth's court.

But where did inspiration come from? It might come from royal construction. Royal arms, initials, and other regal commemorations are found at numerous houses. At Balvenie (Banffshire) there are royal arms, as there are at Muchalls (1619–27), Fraser Castle, and the earl of Huntly's great

Castle. Colliston (Angus) (1621) had the initials IR for James VI, but the inscription at Winton House (1620–30) is even more flattering: JACOBUS PRIMUS BRITANNIAE MAGNAE ET FRANCIAE ET HIBERNIAE REX. Although the new kings of Great Britain produced nothing worth copying in Scotland, their master masons, as we have seen, were active in building or remodelling major mid-seventeenth-century houses.

Theoretically, everyone owed their prosperity, titles, and land to the king. All magnates and merchants might curry royal favour and express their loyalty and respect by emulating royal fashion. There was, therefore, no 'Whig' and 'Tory' architecture as there would be in England in the following century. The new marquis of Huntly, in 'the most splendid heraldic device in the British Isles', commemorated family, king, and religion with the passion of Christ! The Catholic marquis displayed his Catholicism with awesome arrogance, but simultaneously signalled his loyalty to the Protestant crown. Nevertheless those houses which were most classical in the early seventeenth century certainly had the closest royal connections. Lord Edward Bruce of Kinloss was a courtier who frequented the London court. His house at Culross Abbey must rate as the first great Scottish Jacobean country house. The same is seen of even newer men, merchants. Thomas Dalyell was a butter merchant who made his fortune in London, having followed James VI south. James laboured long and hard to open up English markets to Scottish merchants. Purchasing property near Edinburgh in 1612, Binns was remodelled in 1630. Influences of classicism and Jacobean architecture are clearly to be seen.

While the master masons of the King's Works failed to take a lead in producing new classical houses, traditional architecture and sources of inspiration remained. The first earl of Dunfermline was similarly a 'new man' although one who had risen much higher than Lord Kinloss – Dunfermline Abbey had been far wealthier than the abbey of Culross. He administered Scotland in James VI's absence and could scarcely have been closer, politically, to the king. At much the same time as Lord Kinloss's house at Culross, the earl built Fyvie, a distinguished monument of Scots baronial style and a building which is frequently compared to French châteaux – a traditional source of inspiration and certainly the source for James V's Falkland renaissance façade and Huntly's great ornamental windows. At the same time as Binns was being remodelled, Willie the Merchant was having Craigievar built in elaborate tower-house style, but Willie's trading was across the North Sea with Scotland's traditional commercial partners.

If proximity to London was important, so too was proximity to Edinburgh. It is not accidental that Bruce's house at Culross Abbey, the Binns, and Pinkie House were all in the vicinity of the capital. A disproportionately large number of the mid-seventeenth-century houses that no longer followed tower-house architectural styles discussed above are to be found in the Lothians, and the later seventeenth century would witness an increased concentration of new classical country houses there (MACAULAY 1987). Edinburgh had undeniably closer links with London than anywhere else in Scotland, but there was one other important reason for change to be centred here. It was here that the changing basis on which power and authority rested was most marked. And the changes in architecture reflected those changes.

When Mar, Huntly, and Argyll died in the 1630s, they were not just the last of the great feuding earls, they were the last of the great earls who measured their strength in kinsmen and dependants. This trend had begun sooner in England with several results. Households began to decrease in size and the status of servants decreased. Independent lords or their sons were increasingly unlikely to join the households of great dukes as chamberlains, for example. The result was a growing formality in the relations of a household, reflected by increasingly formal spatial arrangements within the house. Such a development, not the need for privacy, lies behind the introduction of corridors. Indeed, rather than increasing privacy, late-seventeenth-century French fashions such as the levée were adopted in England, which made bedchambers even more public places than at the end of the sixteenth century. In its most strikingly rational form at Coleshill, Berkshire (1650), corridors join back stairs to make servants' movements more invisible. The tower-house always had the advantage of numerous turnpike stairs that acted very efficiently as vertical corridors and thus had allowed very exact planning over formal movements throughout the building.

The changing basis of power had other repercussions. By the early sixteenth century in England there was little left of the demesne at great country estates and most rents were collected in coin rather than kind. It was only really in the sixteenth century that feuing land became common in Scotland (SMOUT 1969). Only then did great storage areas begin to become redundant as most of a landlord's tenants paid in cash. Maitland's 'greit and fair' vaults were becoming anachronistic in the early seventeenth century.

Money, not dependants, was the growing source of power. To this should be added royal offices, not only as a source of power, but also of wealth. When James VI made his famous boast in 1607 that he now ruled Scotland with a pen, something his predecessors could not do with a sword, his rule depended more than ever on royal officers and Parliament. The Reformation and removal of the king to London fuelled the demand of the laity to hold office and the increasing need for those offices. James also introduced new offices that he found in England, like justices of the peace, to bring Scotland more into line with England. Wormald (1981, 155) describes it as a 'profound change in late sixteenth century government', and a sign of change was when lesser laymen not only sought offices, but squabbled over them. The change is summed up by the title of Mitchison's book, *Lordship to Patronage, Scotland 1603–1745.* The change occurred in England at least a century earlier (STARKEY 1982) and it changed earliest in Scotland in and around Edinburgh. So marked was this change that Macaulay opens his study of the classical country house in Scotland by noting how general the need was for Scottish lairds to maintain solvency by holding government posts and offices.

This change must have undermined the ideology of personal dominion reflected in the tower-houses. When the earl of Strathmore recognised that feuding and tower-houses were out of fashion, he was recognising the shift in the source of political authority. He was not recognising the growing civility of the Scots. The role of justices of the peace quickly became crucial for settling disputes, but the office was itself a source of dispute. Fletcher (1985, 94) notes that social climbing was endemic, that competition to become 'Your Right Honourable Worship' (i.e. a JP) was fierce, for it brought with it the payment of honour in daily life, even through such small gestures as the doffing of a cap. He is at pains to show that 'the language of honour was the common possession of a whole social class.' It was of vital importance to local office holders in Jacobean England and it was the same honour that was the mainspring of feuding in Jacobean Scotland (BROWN 1986).

New men had been created earlier and had rapidly cemented their power by becoming lairds. New men did the same thing in the seventeenth century, but the basis of power for the landed gentry, local office holding, was now perfectly respectable. Lord Robert Kerr may have regretted the removal of battlements from Ancrum House. His correspondent and friends clearly did not. They recognised that the country gentry squabbled no longer as defenders of their dependants, but squabbled as upholders of royal order. In 1665 the High Court of Justiciary, based in Edinburgh, issued to the MacDonalds of Sleat 'letters of fire and sword' against the MacDonalds of Keppoch. The result was that they 'killed and destroyed many . . . cut off their heads and presented them to the Privy Council to be set in a public place' (LENMAN AND PARKER 1980, 15). One's enemies were now slaughtered in the name of the king, the law, and peace.

Bibliography

Airs, Malcolm 1975. *The Making of the English Country House 1500–1640.* Architectural Press (London).

Airs, Malcolm 1982. *The Buildings of Britain: Tudor and Jacobean.* Barrie and Jenkins (London).

Apted, M. R. 1980. *Claypotts Castle.* HMSO (Edinburgh).

Barley, Maurice 1986. *Houses and History*. Faber and Faber (London).

Brown, Keith M. 1986. *Bloodfeud in Scotland 1573–1625: violence, justice and politics in an early modern society*. John Donald (Edinburgh).

Cameron, Joy 1983. *Prisons and Punishment in Scotland*. Canongate (Edinburgh).

Cockburn, J. S. (ed.) 1977. *Crime in England 1550–1800*. Methuen (London).

Coope, Rosalys 1986. 'The long gallery: its origins, development, use and decoration' *Architectural History* 29, 43–83.

Cormack, Alexander A. 1930. *Teinds and Agriculture*. Oxford University Press (Oxford).

Coulson, Charles 1979. 'Structural symbolism in medieval castle architecture' *Journal of the British Archaeological Association* 132, 73–90.

Craigie, J. (ed.) 1944–50. *The Basilikon Doron of King James VI*. 2 vols. (Edinburgh).

Cruden, Stewart 1981. *The Scottish Castle*. Holmes McDougall (Edinburgh).

Cruden, Stewart 1986. *Scottish Medieval Churches*. John Donald (Edinburgh).

Davies, R. R. 1969. 'The survival of the bloodfeud in medieval Wales' *History* 54, 338–57.

Daview, Stephen J. 1980. 'The courts and the Scottish legal system 1600–1747' in V. A. C. Gatrell, Bruce Lenman, and Geoffrey Parker (eds.) *Crime and the Law: the social history of crime in western Europe from 1500*, 120–54. Europa Press (London).

Dunbar, John G. 1978. *The Architecture of Scotland*. Batsford (London).

Dunbar, John G. 1984. 'Some aspects of the planning of Scottish royal palaces in the sixteenth century' *Journal of Architectural History* 27, 15–24.

Fletcher, Anthony J. 1985. 'Honour, reputation and local office-holding in Elizabethan and Stuart England' in A. Fletcher and J. Stevenson (eds.) *Order and Disorder in Early Modern England*, 92–115. Cambridge University Press (Cambridge).

Gatrell, V. A. C., Bruce Lenman, and Geoffrey Parker (eds.) 1980. *Crime and the Law: the social history of crime in western Europe from 1500*. Europa Press (London).

Girouard, Mark 1978. *Life in the English Country House: a social and architectural history*. Yale University Press (New Haven).

Girouard, Mark 1983. *Robert Smythson and the Elizabethan Country House*. Yale University Press (New Haven).

Gluckman, Max 1956. *Custom and Conflict in Africa*. Blackwell (Oxford).

Hay, G. 1957. *The Architecture of Scottish Post-Reformation Churches, 1560–1843*. Clarendon Press (Oxford).

Henderson, Paula 1985. 'Life at the top: sixteenth and seventeenth-century roofscapes' *Country Life* 177, 6–9.

Hewitt, George R. 1982. *Scotland under Morton 1572–80*. John Donald (Edinburgh).

Houlbrooke, Ralph Anthony 1984. *The English Family 1450–1700*. Longman (London).

Howard, Maurice 1987. *The Early Tudor Country House: architecture and politics 1490–1550*. George Philip (London).

Lenman, Bruce and Geoffrey Parker 1980. 'Crime and control in Scotland 1500–1800' *History Today* January, 13–7.

Macaulay, James 1987. *The Classical Country House in Scotland 1660–1800*. Faber and Faber (London).

MacFarlane, Alan 1981. *The Justice and the Mare's Ale*. Blackwell (Oxford).

MacGibbon, D. and T. Ross 1887–92. *The Castellated and Domestic Architecture of Scotland*. 5 vols, (Edinburgh).

Mitchison, R. 1983. *Lordship to Patronage, Scotland 1603–1745*. Edward Arnold (London).

Newman, John 1985. 'The development of the staircase in Elizabethan and Jacobean England' in André Chastel and S. Guillaume (eds.) *L'Escalier dans l'architecture de la Renaissance*, 175–8. Picard (Paris).

Newman, John 1988. 'The Elizabethan and Jacobean great house: a review of recent research' *The Archaeological Journal* 145, 365–73.

Sharpe, James Anthony 1984. *Crime in Early Modern England 1550–1750*. Longman (London).

Simpson, W. Douglas 1961. 'The tower-houses of Scotland' in E. M. Jope (ed.) *Studies in Building History*, 229–42. (London).

Simpson, W. Douglas 1968. *The Ancient Stones of Scotland*. Robert Hale (London).

Simpson, W. Douglas and R. Fawcett 1982. *Edzell Castle*. HMSO (Edinburgh).

Smith, J. T. 1970. 'Lancashire and Cheshire houses: some problems of architectural and social history' *The Archaeological Journal* 127, 156–81.

Smout, T. C. 1969. *A History of the Scottish People, 1560–1830*. Collins (London).

Starkey, D. 1982. 'From feud to faction, English politics circa 1450–1550' *History Today* November.

Stell, Geoffrey 1977. 'Architecture: the changing needs of society' in J Wormald (ed.) *Scottish Society in the Fifteenth Century*. Edward Arnold (London).

Stell, Geoffrey 1981. 'Late medieval defences in Scotland' in D. H. Caldwell (ed.) *Scottish Weapons and Fortifications*, 21–54. John Donald (Edinburgh).

Stone, L. 1979. *The Family, Sex and Marriage in England, 1500–1800*. Pelican (Harmondsworth).

Summerson, John 1977. *Architecture in Britain 1530 to 1830.* Penguin (Harmondsworth).

Tabraham, Christopher 1986. *Scottish Castles and Fortifications.* HMSO (Edinburgh).

Tranter, Nigel 1962–70. *The Fortified House in Scotland.* 5 vols., Oliver and Boyd (Edinburgh).

Wallace-Hadrill, J. M. 1959. 'The bloodfeud of the Franks' *Bulletin of the John Rylands Library* 41, reprinted as chapter 6 in *The Long-Haired Kings,* 1962, Methuen (London).

Wharrack, John 1920 *Domestic Life in Scotland 1488–1688: a sketch of the development of furniture and household usage.* Methuen (London).

Wormald (formerly Brown), Jennifer M. 1977 'The exercise of power' in J. M. Brown (ed.) *Scottish Society in the Fifteenth Century,* 33–65. Edward Arnold (London).

Wormald, Jennifer M. 1980. 'Bloodfeud, kindred and government in early modern Scotland' *Past and Present* 87, 54–97.

Wormald, Jennifer M. 1985 *Lords and Men in Scotland: bonds of manrent, 1442–1603.* John Donald (Edinburgh).

Wrightson, Keith 1982. *English Society 1580–1680.* Hutchinson (London).

Eleven

The Englishman's Home and its Study

MATTHEW JOHNSON

This chapter reviews the study of 'vernacular' or 'traditional' houses in England, concentrating on the fifteenth to eighteenth centuries. It argues that up to now such study has been narrow in focus and atheoretical in nature. It seeks to explain this theoretical backwardness relative to countries such as the USA and France in terms of the development of the sub-disciplines and, more fundamentally, the social and political context of the study of traditional houses.

This chapter starts with a rather banal question and ends, I hope, on a more profound note. The banal question is this: why is the study of vernacular architecture in England so boring? The profound answer I will attempt to offer is that it is tied in with a cluster of images, traditions, and systems of values, referred to here as the ideology of the 'Englishman's Home', that obscures the difference, the anthropological nature of the study of traditional houses. The meaning of this last statement will, I hope, become clear as the argument of the chapter unfolds.

First, though, the banal question, why so dull? It should be made clear first that this does not refer to the subject matter itself. The raw material itself, the houses and other buildings, are uniquely fascinating given their aesthetic appeal, the depth and richness of the documentary and other contextual evidence to place alongside them, the immediate relevance of their pattern of development to questions of social and economic change, and (last but by no means least) the relative warmth and comfort of measuring up an occupied house as opposed to excavating or field-walking in the rain outside. Nevertheless by the time the fruits of such research reach the printed page the chilly dampness of boredom has set in somewhere along the way. I select at random the titles of some recent papers: 'Crown-post and king-strut roofs in southern England'; 'The axial jowled post in Shropshire'; 'The internal decorative treatment of brick in 16th century Suffolk'; the list could go on. These examples are chosen deliberately because all the papers mentioned actually have something interesting and wide-ranging to say, but their authors have clearly felt it necessary to hide behind a soporific title in order to keep their status as self-respecting students of the discipline in good order.

I want to answer this question of why the insipidness by looking first at some of the underlying assumptions that scholars in this field hold. I will then relate these assumptions to wider aspects of communication (or lack of it) between disciplines such as archaeology, traditional history, and architectural studies, before going on to consider how this situation arose in the first place.

The study of traditional architecture

The study of medieval and post-medieval archaeology in England is characterised by an impressive body of collected evidence that is limited by extreme theoretical conservatism or 'innocence', as the prehistorian David Clarke put it (1968, 20–4), in its interpretation. This is particularly true of the study of traditional architecture in England. Vernacular architectural studies, like historical archaeology in general, blossomed after the war. Since then a plethora of regional and national studies have been produced, again characterised by high standards of recording and primary analysis, but accompanied by implicit and 'common-sensical' theorising. Indeed, much writing is positively anti-theoretical: the largely hostile reaction to Lawrence's paper 'The interpretation of vernacular architecture', is typical (LAWRENCE 1983; MERCER AND HUTTON 1984). This overtly anti-theoretical stance is both unfortunate and misguided. We all use theory whether we like it or not, in the sense that we all bring assumptions and wider values and aims to our work. The only question is whether that theory should be implicit and inarticulate, or clearly and explicitly stated and thought through.

This proposition can be seen when considering previous work in vernacular architecture: different scholars make different sets of theoretical assumptions, though the analysis of these assumptions is rendered problematic by their implicit nature. For the purposes of this argument I shall rather arbitrarily distinguish two major types of approach within this mass of work: typological studies and the economic approach.

Typological studies

Typological studies are defined as local descriptions and classifications of house types, building materials and techniques, and decorative styles, with the intention of producing controls over dating and regional variation. Such work is an obvious and useful first step in vernacular architecture, establishing basic dating parameters and guidelines.

Such studies are epitomised by the work of Cecil Hewitt (1969; 1980). Over the last thirty years Hewitt has built up a detailed typology of carpentry joint forms and other details, based mainly on his work in Essex. While Hewitt's efforts at collation are second to none, and his typologies a huge advance on what went before, his work has been criticised on the basis of its empirical validity, and on the general assumptions underlying the typological method in the first place (MERCER 1975, 95). The major problems with such studies parallel those of culture-historical approaches in archaeology in general: they offer little hold over variability, involve implicit or unverifiable assumptions, and offer little potential for meaningful generalisation. (Indeed, one of the interesting aspects of such work is the degree to which they force would-be critics, such as the author, into a critical position resembling much of the early New Archaeology.)

It is difficult, when using regional classifications such as those of Brunskill (1981) or Harris (1978), to answer basic questions concerning the number and type which exist on the ground. Studies often rely on an unsystematic sample of housing with little explicit concern either over how this relates to the population under study as a whole, or with its randomness. For example, Brunskill's (1978) study of regional house types and building materials is an interesting first step, but is based on a statistically suspect sampling procedure and is of little value without more intensive studies of particular regions. Again, Colum Giles (1986, xix) uses the phrase 'fairly random' in a less than precise manner, while one well-known scholar in this field assured me in conversation that her selection of buildings was totally random; she relied on 'purely chance' contacts through the local golf and Conservative clubs.

Implicit assumptions abound in this approach: for example, the assumption of social emulation, i.e. that stylistic innovation starts at the top of the social scale and then 'filters down', is rarely felt to be in need of qualification or justification (JOPE 1973). Again, typologies are felt to be readily explicable in terms of 'the rise in comfort, accommodation and convenience' of the domestic unit, and 'the concentration of any one type at each time' (MERCER 1975, 1), with often little questioning of what that domestic unit is, how it changes through time and space, and whether culturally-specific notions of comfort, accommodation, and convenience may not vary between periods and societies. The point is not that social emulation does not happen, typologies do not work or that rises in comfort do not occur, but that the reasons why these processes take place need to be explored rather than assumed.

Finally, such studies tend to give a highly particular account of the development of architecture in a particular area which lacks comparative

potential in two senses. First, comparative analysis between regions is
hampered by stress on the unique style of a particular area. This point parallels Binford's claim for archaeology in general, that we should be study-
ing variability rather than similarity (BINFORD 1972, 22). Second, the typology appears to have no relation to the society that produced it: crown-
posts become less ornate, windows move from roll-moulded to ovolo-
moulded type, lobby entries replace through-passages for no particular
reason other than either the internal evolutionary logic of the typology or
some vague process defined as 'fashion'. Houses become 'fetishised'
(PFAFFENBERGER 1988); that is, their changing form is treated as a thing-in-
itself, masking the social relations that in fact cause that form to change.

The economic approach

Studies employing what is called here the 'economic approach' take the
relationship of housing to local economic trends as the central theme.
Again, the theorising of this school is rarely explicit, but the basic assumption appears to be that the numbers and size of a region's stock of traditional houses will tell us something, in a fairly straightforward manner,
about the economic history of the area.

This is undoubtedly an advance on the typological school since buildings
are at least being treated as historical products, indicators of past economic
forces at work in an area, rather than as 'artefacts-in-themselves'. The classic example of this school of thought is W. G. Hoskins' thesis of the Great
Rebuilding and its subsequent modification (HOSKINS 1953; MACHIN 1977;
ALCOCK 1983; JOHNSON 1987).

There are several methodological and theoretical problems with such an
approach, however. The first is the assumption often made of a straightforward wealth/houses relationship. An example is Hoskins' (1953, 50)
discussion of the rebuilding as a consequence of the relationship between
fixed rents and rising corn prices. This has to be qualified in a number of
ways.

First, the number of houses on the ground need bear no direct relationship to past numbers of houses. This is a point made elegantly by Currie
(1988, 6), who modelled the attrition rate of fire on a Cambridgeshire
village and concluded that 'apparent waves of rebuilding may be illusory.
The richest areas may have the fewest old houses.' Any claim of past economic change made on numbers of surviving houses therefore needs careful and critical examination.

Second, any statement made relating wealth and house-building needs
careful consideration both of the classes of people involved and the source
of wealth under discussion. Thus Hoskins (1964; 1968) has argued that
wealth derived from corn harvests will be treated in different ways to
wealth derived from other sources, such as cloth production. He argues
convincingly that the unpredictability of arable farming and fluctuations in

yield make it difficult to invest year-by-year in a new house. Pearson (1985, 116) has argued in the context of the Lancashire Pennines that the situation was more complex than a measure of absolute wealth levels would indicate; security of tenure, social position, and involvement in textile production make the situation far more difficult to disentangle. Machin (1978, 155) has commented that in Yetminster, 'whilst men required money to build . . . the degree of investment was largely determined by the answer to the question "who will be the eventual beneficiary?".' Parallel comments relating differing forms of tenure, in particular copyhold versus freehold, to house-building rates may be criticised on analogous grounds and needs to be similarly qualified.

A more fundamental point, one central to this critique, is that the relationship between wealth levels and house-building is highly problematic in the first place. Whether a household will invest its money in architecture is a decision that will vary from culture to culture and from social group to social group. For example, many peasant societies have a strong ethic against reinvesting surplus money back into the household. Rather, there is strong pressure to dissipate the surplus on feasts, religious celebrations, and similar events, bringing social prestige rather than material wealth back to the family unit (SHANIN 1971, 15). This pressure derives in part from the strongly egalitarian ethic that exists (BAILEY 1971, 19) as well as the different economic logic operating in many peasant communities (WOLF 1966). If we want to understand the decision to put money into houses over other activities, we have to investigate the cultural strength of any 'peasant ethic' of this nature, the subjective level of security as well as the objective level as represented by legal terms of tenure, and the particular world-view or position of the social group or groups doing the building. We need to examine the parallel social and ideational changes accompanying those encompassed by J. T. Smith's (1970, 147) observation that 'in a general way, farmhouses of the 16th to 17th centuries reflect a profound change in social relations involving . . . the disappearance of the peasant in the feudal sense and the emergence of a class of yeomen . . . who, by comparison with their forebears, were free men in an economic as well as legal sense.'

Not only does the economic approach have difficulties explaining why, culturally, a community or social group will make the decision to build, it has problems addressing the question of form. In other words, it can answer the question 'how many?' but not necessarily that of 'why that particular type?'. The way two houses of equal size are laid out obviously varies and it is difficult to account for that variability by reference to economic factors alone. Even rooms given labels referring to economic function such as 'workshops' or 'dairies' beg the question since the functions of these rooms might easily take place elsewhere or be arranged in a different pattern. Rather, we can reasonably expect the way houses are laid out to vary according to the patterns of daily life within them: according to social and cultural factors as well as purely economic ones.

One escape from this problem has been proposed, again implicitly, by Smith and Barley. Peter Smith has argued that plan forms show greater or lesser degrees of evolution according to their distance from London (SMITH 1985, 686–9); Barley (1967, 760) has echoed this view when he ascribes the 'conservatism' of houses in the north and west to 'remoteness and poverty'. Diffusion of form certainly plays a role in traditional architecture (JOPE 1973), but again such an approach fails to answer questions of cultural attitude: why did Wales and the north and west of England choose to remain conservative in plan?; what social factors caused them to lag behind the lowlands?; why did they eventually gave way to the national trend when they did?; and so on.

It can therefore be concluded that economic factors are themselves often only proximal rather than ultimate causes, as Hoskins (1953, 53) himself recognised. We have to question why wealth was accumulated in a particular area or by a particular group at a particular time.

Background

It is important to stress the underlying disciplinary and social factors surfacing in these debates. The typological approach appears very often to be taken by scholars trained in art history and architecture, also by amateurs and local groups. Consequently the interest is in the 'artefact-in-itself' and in the immediate context of the village or town. What I have termed the economic approach has very often been articulated by professionals trained in historical or geographical disciplines. Such scholars very often assume a 'common-sensical' approach to meaning and identify the process of understanding the wider historical context exclusively with the technique of documentary analysis (e.g. MACHIN 1977, 56).

It is also important to stress that such approaches were appropriate to a certain place and time in the development of vernacular architectural studies. The typological approach succeeded in establishing the basic parameters of the objects of study, while economic factors are obviously important and are a logical first place to look for the historical context of housing changes. I am very conscious of only being able to make the above critical comments given a generation of detailed research of a high standard at the level of basic interpretation.

There is much exciting work going on in the study of traditional buildings in areas outside England and outside vernacular architectural studies. There are antecedents in England itself for cultural and social studies. First and most notably is the work of S. O. Addy (1898), based on research in the Sheffield area. Addy noted the distinctive 'Englishness' of the bay system of design, and attempted to relate this to 'Anglo-Saxon' systems of measurement and thought. As a pioneering effort this was a classic work, though it now appears quite ahistorical and unsystematic in nature. Innocent (1917), though interested more in techniques of building construction, accepted Addy's basic thesis. Sir Cyril Fox and Lord Raglan (1951) are usually noted as laying out the definitive methodology for vernacular architectural studies in their three volumes on Glamorgan houses, but that work also contained interpretive elements of importance. Fox and Raglan classified their houses into three phases, medieval, sub-medieval, and Renaissance and, in addition to environmental and economic factors, saw underlying cultural change as driving the transition. In particular they identified what they saw as a rise in the need for material comfort and privacy arising from 'Renaissance' ideas. The architectural result was more segregated house plans and symmetrical façades through time. Unfortunately, they did not go on from this to ask why Renaissance ideas gained in popularity at this point in history and how this might relate to contemporary social change either within Glamorgan or in a wider sense. Raglan (1957) was also interested in social evolutionary theory, and went on to claim, in a paper entitled 'The house: shelter or temple?', that all houses could fundamentally be seen as a union between the Earth Mother and Sky Father. Like Addy, this paper was ahistorical and unscholarly by modern standards, but raised some interesting points (for example relating tidiness and the concept of the sacred) and is worth mentioning.

All these early writers were influenced to a greater or lesser extent by the tradition of folklife studies. I therefore suggest that as the economic approach subsequently developed, and as the study of traditional architecture became more rigorous in its methodology, the intuitive leaps of faith and lack of historical specificity involved in studies such as Addy's or the observations of Ewart Evans (1966) became more readily apparent. Relating houses to economic changes such as harvest fluctuations or local industrial development needed ever-tighter date brackets which the folklife tradition was unable to supply. In addition, houses were seen, quite correctly, less and less as part of a living cultural tradition and more as indicators of past historical change. Consequently such ideas lost currency as the economic approach became dominant.

However, such approaches have been further developed in other countries. In France, the Musée des Arts et Traditions Populaires has produced a fine series of regional volumes (for example BUCAILLE and LÉVI-STRAUSS 1980) whose basic approach claims to be derived from Claude Lévi-Strauss's thought on the transmission of culture in traditional societies. Houses and farmsteads are treated as embodiments of cultural values: their layout, it is claimed, expresses the timeless cultural order of the pre-industrial rural community (LÉVI-STRAUSS 1963) and accounts of housing change have been integrated into wider interpretations of changing material life (BRAUDEL 1973, 192–226). Again, however, the same sorts of problems are readily apparent: it is difficult to find a socio-economic explanation of change through time rather than an ahistorical and often naïve description of the unchanging nature of rural ways of life. Analysis tends as a result to degenerate rapidly into a rather dry typology. In addition, similar methodological problems recur: selection of a sample of farmsteads to study appears, from examining the Musée volumes, to be haphazard rather than truly random.

A stronger body of research has been carried out on the east coast of the United States. Here the influences and interpretations have been more varied, but an underlying stress has always been on architecture as carrying cultural meaning. Upton and Vlach (1986, xxiii), for example, comment: 'the study of intention becomes the ultimate one in vernacular architectural studies, because it is the study of people acting. It shows us people . . . engaged with their surroundings in a critical way, people making their own histories in the face of authorities trying to make it for them.'

Studies of traditional architecture are carried out under the general heading of 'material life' (e.g. ST GEORGE 1988) and have stressed the house as the centre of cultural and social values and activities. The best-known example of such work is Henry Glassie's classic book, *Folk Housing in Middle Virginia*. Such studies have often stressed the central empirical problem of the introduction of the Georgian Order into eighteenth-century vernacular architecture, relating it to social and economic factors via its 'restructuring of architectural authority' (UPTON 1982, 95). Through its stress on cultural meaning in everyday life this work finds a ready home within the study of American material life as a whole (ST GEORGE 1988) and within social history. Isaac's (1983) classic study of eighteenth-century Virginia, for instance, draws on the work of Glassie and other writers to put together an 'ethnography' of everyday life, drawing on the methodology of symbolic anthropologists such as Geertz.

The Englishman's home

> Looking round, with a sudden thought, from a terrace on which I rested for awhile, I realised that there were no small houses to be seen. Apparently the single house, and possibly even the household, had vanished. Here and there among the greenery were palace-like buildings, but the house and the cottage, which form such characteristic features of our own English landscape, had disappeared.
>
> 'Communism', said I to myself.
>
> H. G. Wells, *The Time Traveller*

Part of the answer to the divergent disciplinary development of vernacular architectural studies must be sought in the differing cultural backgrounds within which different scholars work. It is not difficult to see traditional houses and their meanings in terms of a classic piece of ideology in the Marxist sense. The superstructure of late capitalism has a system of

values that is legitimised through the popular image of traditional buildings. This system of values centres around the notion of the 'natural' unit
of the nuclear family and household, for which the traditional house acts as
a metonym: the unchanging nature of the rural community, in which the
lower classes defer to the squire and honest, hard-working yeoman; the
notion of the group of traditional houses clustered round the village green
as an image of quintessential Englishness. This constellation of images
serves to naturalise the structure of gender relations and the family unit
under late capitalism, to give the transient structure of modern class relations an endless historical past, and thus to tie in twentieth-century middle-
class values with a concept of 'Englishness' applicable to all classes and
groups. It also masks the very real conflict tearing at the heart of both past
rural communities and the political present in its image of a peaceful rural
idyll.

Such an analysis bears a lot of truth, and is fairly undeniable as far as it
goes. It also serves as a gloss on the arguments presented above, where it
was seen how the various approaches to traditional architecture have a disciplinary basis to them. Underlying these disciplinary differences, I suggested, was a whole series of notions about the 'natural' and 'common
sensical', such as the desire for material comfort and convenience, and
particularly the desire for privacy. These themes, in their stress on privacy
and consequently individualism, and the primacy of material wants, represent values that may or may not have been present in the past but are
treated as natural and inevitable under industrial capitalism. Consequently
we feel little or no intellectual need to question or theorise them.

This is one reason why so much that is written on traditional architecture
is so dull, because the underlying causes of architectural change that might
be explored are assumed, rather than treated anthropologically. The story
of traditional houses becomes a strongly teleological one, a story with a
definite, preordained direction and outcome, in no need of further ex-
plication or comment.

This point may be clarified by considering the architecture of other
cultures. In study after study (DONLEY 1982; CUNNINGHAM 1964; BOURDIEU
1960; HUMPHREY 1974) fascinating patterns have been outlined relating
domestic space to society, because that society itself is set up as a problem,
an anthropological phenomenon different to us. In short, the established
view appears to be, for example, that the association of women and
women's labour with hearths is a link that needs explanation in East Africa
but can be assumed without comment back home in seventeenth-century
Essex. It follows that when we question these assumptions, we not only
attempt to make studies of traditional houses more anthropological, more
rigorous, and also more interesting, but our work is by its very nature intimately involved in a political challenge of the supposedly natural and
common-sensical nature of those values.

Such an analysis and challenge does not take place within a cultural vacuum. There is the historical tradition of Victorian and later uses of elements of vernacular; the Oxford Movement of the nineteenth century linked this, together with the use of Gothic, with a developed view of the rural past which stressed the values of community rent asunder, in their view, by industrialisation. For such a group the images of traditional houses were part of a conservative reaction against industrialisation and economic liberalism, a strand taken up also by the early non-Marxist socialist movements, most notably William Morris and the Arts and Crafts Movement, but also earlier than this Thomas Paine and other writers stressed the rights of the free-born Englishman (THOMPSON 1963, 77–101). This strand continues in the work of the explicitly conservative architect Quinlan Terry, who ironically stresses the craft tradition in implicitly Marxist terms, bemoaning the alienation of worker from object in modern architecture.

At the same time the urban middle classes have appropriated the meanings of traditional houses for their own dwellings through the use of 'Stockbroker Tudor' and related styles (MILLER 1982). Here again the stress is on tradition, though here it becomes the preserve of the middle classes, opposed to the modernism of institutional and working-class housing. Finally, a further complexity is added by the counterpoint of the Georgian tradition and the centrality of the non-traditional 'stately home' to the rise of the heritage industry (HEWISON 1987). Images of traditional houses have played little explicit part in this, sandwiched between the great houses on the one hand and the recreated working-class communities of the North on the other. At a more local, individual level the meanings of 'old houses' vary along lines of age, gender, and class in a way similar to that described by Yentsch (1988).

Rather than a simple, unified ideology of the middle classes being presented here, traditional houses owe their continuing power and social meaning to their carrying of diverse and often apparently contradictory social messages. They have become part of a wider field upon which each social group can mobilise its view of the world and the historical past. And these social messages are not ones at odds with 'reality', with the meanings involved with the construction and use of the houses from the fifteenth to seventeenth centuries. Just as now their meanings are tied up with the diverse and often contradictory sentiments of middle-class life, so their meanings were then caught up in that web. Just as symbols now acquire their power from being derived from the past, so sixteenth-century symbols derived their power from referring to a medieval past.

The discourse built around traditional houses may have become partly overt rather than purely implicit, but the same process of reassigning meaning continues. Individuals do so, moreover, 'under circumstances directly encountered, given, and transmitted from the past. The tradition of all the dead generations weighs like a nightmare on the brain of the liv-

ing' (MARX 1869, opening passage). It is that tradition, that nightmare, that
archaeologists and historians move within, and it is that tradition and that
nightmare whose historicity we are attempting to understand.

Acknowledgements

I would like to thank Ross Samson for asking me to write this chapter, and
two anonymous referees for acute and constructive criticisms.

Bibliography

Addy, S. O. 1898. *The Evolution of the English House*. Allen and Unwin
  (London).

Alcock, N. 1977. 'The Great Rebuilding and its later stages. *Vernacular
  Architecture* 14, 45–47.

Bailey, Frank (ed.) 1971. *Gifts and Poison*. Blackwell (Oxford).

Barley, Maurice W. 1967. 'Rural housing in England' in Joan Thirsk (ed.)
  The Agrarian History of England and Wales Volume Four: 1500–1640, 696–
  766. Cambridge University Press (Cambridge).

Beaudry, Mary (ed.) 1988. *Documentary Archaeology in the New World*. Cambridge University Press (Cambridge).

Binford, Lewis R. 1964. 'Archaeology as anthropology' *American Antiquity*
  28, 217–25.

Bourdieu, Pierre 1960. *Algeria 1960*. Cambridge University Press
  (Cambridge).

Braudel, Ferdinand 1973. *Capitalism and Material Life 1400–1800*.
  Weidenfeld and Nicholson (London).

Brunskill, R. W. 1978. 'Distributions of building materials and some plan
  types in the domestic architecture of England and Wales' *Transactions of
  the Ancient Monuments Society of England and Wales* 23 (new series),
  41–66.

Brunskill, R. W. 1981. *Traditional Buildings of Britain*. Gollancz (London).

Bucaille, R. and L. Lévi-Strauss 1980. *L'Architecture Rurale Française: Corpus
  des Genres, des Types et des Varientes: Bourgogne*. Payot (Paris).

Clarke, David L. 1968. *Analytical Archaeology*. Methuen (London).

Cunningham, C. E. 1964. 'Order in the Atoni house' *Bijdragen Tot de Taal-,
  Land- en Volkenkunde* 120, 34–68.

Currie, C. 1988. 'Time and chance: modelling the attrition of old houses'
  Vernacular Architecture 19, 1–9.

Donley, Linda W. 1982. 'House power: Swahili space and symbolic markers' in I. Hodder (ed.) *Symbolic and Structural Archaeology*, 63–73. Cambridge University Press (Cambridge).

Ewart Evans, George 1966. *The Pattern Under the Plough: aspects of the folk-life of East Anglia*. Faber (London).

Fox, Sir Cyril and Lord Raglan 1951. *Monmouthshire Houses: A study of building techniques and smaller house-plans in the 15th to 17th centuries*. National Museum of Wales (Cardiff).

Giles, Colum 1985. *Rural Houses of West Yorkshire, 1400–1830*. Her Majesty's Stationery Office (London).

Glassie, Henry 1975. *Folk Housing in Middle Virginia*. University of Tennessee Press (Knoxville).

Harris, Richard 1978. *Discovering Timber-Framed Buildings*. Shire (Aylesbury).

Hewison, R. 1987. *The Heritage Industry: Britain in an climate of decline*. Methuen (London).

Hewitt, Cecil 1969. *The Development of Carpentry, 1200–1700: An Essex Study*. David and Charles (London).

Hewitt, Cecil 1980. *English Historic Carpentry*. Philimore (London).

Hoskins, W. G. 1953. 'The rebuilding of rural England, 1570–1640' *Past and Present* 4, 44–59.

Hoskins, W. G. 1964. 'Harvest fluctuations and English economic history, 1480–1619' *Agricultural History Review* 12, 28–46.

Hoskins, W. G. 1968. 'Harvest fluctuations and English economic history, 1620–1759' *Agricultural History Review* 16, 15–31.

Humphrey, C. 1974. 'Inside a Mongolian tent' *New Society* 31, 45–8.

Innocent, C. 1916. *The Development of English Building Construction*. Cambridge University Press (Cambridge).

Isaac, R. 1983. *The Transformation of Virginia, 1760–1820*. University of North Carolina Press (Chapel Hill).

Johnson, Matthew H. 1987. 'Assumptions and interpretations of the Great Rebuilding' *Archaeological Review from Cambridge* 5:2.

Jope, E. M. 1973. 'The transmission of new ideas: archaeological evidence for implant and dispersal' *World Archaeology* 4, 368–73.

Lawrence, R. J. 1983. 'Interpretation in vernacular architecture' *Vernacular Architecture* 14, 19–28.

Lévi-Strauss, Claude 1963. *Structural Anthropology*. Basic Books (New York).

Machin, Robert 1977. 'The Great Rebuilding: a reassessment' *Past and Present* 77, 33–56.

Machin, Robert 1978. *The Houses of Yetminster*. University of Bristol, Dept. of Extra-Mural Studies (Bristol).

Marx, Karl 1869. *Der achtzehnte Brumaire des Louis Bonaparte*. (Hamburg). *The 18th Brumaire of Louis Bonaparte*, first published in English in *The*

People, 1897. The Socialist Labor Party of the United States (New York).

Mercer, Eric 1975. *English Vernacular Houses: A study of traditional farmhouses and cottages*. Her Majesty's Stationery Office (London).

Mercer, Eric and Barbara Hutton 1984. 'Reply to Lawrence 1983' *Vernacular Architecture* 15, 12–14.

Miller, D. 1984. 'Modernism and suburbia' in Miller and Tilley (ed.), 37–49.

Miller, D. and Christopher Tilley (eds.) 1984. *Ideology, Power and Prehistory*. Cambridge University Press (Cambridge).

Pearson, S. 1985. *Rural Houses of the Lancashire Pennines*. Her Majesty's Stationery Office (London).

Pfaffenberger, B. 1988. 'Fetishised objects and humanised nature: towards an anthropology of technology' *Man* 23:2, 236–52.

Raglan, Lord 1957. 'The house: shelter or temple?' *Archaeologia Cambrensis* 106, 72–89.

Shanin, Teodor (ed.) 1971. *Peasants and Peasant Societies*. Penguin (Harmondsworth).

Smith, J. T. 1975. 'The evolution of the English peasant house to the late 17th century: the evidence of buildings' *Journal of the British Archaeological Association* 33 (third series), 122–47.

Smith, Peter 1985. 'Rural building in Wales' in Joan Thirsk (ed.) *Agrarian History of England and Wales Volume Five: 1640–1750. two: agrarian change*, 686–813. Cambridge University Press (Cambridge).

Thompson, E. P. 1963. *The Making of the English Working Class*. Gollancz (London).

Upton, Dell 1982. 'Vernacular domestic architecture in 18th century Virginia' *Winterthur Portfolio* 17, 95–119.

Upton, D. and J. M. Vlach (eds.) 1986. *Common Places: readings in American vernacular architecture*. University of Georgia Press (London).

Wolf, Eric R. 1966. *Peasants*. Prentice-Hall (New Jersey).

Yentsch, Ann 1988. 'Archaeology is not enough' in Beaudry (ed.), 5–17.

Twelve

Analysing Small Building Plans: a Morphological Approach

FRANK E. BROWN

This chapter introduces a systematic, geometrical technique which can be used to clarify the internal organisation of small, rectangular building-plans. The plans of two modern dwelling-types – the municipal 'cottage' built for the working classes (c. 1919) and the private semi-detached house (1920s and 1930s) – are explored using this method. Through a dialogue between historical evidence and plan-analysis, the principal influences on each design are inferred and their social significance discussed.

This chapter explores the question of the organisation of domestic space, and discusses, by way of some contemporary examples, a particular approach to building-plan analysis. The approach was developed in the field of configurational studies and is known as 'rectangular dissection' (STEADMAN 1973; MITCHELL, STEADMAN, AND LIGGETT 1976). It is a generative process, in which plan layouts are produced by the geometrical process of dividing a basic rectangle, representing the building plan, into smaller rectangles, which may be taken to represent rooms, compartments, and transitional spaces (stairs and hallways). Since this particular method is, by definition, concerned with packings of rectangles, it is not suitable for dealing with plans of curvilinear form. It must be said at the outset, therefore, that it will not provide a means of analysing Zulu kraals, and is not applicable to round-houses. There are other, related approaches, however – most notably Stiny's 'shape grammars' (1975; 1980) – which can be used to tackle curved as well as rectilinear arrangements.

The field where the 'dissection' technique comes into its own is that comprising simple rectangular shapes which contain relatively few component elements. Since a vast number of house-plans, old and new, display precisely these geometrical characteristics, the method emerges as a particularly useful tool for the analysis of domestic space. To judge by Chapman's contribution, it would seem to lend itself as readily to houses of the Bulgarian Chalcolithic as to those of post-war Britain: only among the extremely large, multi-roomed plans of Poljanica is the technique likely to be stretched (see CHAPMAN and my accompanying comment in this volume).

As an incidental point, it should be noted that while the method is based on division or dissection of a simple rectangle, this does not mean that plans of irregular profile have to be discounted. It is perfectly possible to simulate plans with protrusions or extensions by defining in each case an additional rectangle to represent the adjoining void or external space. A void can likewise be specified within the building envelope in order to generate an internal lightwell or courtyard (see STEADMAN 1983, 13–14). Experiments of this kind have in fact been carried out in connection with the nineteenth-century terrace house, and are described in detail elsewhere (BROWN AND STEADMAN 1987, 408–20).

The crucial fact to note is that, viewed as a packing of rectangles, there is only a limited number of forms that a dwelling-plan can take. This limitation is all-important but tends to be masked by extraneous factors, such as differences in detailing, materials, and external architectural features. It is also obscured by dimensional variation among plans. For any given plan 'shape', there is an infinite number of actual plan possibilities, since the size of individual rooms and the overall envelope can vary infinitely. If, however, these differences of relative dimension are ignored, it is possible to reduce all plans of the same shape (or topology) to a single dimensionless representation. This dimensionless representation may be regarded as the canonical version of the plan.

Looking at plan layouts in this way, we can see that the number of possible arrangements is often very small indeed. Figure 12.1 presents the complete range of options for plans of up to four rooms. For one room there is, of course, only one conceivable arrangement. But if we discount Euclidean transformations (i.e. geometrical rotations or reflections of the same layout), then two-room plans are found also to have only one possible arrangement. For three rooms there are two possible options; and for four there are still only six possibilities.

The exclusion at this stage of 'handed' and rotated versions of the same plan is not intended to deny the importance of these differences. On the contrary, the fact that a plan is oriented one way and not another may be highly significant in social terms, as the discussion of the semi-detached house will try to show. The point is that these differences need not, in geometrical terms, be regarded as basic. For the purposes of plan-genera-

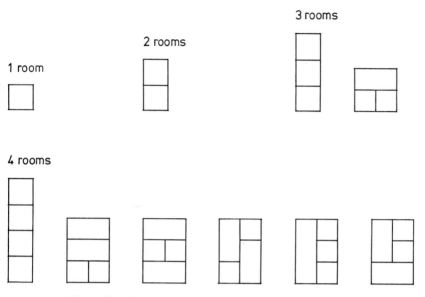

Figure 12.1 All rectangular-dissection plans for up to four rooms in dimensionless representation.

tion, the dimensionless representations given in Figure 12.1 are sufficient basis for an algorithm which will produce all possible arrangements in all possible orientations.

Beyond four rooms, the number of possibilities multiplies dramatically, and we quickly reach astronomical figures. Plans of ten rooms, for example, can be arranged in more than half-a-million different ways. This 'combinatorial explosion' is a familiar feature of such systems, and makes enumeration impractical when many rooms are involved. With very large buildings, however, other structural or organising principles normally come into play: rooms are laid out along corridors or other kinds of circulation route, or they are grouped together in separate blocks or 'wings'. By breaking a plan down into sub-complexes, it may prove possible to generate systematically the plans of buildings with many more rooms than those examined here. This extension of the dissection technique is currently being explored with reference to modern non-domestic buildings. Here, however, we are concerned with small plans only. Most dwellings come into this category, so that in most cases the range of plan options can be enumerated and catalogued exhaustively.

The reason for stressing the issue of complete enumeration is not simply that it raises questions of mathematical interest. (Fascinating though questions of mathematical representation may be, many of these will inevitably

be marginal, if not tangential, to the central themes of archaeological enquiry.) Its significance lies in the fact that, once the complete range of feasible configurations is known, it is very much easier to see what is missing in
any particular context. When a corpus of actual or extant plans is set
against the full spectrum of geometrical possibilities, it is immediately evident which plans did *not* occur. Informed guesses can be made as to why this
was so, and why a particular group of plans arose or was selected at the
expense of other feasible solutions.

These conjectures can then be tested by introducing additional constraints into the process of rectangular dissection – constraints of room
location, access pattern, room dimensions – and observing their effect.
This process of conjecture-and-test may be done fairly rapidly with the help
of an automated system for generating dissections, such as Flemming's
'DIS' programme (1978). Once a plausible set of constraints is arrived at,
i.e. one which produces in a plausible manner the plans actually found, we
are in a position to speculate on whether or not the hypothesised constraints, individually or collectively, have any social meaning.

The procedure is better explained by means of some examples. Two case-
studies are presented here, the subjects of both being historical and fairly
recent (see BROWN AND STEADMAN 1987). One is the working-class 'cottage'
designed by local authorities in the years immediately following World War
I; the second is the familiar semi-detached house, erected in large numbers
by speculative developers in the 1920s and 1930s. As small house-types,
both are amenable to plan analysis by rectangular dissections. Since they
are both modern, a good deal of background information is also available,
making interpretation a less hazardous business than if we were dependent
upon physical evidence alone.

The forces that shaped the municipal 'cottage' are much better documented than those that governed the inter-war 'semi'. The reason is that
the former was consciously designed by professional architects, following
new standards set down in great detail in government reports and pamph-
lets and implemented by way of design manuals. In the case of the developers' semi-detached, on the other hand, internal planning was seldom discussed, but tended to follow certain well-tried patterns and formulae.

For the first example, then, we have an embarrassment of riches and can
use the documentation to specify accurately the constraints that impinged
on plan-layout. With the latter, the constraints are much more open to con-
jecture: this indeterminacy brings it closer to the situation that the archaeologist will encounter.

The working-class cottage, c. 1919

Public housing in this country was really a product of the First World War.
Before 1914, intervention in the housing market had been extremely
limited in scope. Only with the passing of the Housing and Town Planning

Act of 1919 did the provision of housing for the working classes become mandatory. In the years between the wars, local authorities went on to build approximately three-quarters of a million dwellings.

The fundamental aim of the municipal housing programme was to make high-quality, spacious dwellings available to the workers, who would otherwise have been unable to afford them. But the housing that emerged in 1919 was not merely generous in size and facilities, it was also designed according to completely new and different principles. Such municipal housing as there was prior to the First World War had tended to repeat the pattern set by the Victorian terrace: it was built to a narrow frontage with the best living room or parlour at the front and the scullery behind. In the standard byelaw terrace, the scullery was contained within a back extension which could project a long way into the yard. It was the back extension that contained the scullery, and beyond this might be a whole string of storage spaces and sheds, as well as the outside w.c. (Figure 12.2). The main rooms of the house were always in the same position irrespective of orientation. The back rooms on the ground floor were commonly dark, whatever the aspect, through overshadowing.

The new workers' cottage was intended to break with this tradition. By making the frontage of the house much wider, the architects sought to bring sunlight and air into all the principal rooms of the house. Most important of all, the back extension, which was regarded as a particularly objectionable feature, was to be banished. Raymond Unwin had argued passionately against this in his Fabian pamphlet 'Cottage plans and common sense' (1902): 'These projections effectually shade the rooms from such sunshine as they might otherwise get, and impede the free access of fresh air. . . . Every house in a row should contain all its rooms and offices (i.e. w.c. and coal-store) under the main roof, and present an open and fair surface to sun and air on both its free sides' (quoted in SWENARTON 1981, 20). From now on, the self-contained plan was to become the model.

The new design principles were enunciated in the Tudor Walters Report (1918), which included a series of model plans accompanied by detailed recommendations as to external and internal design. These recommendations were repeated with little alteration in the Local Government Board's 'Housing Manual' of 1919, where they were illustrated by twelve type-plans, intended to give a general idea of what was required. Every house was now to be designed to suit its specific site conditions and ensure that sunlight entered the living room. Eight of the type-plans were for self-contained, two-storey cottages, and showed solutions that were appropriate for different orientations (Figure 12.3).

In our experiment, we restricted ourselves to the larger type of house – that with a parlour – and focused on the ground floor layout. Six rooms in all were specified, representing the principal spaces required at ground level. A set of constraints was then drawn up from the recommendations

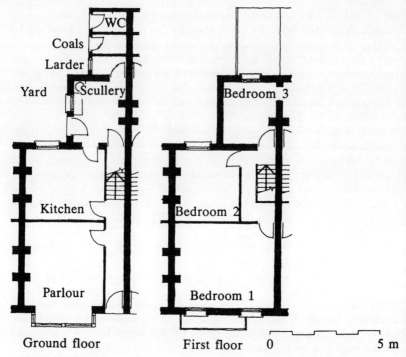

Figure 12.2 Standard terraced house with back projection on both floors (after Burnett).

and requirements of the Manual. These were of two sorts: 1) adjacency constraints, reflecting requirements of aspect (orientation), prospect (view out), and access (internal and external connections); and 2) dimensional constraints. It should perhaps be stressed here, since it is central to the approach, that access relations and other topological characteristics are embedded in the very process of rectangular dissection. Though they not represented visually, e.g. in the form of an access graph, they are, once specified, built into the search procedure of the computer programme. The programme will generate those layouts, and only those layouts, that meet the specifications. By matching topology to geometry, the generative procedure helps us gauge the influence of such things as access requirements on plan form in a way which is not possible when treating these requirements in isolation.

The complete table of constraints is shown in Table 12.1. As will be seen, the living room is given a southerly aspect and is connected to the scullery and the hall. In terms of aspect, the Manual was unequivocal: for the living room, 'The best aspect is south-east, and it must never have a northerly aspect except when sunlight can be admitted at the other end of the room'.

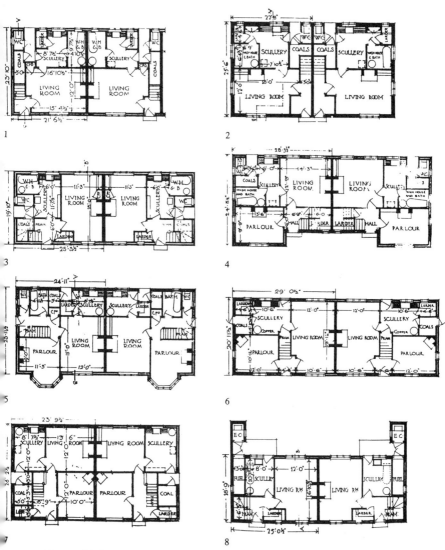

Figure 12.3 Suggested plans for self-contained cottages, from the Manual on the Preparation of State-aided Housing Schemes (Local Government Board 1919).

Internally, the room was to 'be arranged with as few doors as practicable' (1919, 9). In the Tudor Walters Report, it was considered that 'any doors in the living-room beyond the one from the lobby and the one from the scullery are best avoided if a comfortable room is to be secured' (1918, 30).

Table 12.1 Set of constraints for the south-facing parlour house derived from the Manual on the Preparation of State-aided Housing Schemes (Local Government Board 1919).

Space	Adj.[a]	Dimensions (m.)		Area (sq. m.)		Aspect ratio
		min.	max.	min.	max.	
1 Living room	s, 3, 4	3.0	8.0	16.7	30.0	2.0
2 Parlour	s, 4	2.4	6.0	11.2	20.0	2.0
3 Scullery	n, 1, 5	1.8	6.0	7.5	15.0	2.5
4 Hall and stairs	s, 1, 2	1.5	4.0	5.25	8.0	4.0
5 WC and coal store	w, 3	1.5	4.5	5.0	10.0	4.0
6 Larder	n	0.9	1.8	1.1	1.5	2.5
0 Overall plan width		6.0	9.0	53.0	65.0	2.0
depth		4.5	9.0			

a Adjacency constraints: s – south wall, n – north wall, w – west wall.

For the other spaces, the access and adjacency requirements of the Manual and Tudor Walters were likewise carefully followed. Thus, the parlour, though more flexible in aspect than the living room, was considered to be 'very greatly diminished' in value 'if direct access from the front entrance is not obtainable' (1918, 29). And the larder, to be cool, fresh, and airy, was required to be 'on the northerly side of the house' (1919, 9).

The dimensions too were taken as far as possible from the official specifications. Minimum room areas had been set for the living room, the parlour, and the scullery: 180, 120, and 80 sq. feet, respectively. The overall area of the floor plan (latterly 700 sq. feet max.) and the frontage width of the dwelling (20 feet min.) were also strictly regulated. Restrictions on dimension and area, along with aspect ratio (i.e. the ratio of width-to-length of a space), were all included in our list of constraints, as the table shows.

The object of transcribing the constraints from the Manual so precisely and comprehensively was to see how many feasible alternatives there were to the stipulated design requirements: how many plans, that is, that could have been illustrated in the Manual but were not. The results came as a surprise. With the appropriate adjacency and dimensional constraints entered for a south-facing house, the computer programme generated only *one* solution – the one shown in the Manual! (Figure 12.4, cf. Figure 12.3, plan 6 above.)

In case this should be a freak result, the experiment was repeated with a north-facing cottage. But the options were again found to be extremely limited: three plans only were produced, one of which was the type-plan, and another (the third) a slight variation on this. Plan no. 2 involved swapping the positions of the parlour and hall, but as this would mean that the larder would only be accessible from the parlour, it is easy to imagine why

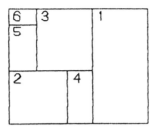

Figure 12.4 The single solution generated by DIS for a south-facing parlour house with front access.

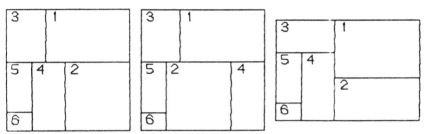

Figure 12.5 The three solutions generated by DIS for a north-facing parlour house with front access.

this arrangement did not actually occur (Figure 12.5, cf. Figure 12.3, plan 7 above).

The interesting point here is that, in the section on house accommodation, the authors of the 1919 Manual were at pains to point out that the typical plans were included 'only for general guidance' and were not intended to hamper initiative or to prevent full expression being given to 'local customs and traditions . . .'. Although they were undoubtedly sincere in this, the choice left open to the designer was in fact so restricted that their injunctions seem ironic. For the south-facing house, at least, the required conditions were clearly so strict that no architect, however inventive, could have found an alternative solution to the one prescribed.

The private, semi-detached house, 1918–1939

Our second example – the private 'semi' of the inter-war period – has many features in common with its local authority counterpart. Like the 'cottages' advocated by the Local Government Board, it was generally of wide frontage, on two floors, and contained all the main accommodation under the one roof. This is not accidental, since private housing of this period was also strongly influenced, both directly and indirectly, by the

Figure 12.6 View of a typical pair of 1930s semi-detached houses,
Radegund Road, Cambridge. Facing: plan of two variants of the 'universal plan'.

recommendations of the Tudor Walters Report and by subsequent legislation.

There were, however, significant differences from the municipal dwelling. The frontage, though wide, seldom matched the standards proposed in the 1919 Manual: the typical 'semi' was about 20 feet (6.1 m.) across the front – narrower than even no. 1 in the Manual (see Figure 12.4). The width was just sufficient to permit two rooms of reasonable size to be placed side-by-side.

In addition, the internal layout was highly standardised. There was no attempt to develop different room arrangements to suit the location and orientation of the building. Instead, much as with earlier terraced housing, the same basic pattern was repeated on all sites. At the front was the main living room or parlour, at the back the dining room and the kitchen. Figure 12.6 shows two variants of what is termed the 'universal plan'.

The question that immediately arises is how determined the plan form

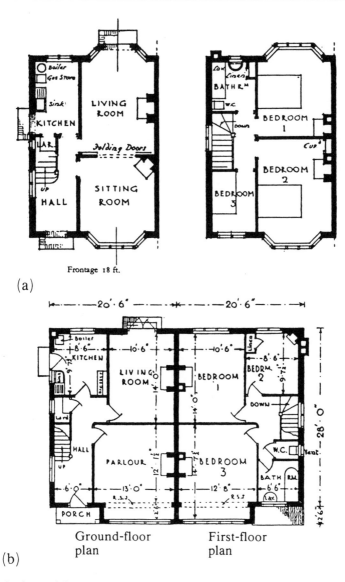

Frontage 18 ft.

(a)

Ground-floor
plan

First-floor
plan

(b)

was by its social programme. There was, of course, good reason for the
developer to repeat a solution once it was found to be marketable. And,
with three ample living rooms on the ground floor and three bedrooms
and a bathroom above, the 'semi' achieved standards that were attractive to
the growing middle-class market and rarely matched in contemporary

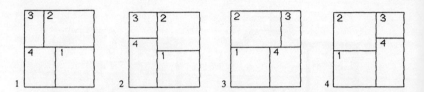

Figure 12.7 The four solutions generated by DIS for the ground-floor plan of a semi-detached house of 6 m. frontage. The full list of constraints is given in Table 12.2.

municipal housing. Nonetheless, it is easy to imagine alternative plan forms that would meet the same standards. The persistence of the universal plan suggests that there may have been other influences and constraints at work besides those of basic amenity. This was tested through plan-generation.

Since there was, in this case, no code of requirements or recommendations that could be consulted, it was necessary for the most part to infer the physical constraints through study and comparison of actual plans. To begin with, attention was focused, as in the previous example, on the ground floor arrangement, and a list of constraints of adjacency and dimension was drawn up (see Table 12.2). The total number of spaces was prescribed on the basis of the universal plan. Adjacencies reflected the fixed positions, as already noted, of the rooms with respect to the exterior (i.e. the living room was at the front, the kitchen and dining room at the back), and the characteristic provision of access to each ground-floor room from a common entrance hall. The maximum and minimum dimensions were derived from actual plans and were made 'loose' enough to embrace all those that were measured.

Table 12.2 Set of constraints used in the generation of ground-floor plan arrangements for the semi-detached house.

Space	Adj.[a]	Dimensions (m.)		Area (sq. m.)		Aspect ratio
		min.	max.	min.	max.	
1 Living room	f, 4	3.0	5.5	11.0	20.0	2.0
2 Parlour	b, 4	3.0	5.5	11.0	25.0	2.0
3 Scullery	b, 4	1.7	4.0	5.0	14.0	3.0
4 Hall and stairs	f, 1, 2, 3	1.7	7.5	5.0	17.0	5.0
0 Overall plan width		6.0	6.0	30.0	75.0	

a Adjacency constraints: f – front, b – back.

The possibilities were tested both for front and side access. Even with only the adjacency constraints entered, the programme produced relatively few options: twenty-four for the former, twelve for the latter – far fewer than for the local-authority house. With dimensions added, the options were reduced still further. For a plan of 6 m. frontage and front access, four possibilities were generated (Figure 12.7). It will be seen that nos. 3 and 4 are simply 'handed' versions (i.e. reflections) of 1 and 2. They do, however, represent distinct plans since, as in the previous experiment, the right-hand wall is assumed to be the party wall. Hence, in 1 and 2, the kitchen and hall (spaces 3 and 4) are against the flank wall of the house, while in 3 and 4, they abut the party wall.

From survey evidence, plan nos. 3 and 4 are far less common than 1 and 2, and no. 1 less common than no. 2. It is no. 2 that was reproduced in row upon row of houses along arterial roads and throughout the English sub-urbs between the wars: this was the universal plan (cf. Figure 12.6 above). The reason for its success in relation to nos. 1 and 3 is easy enough to see: the latter were quite simply less efficient in their arrangement. While not differing greatly in their basic room configuration from plan 2, the internal layout clearly requires either a narrower kitchen (space 3) or an over-sized hallway (space 4). No. 2 evidently offered better value in terms of space utilisation. But why was the 'handed' version of the universal plan (no. 4) so uncommon? The reason is less obvious, but it seems that the key issue was the placing of the entrance hall with respect to the façade of the building. This was explored further by looking at the upper floor arrangement.

Table 12.3 Set of constraints used in the generation of first-floor plan arrangements for the semi-detached house.

Space	Adj.	Dimensions (m.)		Area (sq. m.)		Aspect ratio
		min.	max.	min.	max.	
1 Bedroom 1	5	3.0	6.0	11.0	20.0	2.0
2 Bedroom 2	5	2.7	5.5	8.0	17.0	2.0
3 Bedroom 3	5	2.0	5.0	4.8	9.0	2.0
4 Bathroom	5	1.5	2.7	3.0	6.0	2.0
5 Stairs and landing	1–4	0.9	5.0	2.0	4.5	5.0
0 Overall plan width		6.0	6.0	30.0	75.0	

For the upper-floor input, no external adjacencies were specified. The only requirement was that each of the rooms (bathroom and three bed-rooms) should have independent access from the landing. The maximum and minimum dimensions were again inferred from actual examples, and were made to fall respectively above and below the maxima and minima found in practice (Table 12.3). The number of solutions generated was vast: altogether there were 192 dimensionally feasible possibilities. Unchecked by constraints of 'front' and 'back', plans were produced which were three and four rooms deep.

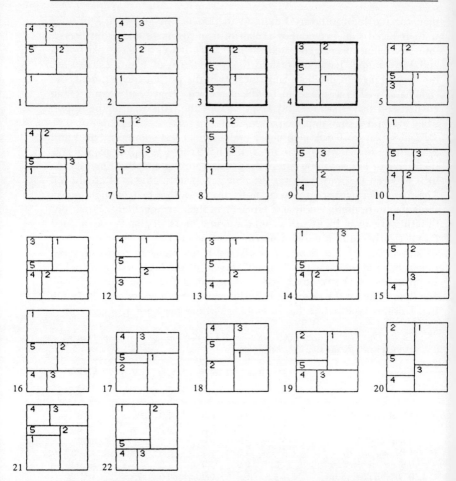

Figure 12.8 Solutions generated by DIS for upper floor of semi-detached house of 6 m. frontage once the staircase and bathroom are fixed against the end (in this case the west) wall. Those plans with three rooms against the party (east) wall have to be discounted since the central room would be without direct daylighting. The standard solutions adopted in practice are shown in heavy outline; compare Figure 12.7. The remaining constraints are set out in Table 12.3.

If we ignore the problem of matching up with the ground-floor plan underneath, all of these solutions are indeed perfectly feasible as long as windows can be placed in the side walls. Most rooms will be less effective, however, if deprived of this: while a bathroom may be totally enclosed, a bedroom without daylight or natural ventilation is unacceptable. Hence,

Figure 12.9 Advertisement from The Daily Telegraph, 1935 for semi-detached Costain houses in Surrey (after Oliver 1981). By omitting the left-hand house, the picture conveys the impression of a detached dwelling.

the greatest flexibility is achieved when the staircase is against the party wall and the bedrooms against the flank wall. If this situation is reversed, i.e. the staircase is placed against the flank wall and the bedrooms against the party wall, then the range of options is greatly reduced, because side lighting is no longer available. Yet this is precisely the situation that arises when the ground-floor entrance hall is located in its familiar position against the flank wall.

Generating the upper-floor plans once again, but with the added constraint that the stair is adjacent to the left-hand (flank) wall, the total number of solutions was reduced to twenty-two (Figure 12.8). Eliminating those that have three bedrooms against the right-hand (party) wall and those where the landing is over- or under-sized, we are left with few practical alternatives. The two standard solutions in the universal 'semi' are shown in dark outline.

Thus, the placing of the entrance hall against the outer or flank wall clearly imposes severe limitations on the plan, upstairs more than downstairs. How was it then that this became the norm in the spec.-built 'semi'? The answer seems to be that it was visual imagery that was all-important. If the entrance halls of the two adjoining 'semis' had been placed next to the party wall, this would have offered utilitarian advantages: it would have afforded better acoustic privacy for the main living rooms and provided the opportunity to economise on drainage and services at the back. But it would also have required the two front doors to be side-by-side at the centre of the building, and this weakens the visual identity of each half of the house.

The developer, in catering for a middle-class market, was well aware that the ideal to which most, if not all, his buyers aspired was the detached house. In practice, this was beyond the pockets of most people, so the semi-detached was a compromise, and the more this could be made to look like a detached dwelling the better. In sales brochures, a 'semi' would often be portrayed with the neighbouring house excluded from the picture (Figure 12.9). With the entrance against the outer rather than the inner wall, each family could also have its own path, its own gateway, as far as possible out of view of the neighbours. Thus, the visual illusion – or allusion – of separateness was complete.

Summary and conclusions

Both of these examples have brought into focus the power of a few variables to shape a building plan. In the first – the municipal dwelling – it was the newly formulated technical and functional requirements that proved critical, in one case literally predetermining the outcome. In the case of the private 'semi', by contrast, functional demands seem ultimately to have taken second place to the question of symbolism and external expression: in the final analysis, it was the social message that mattered most.

It is important, however, to point out that this is not a simple polarity of the utilitarian versus the social. The recommendations of the government manuals and design guides which proved so influential certainly concentrated on very practical concerns: on the provision of bigger rooms, better facilities, and above all, on the admission of sunlight and fresh air into the house. But these criteria are not value-free. They were rooted in very profound fears for social health and social stability. Hence the programme underpinning the design of the working-class house was at once political and ideological: it sought to counter a clearly-perceived threat of social upheaval and to provide a model for housing which would guarantee a healthy environment for the reproduction of family life. In this sense, social values are inscribed within the local-authority house in a far more subtle and far-reaching way than in its private-sector counterpart.

For the archaeologist as for the architect, the crucial link to be forged is inevitably that between the brief and the artefact – in this case the building plan. To make sense of domestic space, it is essential, as shown here, that we first establish the kinds of physical constraints – the limitations, controls – that were imposed, explicitly or implicitly, on the form of the building. These can only be revealed by reference to a comprehensive and exhaustive morphology. To isolate a particular aspect of plan organisation as social or symbolic without reference to the full range of morphological possibilities can be dangerously misleading.

With the help of computer power, the generation of morphological possibilities is now much less arduous a task than it once was. For small buildings of rectangular plan, the method of automated dissection just described can open the way to a much clearer picture of spatial organisation and its social referents.

Bibliography

Brown, Frank E. and J. P. Steadman 1987. 'The analysis and interpretation of small house plans: some contemporary examples' *Environment and Planning B: Planning and Design* 14:4 (special issue on the analysis of building plans in history and prehistory), 407–38.

Flemming, U. 1978. 'Wall representations of rectangular dissections and their use in automated space allocation' *Environment and Planning B* 5, 215–32.

Local Government Board 1919. *Manual on the Preparation of State-aided Housing Schemes*. HMSO (London).

Mitchell, W. J., J. P. Steadman, and R. S. Liggett 1976. 'Synthesis and optimization of small rectangular floor plans' in *Environment and Planning B* 3:1 (special issue on configurational studies in architecture), 37–70.

Steadman, J. P. 1973. 'Graph-theoretic representation of architectural arrangement' *Architectural Research and Teaching* 2, 161–72.

Steadman, J. P. 1983. *Architectural Morphology*. Pion Ltd. (London).

Stiny, G. 1975. *Pictorial and Formal Aspects of Shape and Shape Grammars*. Birkhäuser (Basel).

Stiny, G. 1980. 'Introduction to shape and shape grammars' *Environment and Planning B* 7, 343–51.

Swenarton, M. 1981. *Homes Fit for Heroes*. Heinemann Educational Books (London).

Tudor Walters Report 1918. 'Report of the Committee appointed by the President of the Local Government Board and the Secretary of State for Scotland to consider questions of building construction in connection with the provision of dwellings for the working classes in England and Wales, and Scotland, and report upon methods of securing economy and despatch in the provision of such dwellings'. HMSO (London).

Unwin, R. 1902. 'Cottage plans and common sense' *Fabian Tract* 109. The Fabian Society (London).

Index